A Practical Approach

JOHN COOPER

CENTENNIAL
COLLEGE

Library and Archives Canada Cataloguing in Publication

Cooper, John, 1958–
    Crisis communications in Canada : a practical approach / John Cooper.
Includes bibliographical references.

ISBN-13: 978-0-919852-60-0
ISBN-10: 0-919852-60-2

1. Crisis management—Canada—Textbooks. 2. Communication in
management—Canada—Textbooks. 3. Communication in organizations—
Canada—Textbooks. I. Title.

HD30.3.C66 2006   658.4'056   C2006-906243-9

CENTENNIAL COLLEGE PRESS
951 Carlaw Avenue
Toronto, Ontario
M4K 3M2

Every reasonable effort has been made to acquire permission for copyrighted
materials used in this book and to acknowledge such permissions accurately.
Any errors or omissions called to the publisher's attention will be corrected
in future printings.

Book design and typesetting by Laura Brady

Printed in Canada by Maracle Press

CRISIS COMMUNICATIONS
IN CANADA

*This book is dedicated with respect and thanks to
Yvonne Cooper, Pat Myerson and John Lott
for their wonderful support.*

Contents

Acknowledgements

I wish to thank editor Mark Stanski, Centennial College Press, for his ongoing support and skillful editing of this book. Mark's keenly insightful questions, deft handling of the manuscript and great sense of humour contributed greatly to the final product. As well, I offer sincere thanks to Judy Phillips, whose editing helped create a smooth, seamless text.

For helpful criticism in the early stages of revision, I would like to offer sincere thanks to Nancy Geddie, Public Relations Graduate Certificate Program Coordinator, Niagara College; John Larsen, Principal, Corpen Group; and Joan Campbell, MA, Program Coordinator, Public Relations, Cambrian College. Their suggestions for improvements were invaluable and very much appreciated as this book was taking shape.

I also wish to acknowledge and thank the following people for their support as well as their help in linking me up with great sources of information — and, in many cases, for giving up their valuable time for interviews:

R.K. Brown, RBC Financial Group
Canadian Public Relations Society Inc.
Bob Cohen, Bob Cohen Communications
Maria Cooper

Derek Deazeley, Ontario Ministry of
   Transportation
Allan Dickie

Craig DuHamel, Sunnybrook and Women's College Health Sciences Centre
Larry Farr, Centennial College
John Larsen, Corpen Group
Dr. David Mandel, Defence Research and Development Canada
John McHugh, Avant Strategic Communications
Bart Mindszenthy, Mindszenthy & Roberts
Nadia Norcia, Sunnybrook Health Sciences Centre
Michael O'Connor Clarke, Marqui
Marlane Oliver, 680 News Radio
Kerry Peacock, TD Bank Financial Group
Janice Robertson, Mount Royal College, Calgary
Dr. Peter Sandman
Christine Smith, Centennial College
Robert E. Waite, Canada Post Corporation
Staff of the Whitby Public Library
Rick Winston, Win-Win Communications
John Wright, Ipsos Reid Public Affairs

I

Introduction & History

1 Modern Crisis Communications

Great knowledge sees all in one,
Small knowledge breaks down into the many.

—CHUANG TZU

North American culture is attuned to the crisis. The interest of the public has its source in simple fear of disasters and disorder, in the general anxiety and insecurity that characterizes the modern Internet age, and in voyeurism and a desire to experience dramas vicariously through others. The media have a need to sell news, and crisis is a strong seller. As *Maclean's* magazine's Lianne George noted in its September 29, 2005, issue, "For almost a decade, North Americans have been bracing for one cataclysmic threat after another — superbugs, bioterrorist attacks, apocalyptic plagues. There have been real threats (Y2K, West Nile virus, SARS), but in each case the amount of paranoia surrounding the threat has been exponentially larger than the threat itself. So fear has become the epidemic, and safety, or our perceived lack of it, an obsession."[1] We are, as a community, programmed to react to a crisis. This book will examine the practice of crisis communications in this geopolitical context, drawing predominantly on Canadian but also some American examples.

What This Book Will Do

Imagine a scenario where everything is out of control. Organizations are often a picture of calmness, of routine, of orderly employees going through their daily paces. Beneath the surface, they are driven, often overworked environments where employees scramble to make deadlines, finish tasks and bring "deliverables" to the boss's desk. It's enough in most organizations just to get the day-to-day tasks done without worrying about crises. So when something goes wrong with no advance warning and no immediate answers, people ratchet their activity into overdrive. Junior personnel look to senior personnel for answers and receive blank looks in return; senior personnel turn to their experts and seek something — anything — that will put out the exponentially growing fires that a crisis will create.

This book is about how to identify those potential fires before the first spark is ignited; it's about recognizing the factors that create combustion inside and outside the workplace and generate a crisis, and it's about equipping communicators with the tools to handle a crisis. This book offers a common sense approach to crisis communications. As such, it discusses theories of the ways people view and respond to crises, as well as what communicators need to know to handle them. But the greater emphasis is placed on the practical side of crisis communications. To that end, there are case studies followed by analyses of how communicators succeeded or failed to deal effectively with crises.

Most of all, this book aims for context, for a framework that combines the critical-thinking elements necessary to tackle a crisis. Too often communicators focus on the tactics of handling a crisis and forget to think about the long-term effects of what they do, how a series of tactical moves — whether in planning, writing or contact with their stakeholders (e.g., employees, customers, suppliers, investors, government, lobby groups), the general public, or the media — will eventually position their company in the eyes of the various publics. We will examine how the exigencies of a crisis need not compel a company to abandon the principles that define it during successful and calm moments.

The first part of the book looks at the history of the communications industry, with an emphasis on crisis, and explains the communicator's ideal approach, using modern case studies to illustrate key principles. The second part discusses issues identification and crisis planning. The third part gives in-depth consideration of the nature and information needs of an organization's publics (internal and external stakeholders and the media). The fourth part provides a detailed examination of the tactics and tools for dealing with crisis, focusing on how to create and use communications materials and how to provide leadership for publics. The fifth and final part comprises a number of extensive hands-on crisis communications scenarios for practice.

A History of Public Relations and Crisis

Canadian and American companies in the latter part of the nineteenth century and in the early twentieth century weren't focused on the court of public opinion the way organizations today must be to survive. It was enough that they conducted business, worked to clean up any mishaps they encountered and simply got on with the business of the day. But then North America saw the advent of ubiquitous media — newspapers and radio — along with growth in technology and an increasingly literate populace that could read and form strong opinions. This created an environment unlike any the nineteenth century had seen. These forces forged a new society, one in which information, communication and public opinion became their own growth industries. Human behaviour was generated, formed and refined based on the proliferation of information and ideas. It isn't surprising that public relations is a child of the twentieth century, and crisis communications is a natural, late-twentieth-century evolution of the desire of business, industry and government to fine-tune their ability to be at the top of their public relations game.

The term *public relations* has been around for about a hundred years. Today, it is being increasingly superseded by the more businesslike term *corporate communications*. Most professionals define public relations as the practice of external and internal communications that are used to influence, educate and inform specific publics by a variety of means: writing, publicity, promotion, special events and marketing.

According to the Public Relations Society of America, public relations "has been defined in many widely differing ways … the earliest definitions emphasized the roles of press agentry and publicity since these were major elements from which modern public relations grew."[2] Press agents were the carnival barkers of their time, schmoozing with the public and with the media. Many early press agents were hired by the likes of circus operators such as Barnum & Bailey to drum up local interest in a carnival or circus before it came to a town.

Over the years, their role expanded. Newspapers were cheap, popular and plentiful, and literacy increased; people tuned in their radios and, later, turned on their television sets. Information became the overriding concern of business. The profile and success of a company was defined by how well the publicity and public relations representatives did their jobs.

Communicators worked with politicians to calm the troubled waters. In the movies of the 1930s and 1940s, they are depicted as the shadowy figures manipulating the media behind the public's back. If a company's negligence caused a death, the PR person worked to rebuild a company's reputation, usually through media contacts.

Today, communicators are sometimes seen as the forces that, through the use of company-sponsored scientific studies and corporate good deeds, work to convince the public, for example, that cigarette companies are responsible corporate citizens who are not trying to get children hooked on nicotine; that burning coal is not contributing to global warming; or that the chemicals in the water are not going to cause cancer. But the public relations professional also promotes positive values, good works in the community and a caring attitude toward an organization's publics and clients.

EDWARD L. BERNAYS: THE FIRST PROFESSIONAL COMMUNICATOR

Any book about communications must make mention of Edward L. Bernays (1891–1995), the world's first truly professional communicator and its original theoretician. Although it could certainly be said that people have been communicators for thousands of years, Bernays turned it into something approaching an art.

Bernays was famous for creating the term *engineering consent,* a process that allowed one to influence and control masses of people, supposedly without them even realizing they were being manipulated. At the heart of this process was the understanding of the motivation of a group of people and how people tend to think in a group (often called "groupthink motivation"). In today's corporate communications world, communicators think of engineering consent in a less deliberate and conniving way. They need to know their publics, and they need to target their messages to those publics appropriately so that they can subtly change either their publics' opinion of the organizations or their behaviour toward the organization or product. Communicators want to provide their publics with the information to allow them to make informed decisions.

The legacy of Bernays continues to this day. He became famous for employing third-party authorities, enlisting experts to support his messages and then watching as people's opinions and behaviour changed in favour of his clients. Those messages always addressed the bottom line, answering the question, "What's in it for me?" Corporations that employed these strategic appeals to their customers' needs benefited greatly in terms of increased sales and customer loyalty.

> Any effective communications initiative focused on a crisis must have the promise of simple, straightforward benefits for its end users, both within the organization and outside it.

This approach worked with the promotion of bacon. Bernays surveyed doctors about eating habits and found that doctors were in favour of patients having a hearty breakfast. Bernays used this hook (a key point used to engage the various publics' attention) to promote his client's product: bacon. Bernays recognized that the important element in his appeal was to go beyond promoting the product itself by also selling an idea about a product, taking the message from the tactical to the strategic, from "this product is good for you" to "this product is part of a process of feeling good about yourself." The employment niche he created for himself and for those who followed was of the expert who understands people and who can successfully predict how a message will be received by a certain section of the public.

Today we see experts and authority figures everywhere — from September 11, 2001, when military experts and experts on terrorism filled television screens across North America, to emergency response experts (e.g., Hurricane Katrina in 2005), health experts, fitness experts and political experts. The list is endless — with each expert promising the view of "where we go from here," a slice of the future, as it were. Crisis communications has found its niche in a world racked by instability, uncertainty, changing patterns of political and social behaviour, and high-speed communication. Organizations need crisis experts who can help them plan for the possibility of things going wrong.

EDWARD L. BERNAYS, PROFESSIONAL COMMUNICATOR: CURRICULUM VITAE

- U.S. Government. Bernays served with the Committee on Public Information to promote World War I as the war that would "make the world safe for democracy."
- American Tobacco Company. In what would now be considered politically incorrect, Bernays encouraged women to smoke by sending out svelte, successful-looking young women to puff away on the streets of major cities, linking smoking with female empowerment during women's rights marches: the Lucky Strike cigarettes were held up as torches of freedom.
- General Electric. Bernays created a worldwide media event with GE's sponsorship of the light bulb's fiftieth anniversary celebration, called "Light's Golden Jubilee," in 1929.
- Authored the books *Crystallizing Public Opinion, Propaganda* and *Engineering Consent.*

"The conscious and intelligent manipulation of the organized habits and opinions of the masses is an important element in democratic society. Those who manipulate this unseen mechanism of society constitute an invisible government that is the true ruling power of our country. We are governed, our minds are moulded, our tastes formed, our ideas suggested, largely by men we have never heard of ... in almost every act of our daily lives, whether in the sphere of politics or business, in our social conduct or our ethical thinking, we are dominated by the relatively small number of persons who understand the mental processes and social patterns of the masses. It is they who pull the wires which control the public mind."[3]   — From *Propaganda*

In today's world we have the Internet, instantaneous communications, hundreds of television channels, influences from various sources, and increasingly sophisticated media consumers. One might feel that the quote from *Propaganda* sounds outdated. Yet, we must admit that we are influenced, perhaps in subtle ways, by what we are told and how it is told to us. It could be argued that we are conscious of the influence that takes place and that when we act, we do so on the basis of this knowledge. It doesn't always strike a positive chord with people, for who wants to be manipulated?

A lot of what Bernays did is old hat now, but its significance endures. Social scientists, university researchers, market research experts, psychologists and behaviourists looked to the foundations that Bernays established to find ways to better understand human behaviour; these foundations set the stage for surveys, polls, questionnaires and other means used to identify response and behaviour patterns and plan for how people might act in the future. For crisis communicators, Bernays's work demonstrates that there are principles governing how people are likely to react in a crisis, giving solid ground to the options provided to clients. These principles allow communicators a measure of confidence in predicting how their publics respond to crisis and, more important, how they respond to communications approaches to crisis.[4]

NEGATIVE IMPRESSIONS OF THE COMMUNICATOR'S ROLE AND OF SPIN

Negative impressions of the communications industry began with Bernays and exist to this day, despite its emergence from its theoretical foundations into a profession moderated by much new thinking, sophistication and the ethical influence of professional associations and post-secondary programs. One such negative impression has to do with the liberal use of the term *spin* by both the industry and the media. Spin refers to the less-than-honest and forthright presentation of information during a crisis or scandal by an organization's communicators, who are sometimes called "flacks" or "spin doctors."

© Darrin Bell and Theron Heir/Dist. by United Feature Syndicate, Inc.

Communicators work hard to build a positive image for themselves. Why? Because the vestiges of past perceptions of their work still linger. Images of communicators as artists of deception for the corporate world are prevalent in our culture. The communicator's work cannot be of much value if the very name of his or her profession is synonymous with deception.

The communicator's role is to present the organization, and its people, actions and ethos, in as positive a way as possible to the organization's publics. But in doing so, communicators do not fabricate the truth nor can they attempt to do so, history tells us, without long-term loss of credibility for themselves, their profession, and their employers.

WHAT IS CORPORATE SPIN?

First used by speechwriter and columnist William Safire in a 1986 *New York Times* column, the term *spin* was described by Safire as being derived from the phrase "spinning a yarn" — being deceptive.[5] In a paper titled "The Anatomy of Spin: Causes, Consequences, and Cure," Kenneth S. Hicks of Rogers State University claims, "Spin emanates from public relations, but is a particular manifestation of rhetorical behavior that occupies a gray zone between public relations and propaganda." Referring to Safire, Hicks says, "Safire further mused that spin has more recently become a noun, and that spin now means that a person has 'angled' a story 'to suit our predilections or interests.' Elaborating, Safire noted that the 'phrase spin doctor was coined on the analogy of play doctor, one who fixes up a limping second act, and gains from the larcenous connotation of the verb doctor, to fix a product [in the same] way a crooked bookkeeper "cooks" books.'"[6]

Former U.S. president Bill Clinton's statement in the Monica Lewinsky affair that he "did not have sexual relations with that woman" is a now-classic attempt at spin; he played off the legal and technical differences between oral sex and intercourse (he engaged in the first but not in the second) to take his case in a direction that would emphasize that he was not guilty of any wrongdoing.

Communicators are wise to avoid using spin: it often treads dangerously close to attempting to hide the truth or lying. Spin is often viewed by an increasingly sophisticated public, as well as by the media, as a cover-up that wastes time instead of buying it for the communicator's employer. Moreover, the level of sophistication in most commentators, stakeholders and the public is such that they can see through the spin.

Think of watching a magic trick. If the magician knows that the audience knows how the trick is done, why bother doing the trick at all?

THE ESTABLISHMENT OF MODERN PRACTICE

Potential communicators continue to enter the field because many believe they can combine a love of ideas and words with an occupation that offers exciting and interesting work and, for many, something new every day. Eighty per cent of what communicators do involves writing, and most who come into the field either already have sound writing skills or are working on them.

Full-time positions for communicators began appearing in the 1970s and 1980s, when corporations recognized they needed specialists who could do several things:

- Write on many levels and for various products, reaching people both within the organization and outside it;
- Communicate with the media and with the organization's publics, including special interest groups (often called stakeholders) and government;
- Focus specifically on building and maintaining the organization's profile with its publics;
- Research and understand what the organization does and put it into context in relation to the industry in which it operates and the greater economic and social communities in which it is situated, and also clearly explain the organization's role, mandate and direction;

- Develop and deliver special plans for handling various situations, including crises;
- Keep track of issues affecting the organization's public profile by monitoring the media and other sources of information, and then provide advice and guidance to senior people within the organization.

In short, corporate communications is the practice of safeguarding an organization's reputation. It promotes understanding of an organization's goals and builds support for those goals among the organization's publics. It does this through a series of ongoing activities designed to build and maintain a positive profile of the organization, from meeting with the general public, government and media to issuing news releases, holding press conferences and monitoring public perception of the organization.

A SELF-POLICING INDUSTRY: ETHICAL STANDARDS

The industry is responsible for policing itself. Organizations and the communicators delivering their messages must ask, "Are we doing the right thing?"

Associations such as the Canadian Public Relations Society (CPRS) represent the industry, and many communicators recognize that joining a high-profile organization such as CPRS is essential to enhance their credibility as professionals and build on their foundation of skills. Organizations such as CPRS make it a part of their mandate to set a benchmark for proper public relations behaviour. They do so by accrediting their members through a series of strict examinations, providing advice on ethical behaviour in the industry, and ensuring that members adhere to a common set of professional standards. The society outlines a nine-point code of professional standards for its members:

1. A member shall practice public relations according to the highest professional standards.
2. A member shall deal fairly and honestly with the communications media and the public.
3. A member shall practice the highest standards of honesty, accuracy,

integrity and truth, and shall not knowingly disseminate false or misleading information.

4. A member shall deal fairly with past or present employers/clients, fellow practitioners and members of other professions.

5. Members shall be prepared to disclose the names of their employers or clients for whom public communications are made and refrain from associating themselves with anyone who would not respect such policy.

6. A member shall protect the confidences of present, former and prospective employers/clients.

7. A member shall not represent conflicting or competing interests without the expressed consent of those concerned, given after a full disclosure of the facts.

8. A member shall not guarantee specified results beyond the member's capacity to achieve.

9. Members shall personally accept no fees, commissions, gifts or any other considerations for professional services from anyone except employers or clients for whom the services were specifically performed.[7]

(Reprinted with permission of the CPRS.)

Crisis

Crises — and their handling — have a long history, and people's approaches to crises have varied over the years. Generally, organizations haven't taken responsibility for their crises and have tried to slough them off onto someone else. Or they have simply ignored them, hoping the crises would simply pass on their own, leaving business to continue as usual.

The *Oxford Dictionary* defines *crisis* as a "turning point ... a time of danger or suspense in politics, commerce, etc."[8] *Funk and Wagnalls Dictionary* defines it as "a crucial turning point in the progress of an affair or of a series of events, as in politics, business ... a critical moment."[9] The U.S. Navy defines it as "an incident or situation involving a threat to the United States, its territories, citizens, military forces, possessions, or vital interests that develop rapidly and creates a condition of such diplomatic, economic, political, or military importance that commitment of U.S. military forces and resources is contemplated to achieve national objectives."[10] Organizations will slant the definition to reflect their own activities.

For communicators and the organizations they work for, a crisis is any event, real or imagined, that might dramatically affect the way people feel about and behave toward that organization. Crises can range from natural disasters, such as Hurricane Katrina, which wracked New Orleans in 2005, to human error, whether it's improper programming of a computer system, an employee's sloppiness in doing his job or the malfunction of equipment. A crisis is an issue that has passed beyond the company's control because of a specific catalyst (investigative journalism, a whistleblower, an on-the-job injury) or because the time limit for dealing with an issue has passed (for instance, a workers' strike in response to long unaddressed worker-safety concerns).

The people who constitute an organization's publics react in startling ways, and communicators may scramble in a mad dash to find the right answers, complicating the process of resolving a crisis. Or they may deliver pat, generic homilies to explain away the situation, leaving stakeholders and others to scratch their heads or rise up in anger. Sometimes communicators say nothing, hoping the situation will simply go away.

But long before a crisis happens, crisis communications planners should ask, "What if the worst happens? What if this issue grows out of control?" By addressing it beforehand, communicators are doing their due diligence, working to acknowledge weaknesses, vulnerabilities and problems — unpopular topics with time-deprived business people driven to pursue profits ahead of all other considerations. The communicator pauses to consider; disaster may strike, a mistake may be made, a life (or lives) may be lost and business may go into a tailspin. Communicators' responses in a communications crisis will shape the way their organization is seen, how it conducts business and how it sees itself. It can mean the difference between success and failure of the organization in both the short and long term.

CRISIS COMMUNICATIONS

Crisis communications, a specialized area of corporate communications, is linked to issues management (the practice of examining where everything from corporate practices and events to opinions of stakeholders and consumers' ideas about an organization may lead). Issues are examined in detail in Chapter 3. For now, an issue is best thought of as any question that may be asked about an organization that might provoke debate and polarize its publics. Are the hiring practices and wages fair? Are the suppliers reputable? Are all of the suppliers legitimate and honest? Are the company's dealings with farmers in developing countries fair, and how will consumers feel if they became more aware of these dealings? Answering questions such as these help communicators uncover issues, any of which can turn into a crisis in an instant with the introduction of the right catalyst. Issues can be thought of as the boiling pot shortly before it boils over. Issues managers ask, "Where are our practices taking us, and how will our future be affected?" Crucial to the approach of issues management is the idea that the issue itself is a factor that the company can manage or control.

This is one of the major reasons why thinking about the crisis before it hits is essential. In his 1986 book *Crisis Management*, Steven Fink talks about the prodromal stage of a crisis, when what appear to be insignificant events are the distant early warning signs of a potential crisis.[11] Communicators learn to recognize these signs by being sensitive to their organization's environment and by planning well in advance for what *might* happen. Organizations need professionals who can take a step back and ask, "What if something happens? What will we do?" and determine the steps necessary to address the event and to communicate those steps in a way that will salvage the company's reputation. Communicators look at issues that arise and see whether they might develop into crises, then plan for that potential. For example, a communicator who works for a manufacturer that relies on raw materials shipped from a part of the world that is wracked by internal political struggle, might ask him- or herself:

• What if there's a change in government in the country where our suppliers are located? How will the company handle that?

- What are the first questions our customers might ask?
- What about human rights organizations that might question our dealings with this country?
- What do we need to do to reduce the risk and avoid a crisis in the first place?

Planning begins around these basic questions, and the steps worked through to answer every question that might arise.

> The practice of crisis communications is the practice of managing the flow of information to and from the organization and all people with an interest in that organization, however remote, in a time of crisis.

COMMUNICATORS' ROLES DURING CRISIS

Communicators play several roles. On the strategic side, they plan for crises and advise senior management on how and when to communicate. On the tactical side, they write the products needed to flow information to publics during a crisis. They also put the crisis plan into action and respond to inquiries about the crisis while it is happening.

Most organizations have limited resources set aside specifically for dealing with crisis communications. Most do not have communicators who are crisis experts and will hire outside firms if the communicators they do have are overwhelmed or out of their depth. Yet, it is important for communicators within the organization to be able to plan for and deal with a crisis. Bringing in a specialist means a delay while that person is brought up to speed and integrated into the communications department and executive group. The costs may be prohibitive. Even if there is time and money to outsource, communicators within an organization need to be effective deputies during a high-stakes crisis — the situation most likely to motivate outsourcing.

Most communicators are strong generalists who can handle the regular corporate communications activities of writing, media relations and planning. But they also need to spend time thinking about what the company does, how it is perceived and how its image could change if there were an error, accident or disaster.

The communicator must also think about how to pull information together and deliver it to people both inside and outside the organization. In the planning stages, crisis communications may only take up part of the day or week, but when a crisis hits, it will be a round-the-clock endeavour for as long as the crisis lasts. Good preparation often means a shorter crisis. Crises may demand only short, intense bursts of activity for a few days or sustained exercises that last months.

Crisis Communications Strategies

How an organization responds to a crisis is essential to its recovery, and some strategies, if poorly chosen, may aggravate an already dangerous situation. The following are the major overarching strategies executives and communicators choose from.

Forgiveness strategies are implemented when an organization has made a mistake or is otherwise at fault. An example of such an approach is the January 1986 *Challenger* space shuttle disaster. After the shuttle broke up after liftoff, NASA adopted a forgiveness strategy for handling the disaster. NASA admitted it had made a mistake and, most important, promised and delivered on program changes to ensure that no similar mishap could happen again (though NASA would continue to face problems with its shuttles, most recently during the break-up of the *Columbia* space shuttle on re-entry in 2003). Forgiveness strategies allow an organization to "come clean" and to prepare and deliver sweeping changes in its organization, policies and practices to improve its position with its publics. This strategy can have long-term positive effects. It allows companies to rethink, plan and implement changes.[12]

Sympathy strategies are employed by organizations as a means of portraying themselves as victims in a crisis. When cyanide-tainted Tylenol killed seven people in the Chicago area in 1982, Tylenol maker Johnson & Johnson employed a sympathy strategy early on, stressing to the public that the company, having no prior knowledge that anyone had tampered with its medicines, was also a victim. The effects of this strategy are short term, as the public's sympathy for organizations tends to be short. In the Tylenol case, the company soon moved to a forgiveness strategy, accepting full responsibility, compensating families and implementing new packaging standards for its products.[13]

Avoidance strategies are used when companies do not want to take the blame and so shift it elsewhere. In 1993, the American hamburger chain Jack in the Box experienced a crisis because of cases of E. coli that were attributed to burgers purchased at a Seattle Jack in the Box restaurant. Three children died after eating the burgers. The company used an avoidance strategy, claiming that the source of the problem was elsewhere (in this case the meat supplier) before moving to a forgiveness strategy and implementing changes to more effectively screen its food products to ensure a higher level of safety. As with the sympathy strategy, the effects of the avoidance are short term and can be used only to buy time as an organization brings in a plan that will address the situation effectively.[14]

Attachment strategies are effectively used in spreading out the responsibility for taking action in the wake of a crisis. In 1979, following a train derailment in Mississauga, Ontario, in which more than 200,000 residents were evacuated after clouds of toxic chemicals spewed into the atmosphere, the City of Mississauga, Province of Ontario, and Canadian Pacific Railway took joint responsibility in resolving the crisis and planning for more effective control of the movement of dangerous goods by rail, as well as requiring emergency evacuation plans in the future.[15]

Each of these strategies has its uses for a given crisis, but the biggest challenges during a crisis are meeting deadlines and ensuring accuracy of information. When the media and the public relay a sense of reassurance about the organization, through positive media stories, fewer angry calls to the customer service lines and the resumption of normal sales levels — communicators can rest assured that they have done their jobs well. Creating this reassurance and trust in media and the public depends more on these two factors — speed and accuracy — than on any others.

Communicators Approaching Crisis

This book advocates a move beyond specific strategies and tactics. In fact, the book's first goal is to ensure that new communicators are able to do more than simply adopt reactive postures. Even a good strategy, if it is the only one a company's executives are comfortable with, is no more than a reaction. Communicators themselves (whose business is to always focus on the overarching goals of any particular communications) do not generally stand back far enough from their own exhilaration, ingrained habits and nearsightedness to truly use a plan of action, or even all of their creativity. Rather than setting out a particular set of universal principles or theories, this book encourages readers to learn how to think creatively to apply strategies and tactics to various situations.

PROACTIVE VERSUS REACTIVE

The essence of crisis communications is proactive thinking. Only forethought and preparation enable a spokesperson to do anything more useful when faced with the breaking crisis than say "No comment" or "We have no information at this time but hope to have answers as soon as possible." Reactive approaches to crisis put a company into a mode of action or inaction that is uninformed, inflexible and often irresponsible: spokespeople do not have information; no measures have been planned for key personnel to assemble and present information; and the company's response is unintelligent, its assessment of its responsibility and the solution it needs to implement oversimplified and inadequate.

Issues identification and management is thus the key component of a common sense approach to crisis communications. Effective communicators are interested in tomorrow's problem *today*, and make that problem a regular part of their workday. New communicators can develop their understanding of issues management by learning how to study a company's practices and by monitoring media channels. But there is another dimension of proactive thinking that is even more practical and tactile. This way of thinking is less theoretical and speculative — it doesn't come out of brainstorming sessions, focus groups or academic conferences on media and consumer behaviour. Simply put, it's the experienced communicator's visualization of how a certain crisis starts, develops and dissolves in the face of a well-executed communications plan. The communicator looks ahead and imagines all the deadlines, meetings, writing tasks and press conferences; he or she also imagines the many stresses on stakeholders, company management, staff and fellow communicators on the first through to the last day of the crisis.

This second dimension of proactive thinking, the experienced communicator's advanced view of events as they will likely unfold, comes only from practice. In the next chapters of this book, you will begin to practise. For now, the best way to appreciate the value of this viewpoint is by imagining taking up a risky sport such as rock climbing, and then taking that sport to the competitive level after numerous climbs and a few frightening, possibly life-threatening, falls.

Before tackling a challenging cliff, you would practise, alone and with your team, learning all the tough points, where the footholds are most scarce. You would talk those points over with your team exhaustively, sharing information and getting tips from the more experienced teammates. Next, you would strategize together, visualizing each part of the climb, seeing yourself at the goal: the top of the peak. Your strategy would contain tactics for handling each phase, such as rest and catch-up periods for members on the rough patches. Your team also would think about what would happen if a teammate fell, keeping in mind where everyone else would be on the cliff, especially during the rough patches. As individuals, you have all practised dangling by your line, and you know the fear, and how long it takes to drop the panic and start working back up to the rock. You know your team is ready to hold you.

If the team has a fall during the competition, your team will later review each crucial step of the climb, and you will all be honest about whether the fall was preventable. Was the team going faster than one member could handle at that point? If the climb is strong, you discuss everywhere you might have had a problem but didn't; you'll ask, "What did we do right? What can we do better next time?"

This analogy includes both dimensions of proactive thinking. The team discussion of the climb is akin to issues management, while learning the minute details of the climb and the practice of dealing with those details, right down to the potential fall, are akin to the experienced communicator's hands-on perspective, the feeling-out of a crisis in advance.

Like an experienced rock climber, a proactive communicator is ready to tackle a topic, thinking strategically (what is my organization's overall goal, and how can I help to achieve it?) and about tactics (what steps do I take, what products do I produce, what processes do I follow to make that goal a reality?). Good proactive communicators walk themselves through a plan.

By contrast, a reactive communicator, like a climber who panics when he or she can't find a foothold, scrambles for the first grip within reach without thinking ahead to the destination or even the next handhold. He or she grasps at information, wondering whether the facts planned for release are definitive or the solution a sure one. If the reactive communicator manages to see the company clear, credit for a job well done is not due, though he or she might earn a pat on the back for being just plain lucky.

BEYOND TACTICS: THE SEAMLESS APPROACH

Communicators often think of communications in a component, or tactical way, by thinking of those steps needing to be taken to get out of trouble that day; by, one day at a time, developing a set of messages to get ideas across and the means to communicate them — news releases, speeches, backgrounders, fact sheets, media lists, communications plans and events. The various stakeholders, whether internal (fellow employees and senior management) or external (the media, the general public, associations, and stakeholder groups), are thought of separately. Ideas are drafted and implemented in a step-by-step way that fails to link these tactics or publics together into a cohesive whole.

What is needed, however, is to develop a seamless way to look at issues and crisis communications.

Communicators want to use common sense —

- To use a plan effectively, pulling in the right personnel to handle it;
- To think about customer service and how it affects the way they handle crises in their organizations;
- To see that they have a variety of publics that they have to serve. These publics are not only those on the outside of the organization; they also reside within the organization, and communicating properly with them is just as important as getting the right message to external stakeholders.

KEY GROUPS AND THEIR IMPORTANCE TO COMMUNICATORS

MEDIA: Media include newspapers, radio stations, magazines, special interest publications and television stations that report on subjects of interest to their audience. Most media also operate websites, so that their information is often up-to-the-minute. The media filter the information a company provides, reworking it in a way that will appeal to their target audience.

PUBLIC: The general public — made up of the average citizen — may have a strong interest (especially if he or she is a client of the company or buys its products) or a marginal interest in the company.

EXTERNAL STAKEHOLDERS: Special interest groups, associations or community groups may have a stake or an interest in what a company says. They are especially important in helping to form, refine and change opinions about the company. Other external stakeholders include:

- THE INDUSTRY: The company's own industry — its workforce as well as industry associations — will take an interest in what a company does, whether it is announcing a new project or responding to a crisis.
- GOVERNMENT: Governments (municipal, provincial, and federal) play a role in regulating industries or setting standards for how companies operate. They will be focused on how a company does business and on how it responds to crises.

INTERNAL STAKEHOLDERS: Employees within the organization will have a keen interest in the direction the company is taking, whether it's in or out of a crisis. Internal stakeholders formulate opinions, drive rumours and react to crisis situations — and are often at a disadvantage in knowing how a company is handling crisis issues. It is therefore essential that communicators keep them informed.

Most of all, communicators want to make sure that every team within their organization that deals with the crisis is communicating with every other team. This sometimes is easier said than done. Generally, organizations tackle problems by breaking up tasks and assigning them, without bringing the separate teams to the discussion table regularly to share information and discuss progress and next steps.

Bringing the various teams together allows the organization to identify its strengths, which in turn allows them to come to the forefront during a crisis. For example, a spill of toxic chemicals in a plant will trigger a response from key areas within the company: the shop floor where the spill occurred; the communications department, where communicators will pull together the necessary facts and prepare a statement for the company's president; the president's office, where the most senior personnel will be the official spokesperson when delivering information; the plant's workplace safety office, where the appropriate representative will report on the safety record of the plant and the steps being taken to clean up the spill; and human resources, for information on the condition of anyone injured as a result of the spill.

All these teams working separately could serve up five versions of the same event. That's where the communicator comes in, pulling together information from each area and effectively becoming a "one window" source of information. But it's essential that all parties be brought together at one table, to discuss the situation, contribute information and, where appropriate, help decide on a message that is free of contradiction. This allows for discussion that is far-reaching and goes beyond the immediate question of "What is the company doing about the spill?" It will answer other questions important for reinforcing the company's image:

- When did it last have an accident?
- Is the spill a threat to the community?
- What safety measures are in place?
- What caused the spill?

The more questions communicators can pose to themselves — and answer sufficiently — the better prepared they will be when the media and stakeholders call the company. They will be thinking not just of the products they created but how those fit together into the overall goals. Communicators' *final* goal is to resolve the crisis and have the company come away from it with, at minimum, a break-even position in terms of its reputation with its publics. The seamless approach is one that constantly reconsiders the question: "Are we moving toward our goal of resolution?" and not simply, "Did this news release read correctly?" The component, product or tactic (such as a news release) is simply one part of the seamless movement of information and activity that gets communicators closer to their goal.

Conclusion

We live in an era of information and public opinion. Today's communicators wear many hats: they write products, explaining the organization's role and mandate to its publics; build and maintain the organization's profile; monitor issues affecting the organization; and develop and deliver plans for handling various situations that may arise. Communicators must do all this in an ethical manner; doing so will go a long way to shedding the negative image they often have as being masters of spin.

Crisis communications is a specialized area of corporate communications, but very much a part of any communicator's job. When a situation arises that can dramatically affect the way an organization's publics feel about it, that organization has a crisis on its hand. Communicators can do their due diligence by addressing issues before they become crises. Asking the right questions and carefully considering the answers help communicators uncover issues, any of which can turn into a crisis with the right catalyst. If a crisis does arise, communicators' responses to it will shape the success or failure of their organization. A company need not abandon the principles that define it during calm moments. The key is in preparation, with good preparation often meaning a shorter crisis.

The effective communicator looks ahead, being *pro*active rather than *re*active. Instead of relying on a set of inflexible principles, communicators must think creatively about whatever situation arises. They do this not by simply following a series of strategic principles or tactics but by implementing a seamless approach to looking at issues and crisis communications, one that constantly looks ahead to the final goal of resolution. But what exactly does this approach involve? This is the discussion of the chapters that follow.

Key Concepts

CRISIS: A crucial turning point in the progress of an issue or a series of events that affects the credibility or profile of an organization.

DEADLINES AND ACCURACY: Both aspects are critical during a crisis. Timing is crucial in terms of preventing further damage and in setting out the organization's approach to handling the crisis. It is essential to be "in at the front end" of the crisis to establish the organization's leadership role in handling it. Of equal importance is ensuring that the information relayed is accurate and reliable.

ENGINEERING CONSENT: A term coined by Edward L. Bernays to refer to understanding the publics' motivation and using that knowledge to control their behaviour.

ESSENTIAL TASKS OF COMMUNICATORS DURING CRISIS:
• Understand the organization, its philosophy and its current response mechanisms and capacity for managing in a crisis;
• Plan strategy;
• Assemble a crisis team;
• Provide a flow of information to publics with regular updates.

FORGIVENESS STRATEGY: A strategy aimed at winning forgiveness from stakeholders and creating acceptance for the crisis, while allowing the organization to take steps to rectify the situation.

PUBLIC RELATIONS/CORPORATE COMMUNICATIONS: External and internal communications that are used to influence, educate and inform specific publics. Communicators seek to develop an understanding of their organization's aims and goals (and to build support for those goals within those publics) through an ongoing series of activities.

STANDARDS: A set of professional standards, including honesty, accuracy, integrity and truth, to which communicators are expected to adhere.

2 | Crisis Communications Then and Now

TWO CASE STUDIES

In Chapter 1, we looked at Edward L. Bernays, who laid the foundation for modern public relations. We'll now consider two crisis communications cases, comparing a seminal case in crisis communications history with a much more recent one. The first, the most famous crisis communications scenario of them all, is widely considered to have laid the practical groundwork and set the benchmark for proactive corporate communications: Johnson & Johnson's Tylenol crisis of 1982. The second case examines the extent to which experienced communicators working decades later (many of whom have graduated from post-degree programs in communications) needed to think creatively and reapply received wisdom. Even with sound theories, communicators deal with hazardous situations that can lead them to panic just as any stakeholder might, to be short-sighted and to fall back on instincts in the face of extremely demanding communications scenarios.

This chapter examines —

- The key tasks of handling a crisis;
- The need to apply and sometimes innovate upon received wisdom;
- The extent to which crisis communications has changed.

Case Study:
Johnson & Johnson and Poisoned Tylenol —
A Grandfather of Crisis Communications Management

CORPORATE GLANCE: JOHNSON & JOHNSON

Johnson & Johnson is a world leader in pharmaceuticals. Its Tylenol brand of acetaminophen was sold to more than 100 million customers in 1982. Those were impressive numbers for a product that was a market leader and would have earned it a top spot in the Fortune 500 all by itself.

Founded in 1886 as a maker of surgical dressings, Johnson & Johnson (J&J) over the years grew and diversified, producing a range of products and boasting operations in 57 nations and sales in 157 countries. In addition to Tylenol, its products include Acuvue contact lenses, Band-Aid bandages, Clean & Clear facial wash, Johnson's baby products, Neutrogena skin products, and a range of pharmaceuticals and orthopedic devices.

By 1982, Tylenol accounted for:
- 19 per cent of J&J profits for the first three quarters of 1982;
- 13 per cent of the company's year-to-year sales growth;
- 33 per cent of J&J's year-to-year profit growth.

One cautionary note, though: while J&J's approach to this crisis has become the most famous textbook case for how to handle a crisis, its fame rests largely, but not solely, in the circumstances: death, widespread panic, and anxiety. Organizations up to the time of the J&J crisis had handled crises (such as the Ontario government's handling of the Mississauga train derailment of 1979, discussed in Chapter 7) and handled them well. But J&J's crisis management created another breaking moment — a point at which communicators recognized the future potential for large-scale reputation damage and the need to focus on damage control.

Up to that time, many organizations found themselves handling crises that entered the public arena, but society's expectations were different. The public often felt that the corporate crisis was something separate from public interest. Industry regulations and the level of corporate accountability were lower. Companies at the time just didn't have to say as much about what was happening to them as they do now. It wasn't until the 1970s and 1980s that the public, through consumer groups, regulatory watchdogs and the media, turned a probing eye on industries and businesses and began asking the hard questions about corporate responsibility.

But the very universal nature of the crisis — its criminal aspects, the prospect of widespread death delivered through a well-known, trusted product that was supposed to help people, the relative helplessness felt by members of the public — all garnered for J&J an unprecedented amount of attention, thrusting the company into the spotlight. It was a nationwide, high-profile, full-blown crisis the likes of which hadn't been seen before.

THE CRISIS

In the fall of 1982, it was discovered in the Chicago area that capsules in bottles of Tylenol Extra-Strength had been replaced with cyanide-laced capsules, the bottles containing the deadly capsules resealed and placed back on store shelves. Seven people died. J&J and its subsidiary responsible for making Tylenol, McNeil Consumer Products Company, were faced with the worst crisis of the company's history.

J&J learned of the tragedies through a Chicago news reporter. A crisis was sparked that marked the first serious inkling of a major sea change in the media. It also followed a pattern of public behaviour, typified by a thirst for information that was established in Edward L. Bernays's time: if something goes wrong, people want to know about it. Today, more channels, more electronic media, and instant access to information means that 24 hours a day, seven days a week, the media are watching, gathering information, assessing, bouncing their perceptions and information off other sources and building a case about an issue. In 1982, even before the advent of the Internet, news moved quickly. For organizations, the speed of information also meant that a crisis, normally an internal issue that *may* have affected external clients, would become a public issue. A company in the midst of a crisis that once would have appeared only in the business pages could now expect to have its image, credibility and reputation plastered on the front page of newspapers, analyzed on the six o'clock news and talked about on current-events shows. At the time, J&J didn't know just what kind of a precedent it was setting.

TIMING AND AVAILABILITY

In 2004, criticism was directed at U.S. president George W. Bush in the wake of a December 26 earthquake and tsunami that killed more than 100,000 people in southern and Southeast Asia. Despite pledging US$350 million in aid, Bush was criticized for taking a full 72 hours to respond to the tragedy. In Canada, then prime minister Paul Martin was likewise criticized for continuing to vacation in Africa instead of flying home immediately after the devastation was reported. Both delays resulted in negative media attention for the two leaders, and both leaders fell dramatically short of the public's expectations.

The philosopher Spinoza said, "Nature abhors a vacuum." The media, too, abhor a vacuum — an information vacuum. As with many crises, the media were the first to see what was happening with the Tylenol story and they began to fill the information vacuum. Sometimes that vacuum, or information gap, is filled with pure speculation and sensationalism. Such filler is far from harmless: when speculation grows rapidly upon itself, the stage can be set for devastating change in an organization's image.

"Poisoned Tylenol" was the catch phrase that would set off panic among the public. Driven by a need to contain false information, reduce panic and take action to protect the public, J&J created a seven-member strategy team. Company chairman James Burke established two goals: to protect consumers and to save the product.

WHAT THE MEDIA SAID ABOUT TYLENOL

Initially, the media focused on the human face of the crisis, outlining in detail the horrifying deaths of innocent people, particularly the children who had died. Headlines in national print media were potent: "Poison madness in the Midwest," "The Tylenol Scare," "Tylenol, Killer or Cure?"

More than 100,000 news stories ran in American newspapers, along with hundreds of hours of television coverage at both the local and national levels.

As a result, more than 90 per cent of the U.S. population was aware of the crisis within its first week. Some analysts say the Tylenol story received the most news coverage of any topic since the 1963 assassination of John F. Kennedy.[1]

MEDIA AND SENSATIONALISM

In handling a crisis communications story with a strong human element, the media often lead with the sensationalized hook, filling in with more balanced information in later coverage.

In early 2005, *60 Minutes* reported in a story on Internet search-engine giant Google that "Googling" a person or topic will almost invariably pull up a series of hits that are overwhelmingly negative or sensationalistic.[2]

WHAT JOHNSON & JOHNSON DID TO CONTAIN THE CRISIS

J&J took several steps to handle the Tylenol crisis. It —

- Formed a crisis management team;
- Took the approach of "people first, product second," establishing the public's well-being as its first goal and building its strategy around this goal. While reputation management was important, the primary focus was on ensuring the safety of consumers, *then* protecting the image of the product. This was in keeping with the company's credo, "We believe our first responsibility is to the doctors, nurses and patients, to mothers and fathers and all others who use our products and services."
- Created a series of key messages that underscored the company's credo of people first, and it delivered those messages through media interviews, on television, in press conferences and in print advertising;
- Told consumers, through the media, to stop using Tylenol products, and to refrain from use until the company established the root of the tampering;
- Withdrew all Tylenol capsules from the Chicago area;
- Took all Tylenol capsules off store shelves after more contaminated bottles were found. The company recalled 31 million bottles of Tylenol, valued at US$100 million in retail value, and it told the public what it was doing;
- Issued a national media alert that included a 1-800 consumer hotline as

well as a toll-free media line. Every day, the company updated its media line with taped messages;

- Held national press conferences. Additional coverage was gained through shows such as *60 Minutes* and *Donahue*, where senior executives talked about what the company was doing and why it was taking such a drastic course of action;
- Offered financial assistance and counselling to families directly affected by the poisoned capsules;
- Created a now-industry-standard triple-sealed safety package within six months of the crisis — a move that established the company as a caring innovator.

THE RESULTS

The result of J&J's crisis communications strategy was that the company itself was seen as a victim of a crime. The public and media lauded J&J's concerns about safety and its quick action in addressing the crisis. They also recognized the cost to the company, which ran into the tens of millions of dollars. Analysts have lauded J&J for the company's quick action in the face of what was considered a terrorist act, the act of turning a controlled situation into out-of-control chaos. Thus, J&J's main actions have come to be seen as a checklist of basic steps in crisis communications:

1. Work quickly but effectively to identify the issue;
2. Pull together a team;
3. Establish a plan with simple, well-defined goals and key messages;
4. Take action;
5. Communicate with stakeholders and the media and provide regular updates;
6. Follow up;
7. After the crisis is over, evaluate the success of the crisis management actions.

The Tylenol case attracted a great deal of attention from numerous sources. One was the U.S. Department of Defense, which analyzed J&J's approach in its development of effective crisis communications training materials. In a piece for staff handling of crisis situations, the U.S. Department of Defense called J&J's strategies strong and enduring examples of forgiveness and sympathy strategies. The two components within that forgiveness framework were *remediation* and *rectification*. According to the Department of Defense analysis, remediation is offering compensation to help victims of the crisis (in the form of counselling and financial assistance, demonstrating to the media and public a proactive approach). Rectification is taking action to prevent a recurrence of the crisis (the triple-sealed packages).[3]

LESSONS LEARNED

Before the Tylenol crisis, Johnson & Johnson did not have a crisis communications program in place; the company learned about crisis communications the hard way. Yet, its efforts in putting people first and its product second, and in being responsive and direct, worked. Being sympathetic and proactive allowed the company to thrive to the point where it is again a market leader.

Before the crisis, the company handled its media relations primarily through advertising and marketing. Although it tended to respond to the crisis also through advertising, the image of its chairman personally taking responsibility for the crisis helped re-establish the company's positive image in the public's eye.

Communications planning became *de rigueur* after the Tylenol crisis. Public relations vice-presidents were suddenly saying to their presidents, "Let's consider the downside to whatever we might do. Let's look at a 'what if' scenario and see if we can come up with ways to maintain a positive company image."

At that point, the foundation for modern crisis communications was laid. The practice would draw on the same people who handled writing and planning and often the same people who did the day-to-day public relations work. They would now be called on to create crisis plans as well. But now the practice would also draw on outside consultants who could walk companies through scenarios to prepare them for the worst.[4]

Before we look at the Royal Bank of Canada (RBC) crisis of 2004, we need to appreciate that long before this case, planning for a crisis was considered essential to many organizations. Despite the enlightened approach of modern companies and the skills of the communicators they employ, both planning for a crisis and managing communications in the thick of one will always be a hit-and-miss proposition. RBC's crisis took place more than two decades after the Tylenol crisis; countless companies had experienced crises and had planned for their management, or learned from their mistakes. If there is one guiding precept of this book, it is that crises are never homogeneous, no matter how many patterns may be observed. An appreciation of past public relations cases provides models that can be used to create best-fit plans for crisis management within an organization, but once a crisis is sparked, communicators must rely on their flexibility and creativity — generally under intense pressure and scrutiny — and a feel for the events as they unfold.

Case Study: The Royal Bank of Canada Crisis

THE CRISIS

In the summer of 2004, more than 2.5 million RBC clients were without full access to their accounts. The bank told people that it was the result of a computer upgrade that didn't work. Essentially, what should have been a routine programming update resulted in transactions made on May 31 and June 1 (from deposits and withdrawals to payments) not being reflected in client account balances. Human error, a glitch in operations, an oversight by IT personnel? Whatever the cause, a system program that should have been seamlessly integrated and effective just didn't take.

David Moorcroft, senior vice-president of corporate communications at RBC, called it "the perfect storm of technology" in an interview with the *Toronto Star*. Perfect storm is the nautical term for a confluence of winds and waves that come together to create a storm of tremendous proportions.

"An unlikely combination of errors and events came together at the same time," said Moorcroft of the RBC crisis. Everything from incorrect keystrokes to the failure to conduct quality-assurance tests to implementing the programming change at the beginning of the work week instead of on a Friday (which would have given the bank the weekend to fix the problem) caused the crisis to escalate. RBC had to go back and manually correct each transaction. This caused days of delay and further error. From a public relations perspective, that perfect storm created anger, anxiety and resentment among clients in an industry that prides itself on customer service and that deals with money, something crucial to any client's well-being. The lack of high-profile leadership in the form of RBC Financial Group president and CEO Gordon M. Nixon (he was not front-and-centre when the crisis broke) added to the anxiety. Still, RBC's communications group was confident it could handle the crisis.

CORPORATE GLANCE: ROYAL BANK FINANCIAL GROUP

In an era where customer service is everything, Royal Bank Financial Group had reason to be concerned about the computer glitch. An umbrella organization for subsidiaries with five major lines of business in personal and commercial banking, wealth management, insurance, corporate and investment banking, and securities custody and transaction processing, the company is a leader in diversified financial services. It's also Canada's largest bank (by market capitalization and assets). It holds top-ranking industry positions in personal and commercial banking, and continues to rank highly in securities underwriting, wealth management and insurance. The organization has —

- 12 million business, personal and public sector clients in 30 countries
- 1,311 branches and other units, and 4,151 banking machines
- 2.5 million online clients and 2.4 million telephone clients[5]

"[On] day one, our best information indicated that the problem would be corrected by end of day," says Ken Brown, RBC Financial Group's senior advisor, Corporate Communications. "Any impact on clients at that point would be minimal. What we did was communicate with our employees; we updated our website so that appropriate information was there for our clients; we provided appropriate Q&As for our folks at Royal Direct telephone banking [where most of the client questions would be directed] and we responded reactively to media — and there was one media call that day."

The media duly reported on the situation, emphasizing the human element and the effect the glitch had on paycheques going into bank accounts. The *Toronto Star*'s June 9 banner read, "Royal Bank stumbles through computer crisis," while the *Globe and Mail*'s of the same day stated: "RBC faces worst tech nightmare."

MEDIA SAMPLING: THE CANADIAN PRESS, JUNE 3, 2004

THE HEADLINE: "Tens of thousands of payroll deposits delayed by Royal Bank computer backlog."

THE LEAD: "Tens of thousands of Canadians whose pay day was on Thursday were affected by a processing delay at the Royal Bank of Canada, which is still working to catch up on a backlog created earlier this week by a computer software glitch."

THE RBC MESSAGE (Gay Mitchell, executive vice-president, RBC Financial Group): "It's been very frustrating for our customers and inconvenient and we're really very sorry for any inconvenience it has caused. Our customers' business — their money — is safe and secure and there has never been any question of that throughout this."

Initially, some media commentators criticized CEO Gordon Nixon for being "missing in action" during the first crucial hours of the crisis. This perception emphasizes the need for senior people to be seen at the helm and in control during the crucial first hours of a company crisis, at the front end. We saw this in the Tylenol case, when Tylenol's chairman, James Burke, positioned himself as the corporate spokesperson right from the start — the right move for Johnson & Johnson.

RBC TAKES CONTROL

So, how did RBC respond to the crisis? Once a series of identical complaints from customers had been logged and a call was placed to head office, RBC's key senior communicators and executives met to put their plan into action.

This ready crisis plan was used to plot the steps necessary to tackle the crisis, and focused on getting information to clients and media, and demonstrating that steps were being taken to bring the situation under control.

According to Ken Brown, the first step was establishing the necessary information channels between the important divisions of the company. Executives had to be accessible to the bank's communicators. Customer service people taking calls from and meeting with the public, as well as the IT people working on the software problem, had to be able to convey their feedback and progress to the communicators and executives. Only by rapidly creating these channels could the communicators create a reliable and timely flow of information to external publics. Amid a flurry of media interest and anxious customers, RBC sought to provide a flow of information to its publics. Its communications team went to work; a core group of five employees worked on preparing the communications materials.

The company began issuing news releases through Canada NewsWire, a national newswire service, on June 2. The first news release stated: "A processing disruption, which resulted in some RBC Financial Group client transactions not being reflected in account balances, is being resolved." It provided a time-sensitive update, stating that, as of 2:30 p.m. on June 2, "account balances for RBC clients in Canada have been updated to reflect all transactions of May 31." It promised that errors would be fixed for June 1 and 2, and RBC issued a formal explanation from RBC executive vice-president Rod Pennycook:

> We recognize this has caused not only our own clients but also clients of some other institutions considerable inconvenience and for this we sincerely apologize ... We are now completing the process of rechecking and verifying transactions that took place between May 31 and June 2.[6]

Pennycook's statement ended with a promise of continued service delivery: "We have continued to serve our clients through normal channels including branches, ATMs, telephone and online banking for most of their financial needs."

For the next several days, the bank continued to update employees and add information to its website. After June 2, it was apparent the problem wasn't going to be fixed quickly.

"At that point, it went from being more of an issue to being a crisis," says Brown. "We continued updating our sites and we created a special micro-site on processing disruptions on the RBC website with specific information for clients regarding the processing disruption. We engaged other financial institutions to get their cooperation to reverse service fees for their clients who may have been affected."

Beginning on June 1 and continuing for several days, the media went to organizations most directly affected by the RBC crisis (including the Ontario and New Brunswick government staff) for commentary but balanced the story with the key messages delivered by RBC officials. The media followed up with articles that outlined the steps the bank was taking to rectify the situation.

On June 3, the bank sent out another news release, stating that accounts had been updated to reflect transactions through June 1. "Verification of all June transactions is continuing ..." said Pennycook. Pennycook's message encompassed a thank you to customers for their patience:

> We appreciate that our clients have been extremely patient and want to assure them that their money is safe and secure ... Our systems are running well and are making good progress. In addition, we are continuing to be extremely thorough to ensure that all transactions are correctly reflected in client account balances.[7]

On June 4, RBC's news release promised extended hours: "In order to be as accessible as possible to clients who may be experiencing difficulties as a result of this disruption, many RBC branches will be operating under extended hours today." The news release, like the previous releases, provided a website address; in additional, it promised signage at all banks directing customers to those branches with extended hours. RBC realized that during a crisis involving a service interruption, it is often important to introduce increased service levels in as many ways and areas as possible.

FURTHER MEASURES

The company also placed a notice in print media, signed by executive vice-president Gay Mitchell and headlined "To our valued clients and clients of other financial institutions." Its three top messages were—

- "Your money is safe";
- "You won't be charged" (overdraft fees would not be charged because of the disruption);
- "Accessing cash" (money would be available to clients).

On June 8, after most client accounts were up-to-date, Gordon Nixon issued an apology, printed in major newspapers. Carrying the corporate logo of the RBC Financial Group and titled "An apology from RBC Financial Group to our clients, and clients of other financial institutions," it read:

> On behalf of RBC Financial Group, I apologize for the inconvenience and frustration we caused during RBC's processing disruptions last week. Our first priority was to fix the problem. The problem is solved, but we will not consider this issue behind us until we have resolved the consequences for you, no matter where you bank.
>
> We promise to refund banking service charges, fees, overdraft interest or associated past due fees you may have incurred as a result of our disruption. For RBC clients, if you see such a charge that has not been reversed, please bring it to our attention. Clients of other financial institutions should bring any such charges to the attention of their institution. Your financial institution will correct the problem and be reimbursed by RBC.
>
> I would like to thank our clients and clients of other financial institutes for your patience and understanding. I would also like to thank all the other financial institutions in Canada for their cooperation. And I would like to thank every one of our employees for their hard work and commitment.[8]

Nixon also engaged in interviews with a wide range of media between June 8 and 10. He appeared to ask as many questions as he answered but underscored the bank's forgiveness strategy by saying he was certain that customers would forgive RBC for the glitch. "Are there other protocols or processes that would somehow have generated a different result? What could or should have been done that might have ... prevented this from occurring?" he asked in a June 10 Canadian Press interview. There was a rationale behind it: asking questions demonstrated that the company was in touch with all the issues its publics were worried about and that it was as interested in finding solutions as its customers were. Moreover, the successful execution of a forgiveness strategy requires that the company demonstrate, by words and actions, that it is willing to reflect and reform, in addition to restoring normal business and offering compensation. RBC was getting ready to tackle the next steps, and that was the introduction of a formal "Make it right" claims program on June 18. It hired Crawford Adjusters Canada to provide claims administration services. Customers were given an opportunity to obtain claim forms through any RBC branch or business centre; they were also advised of a toll-free number to call and provided with an email address for information on making a claim.

According to Ken Brown, by Thursday, June 10, the crisis was effectively over — the media calls on the crisis ended, the company had done its due diligence in fixing the problem, and the president and CEO had issued a public statement and conducted interviews proactively to deliver positive messages.

One technical publication took some swipes at RBC. ITBusiness.ca warned in a June 10 article by Fawzia Sheikh that "although RBC Financial Group finally outlined details of the technology failure that for days kept money out of millions of Canadian bank accounts, a marketing expert [IBM] warned the bank has only days to do a better job of smoothing things over with customers."[9] But the company was essentially in the clear as far as the public relations aspects of the crisis went. RBC recognized the problem, had worked to solve it and had promised its publics that it would take action to ensure a similar problem would not happen again. From a public relations perspective, with the exception of the late showing of Nixon, the company had handled the situation well.

On June 18, RBC Financial Group issued a release announcing the establishment of a "formal process to review claims for costs or losses incurred as a result of its recent processing disruption."[10] Whereas earlier releases quoted a vice-president, this news release followed the lead of the newspaper advertisement and quoted Nixon: "With the processing disruption behind us, our primary objective now is to make it right for those who were directly impacted. I want to thank those who were inconvenienced for their patience and understanding, and once again offer them my sincere apology."[11]

After the crisis was over, it was time for critical analysis. To that end, the following month, the company conducted a technical post-mortem of the crisis. As reported by the *Toronto Star*'s Erik Heinrich, it involved a third-party analysis by IBM Global Services. IBM Global Services concluded that "the bank had adequate protocols to prevent this kind of error, but that the bank's information technology department failed to follow them. Moorcroft won't say if heads rolled, but he says the bank will make sure staff do not deviate from existing protocols."[12]

FOLLOW-UP AND EVALUATION

Follow-up and evaluation is an essential final phase of crisis communications. Follow-up is at least a two-part process. First, the organization must ensure that all stakeholders have been looked after and the best possible outcomes have been achieved. For Johnson & Johnson, this meant ensuring that the families of the victims were compensated and received counselling. Second, the organization must carefully study a crisis after it has passed in order to review performance and learn from both failures and successes.

RBC's Ken Brown says the company studied its performance carefully to see how well it did. The results:

- RBC received a high level of media coverage: 142 million impressions (often called "hits"), which was greater than any single event affecting the Canadian financial service sector in more than two years;
- Of the coverage, 20 per cent occurred within the first 72 hours;
- Favourable or neutral exposure accounted for 70 per cent of total coverage.

POSITIVE MESSAGES	COVERAGE (%)
Clients affected will be reimbursed for charges	43
RBC apologizes for the problem	28
The money of those affected is safe and secure	24
RBC's computer systems remain safe and stable	2

NEGATIVE MESSAGES	
RBC has missed its own targets	7
RBC lacks adequate customer support	4
Executive management absent during crisis	3
RBC officials have been silent on the issue	3

The positive messages were repeated in the coverage RBC received; the key messages of taking care of clients, ensuring the security of clients' money and apologizing for the mishap went over very well.

How did the messages play out? An RBC-commissioned public opinion poll found a high level awareness of the mishap, at 89 per cent of those polled; 91 per cent believed the disruption could have happened in any financial institution; 52 per cent believed the disruption was a one-time glitch; and 89 per cent expected to keep or maintain their business with RBC.[14]

They were all respectable numbers, and they confirmed for Brown and RBC that the bank had handled the crisis well overall, despite having made mistakes.

COMMON SENSE PRINCIPLES CULLED FROM THE RBC CRISIS

So, how did the staff of RBC handle themselves during this perfect storm?

In general, RBC responded to a unique crisis in accordance with all the principles of good communications practices that Johnson & Johnson had established in its Tylenol crisis. Most important, RBC took responsibility and developed a message for its publics that was direct and forthright and which did not shy away from the problem. These alone are perhaps the most essential principles of effective modern crisis communications.

Let's look at these and other key principles that were reflected in RBC's actions:

1. **Acknowledge the crisis, and do so as soon as possible.** RBC's statement in its first news release of June 2, only 24 hours after the first phone calls came in, reported the problem in clear terms and made a promise to deliver specific results by the next day. Sometimes the handling of a crisis depends not so much on providing a lot of information but on how and when key information is provided. Timing is crucial, both in terms of repairing damage and in setting a course for being seen to be taking charge.

   Crisis acknowledgement is a way to focus a company's external publics — and its employees — on the main issue instead of on tangents, speculation or spin. It means the company is not trying to hide anything, exaggerate or underplay its involvement or responsibility. Simply taking this first step puts communicators on a course for tackling a tough problem rather than thinking and acting solely in terms of the perceived culpability of the organization.

2. **Put people first.** "Our focus was to deal with the technology issue, but first of all to deal with our clients — keeping them up-to-date and making sure they were able to get cash," says Ken Brown. "Some media wanted to get into the nitty-gritty on the technology side. We didn't want it to become a technology story; [we wanted to say,] 'Your funds are safe, the problem's been identified, we're just catching up on the backlog. The first and foremost priority is looking after our clients.'" Indeed, customer service had to come first; any company knows that what will matter to its client base is that the service provided to them will not be disrupted for long. On its website, RBC expresses its vision as: "Always earning the right to be our clients' first choice." That vision is necessarily underscored in the approach the company takes to its handling of crisis communications.

3. **Decide on the key messages.** Make sure the company's message is clear and people-focused, and promises action. RBC's message of acknowledging the inconvenience, clearly apologizing and stating that "our customers' business" comes first was well received by both the media and the public.

4. **Take responsibility for, and ownership of, the crisis.** Taking responsibility for a problem doesn't mean the company is also accepting blame for it.

It means the company is doing something about the situation. Taking responsibility for a problem delivers a clear message to the company's clients and to the community at large that the company will take care of problems resulting from its participation in the lives of its clients and in the communities affected by its operations. RBC was careful to express those notions of responsibility in Gordon Nixon's print advertisement, in which he said that RBC was concerned about rectifying unrecorded transactions for everyone, whether RBC bankers or not. He made sure to say that non-RBC customers would be compensated by their own banks, at the expense of RBC.

Taking *ownership* is taking responsibility a step farther. It means that key people monitor the ongoing problems and the implementation of the solution, right up to the follow-up process, to ensure that publics are satisfied and that relationships have been cared for. This requires that the crisis team be broadly empowered to ensure a solution is working and is being communicated to stakeholders properly. Ownership means having the knowledge, experience and power to do a job without requiring a lot of reviews and approvals from upper and lower levels of management that would slow down what must be an agile communications function. RBC corporate communications staff members were able to confidently develop messages, set up media interviews, and research and deliver information in a way that helped boost the company's image.

5. **Deliver solutions from the top.** The apology printed in major newspapers on June 8 was signed by RBC's president and CEO. Leadership means the person at the top takes responsibility for the crisis and does not delegate that task to subordinates. Ken Brown admits that the first advertisement, signed by Gay Mitchell, generated some criticism. In retrospect, the advertisement should have been signed by Nixon.

6. **Make a promise to deliver on.** RBC put itself in a position to be held accountable for its actions. It committed to creating results for customers, often giving itself deadlines and thereby providing customers with expectations by which to judge. Doing this reinforces to customers the company's desire to satisfy them, and it places the company on a schedule and gives it goals to follow through on.

7. **Acknowledge harm or inconvenience to stakeholders, and thank them for their patience and understanding.** Nothing connects a firm with its stakeholders more effectively than bringing common ground into the picture. Common ground is created by sympathizing with customers as people who have a right to be upset because of the effects of the crisis on them. In finding this common ground, spokespeople present the company goals of a return to profitable business as being identical with compensation and return to good service in the minds of internal and external stakeholders.

HOW DOES RBC'S CRISIS DIFFER FROM JOHNSON & JOHNSON'S?

The Royal Bank of Canada's crisis flashpoint certainly bears little resemblance to that of Johnson & Johnson's. RBC's service meltdown was not the result of a software saboteur or a terrorist. RBC had a problem with its technology, compounded by failures to follow safety protocols within its own IT department. What was it up against that differed from the Tylenol case? Remember, the bank found that millions of customers were not receiving full service. To what extent could and did RBC follow Johnson & Johnson's model? Could RBC expect to use as successfully a forgiveness strategy?

© Mark Heath/Dist. by United Feature Syndicate, Inc.

For starters, this breakdown in service flew in the face of basic precepts that go with the corporate world, including the goal of a 99.9 per cent efficiency of systems, which means that systems can be down for only hours a year. The problem, too, was compounded by its occurrence on the heels of other problems in other businesses. These ranged from Air Canada's crisis with its reservations and check-in system in August 2003 (caused by the Blaster virus) to TD Bank Financial Group's motherboard-generated computer problems that threw its debit-card system for a loop in 2001. Then there were trading issues at the Toronto Stock Exchange that caused software to crash in 1997 and a 1996 software crisis for the Canadian Imperial Bank of Commerce in eastern Canada.

After a succession of similar crises in the same industry, stakeholders may justifiably level their frustration with the vulnerability of that industry at the very next victim, blaming *it* for failing to take adequate measures to protect itself from a clear and present threat. People's expectations for an industry, or for a single organization, are one of the main factors that precondition a crisis. In the case of RBC, the consumer expectation is continuous service. Consumers expect RBC to protect itself from software malfunctions after having seen other firms in the industry suffer problems. Unlike Johnson & Johnson, RBC had examples to learn from and the time and resources to protect itself. The RBC computer glitch would have been a different and possibly less serious crisis had public expectations been different.

Given the environment in which it was operating, RBC may have failed seriously in issues identification. It had sufficient time and ample case studies, old and current, to tip it off. Surprisingly, this failure to follow the procedures that would ensure smooth operations is a defining aspect of this and many modern crises. It's strange, considering that all businesses today are so dependent on the hardware and software that support every aspect of their operations, that in many cases, banking services included, business itself is largely intangible, comprising electronic files and data. Therefore, safety and prevention protocols for software, databases, and so on should be part of any company's strategy for prevention, and it should be recognized as a possible issue in most any communications department. Furthermore, RBC has 35 communicators working in several layers of its operations, including the executive level. Why weren't the IT protocols followed by an organization so invested in effective communications and, presumably, crisis planning? It might even appear that the communicators at RBC do not normally take responsibility for problems in core business functions but only for effective communications with stakeholders once a crisis hits.

It is important, then, to appreciate that not all companies integrate communications factors into other primary business functions to the same degree. Indeed, the degree to which communications are integrated into a business says much about how essential a function it is held to be at a given firm. At RBC, where communications are an essential function with a role that includes advising on business operations, fault can be found in issues identification and, by extension, crisis planning. But it is also important to mitigate this by saying that no company can see itself with perfect clarity, no matter how many talented professionals are on the payroll. Ironically, companies often see themselves in greatest clarity at times of crisis.

For communicators, there is therefore an implicit decision to be made about auditing their own practices. When and how thoroughly need this be done? This is akin to deciding how often to get a physical examination at the doctor's office — when we are ill, when we are healthy, or just once a year? What about a high-performance athlete, an elderly person diagnosed with heart disease who still enjoys running marathons? What extra tests are added to the checkup? If a company maintained an endless vigil over all its operations, it could not function well, nor would it necessarily gain more perspective or a better vision of itself. Good issues management is not about seeing all possible futures but about trying to find the blind spots that could be truly dangerous to a company's image and operations.

Conclusion

Since the 1970s, the corporate attitude to crisis has changed: no longer is a crisis seen as something exclusive to the company, affecting only the company and perhaps some of its external stakeholders. Before 1970, the general feeling was that the corporate crisis was something separate from the public interest, but increasing industry regulations and a higher level of corporate accountability began to change this attitude. The advent of consumer groups, regulatory watchdogs and greater media scrutiny also meant that corporations had to become accountable for their actions. This in effect was the beginning of modern crisis communications. The people who handled writing and planning in an organization, and often those in public relations, were now also responsible for creating crisis plans. As the examples of Johnson & Johnson's poisoned Tylenol and the Royal Bank of Canada's computer glitch have shown, there are several steps communicators must take when their organization is faced with a crisis:

1. Work quickly but effectively to identify the issue;
2. Pull together a team;
3. Establish a plan with simple, well-defined goals and key messages;
4. Take action;
5. Communicate with stakeholders and the media and provide regular updates;
6. Follow up with media and stakeholders;
7. After the crisis is over, evaluate the success of the crisis management actions.

Key Concepts

KEY MESSAGES: Messages delivered to media and the public that underscore the organization's vision and mandate. In Johnson & Johnson's poisoned-Tylenol crisis, those messages focused on putting people first and the product second. The company based its concerns on protecting the health and well-being of its consumers before focusing on protecting and rebuilding the image of its product.

OWNERSHIP: Taking ownership of the crisis; take responsibility for bringing it to an end.

RECTIFICATION: Taking action to prevent a recurrence of the crisis.

REMEDIATION: Offering compensation to help victims of the crisis; this could be anything from counselling to financial assistance.

SENSATIONALISM: A sensationalized or negative angle with which the media often lead a story, bringing in more balanced information in later coverage.

Part I: Interview and Exercises

KERRY PEACOCK,
Senior Vice-President, Corporate and Public Affairs, TD Bank Financial Group

Kerry Peacock has served as senior vice-president, Corporate and Public Affairs, at TD Bank Financial Group since September 2001. Her mandate is to ensure that the bank's reputation is protected and enhanced through effective communications to both internal and external stakeholders. Peacock previously served as vice-president of internal communications with TD; she holds a Certified General Accountant designation and has a Master of Business Administration from the Richard Ivey School of Business. She was named a Dobson Fellow for 2005 by the Dobson Centre for Entrepreneurial Studies at McGill University and serves as a director of First Nations Bank of Canada and of Toronto's cultural and entertainment complex, Ontario Place.

ON HANDLING CRISES AT TD

"The bank has a business continuity management system in place: every area has a plan that asks, 'If X happened, what would you do?' We plan for it now, so that we don't have to plan later, when time is a factor. This means that when a crisis breaks, it's dealt with in an almost automatic way. For instance, if there's a power outage, we know how to deal with it — a structure is in place. We also have a crisis management book, which includes templates of the crisis communications plan and news releases, key client contact information and key messages for up to 10 scenarios. It's a tool kit we update regularly. And we hire outside firms to come in and run exercises with the executive team and the technology personnel. In these exercises, a crisis situation is simulated and participants are required to respond as they are expected to if the event were real — walking through the crisis management of it."

ON IDENTIFYING ISSUES

"Environmental scanning plays an essential role in determining whether there is a crisis. The bank has an internal process that alerts staff when we need to escalate our response to a crisis level. In fact, we use crisis response tools in many day-to-day activities. For instance, let's say a customer phones the call centre about an error on his or her account statement. It might turn out that a staff member made an error in posting and so the statement is easily corrected, but it might be that something is wrong with the system and thousands of statements are incorrect. The call centre staff are checking and asking, 'How big is this problem?' Another part of environment scanning involves learning from others — for instance, computer problems encountered by other major corporations — and saying, 'That happened to them and here is how they responded … what we would do?' We need to look at what *we* do and how *we* need to do it and not simply say, 'Well, that's *their* problem.'"

ON WORKING WITH DECISION MAKERS

"When a crisis breaks, communicators must have access to the organization's decision makers. This means that those decision makers must have an appreciation for the role communicators play during a crisis. They must also recognize that a crisis communications plan is something that needs to be in place in advance, not written during a crisis.

"Communicators sometimes need to work through influence — to say to the decision makers: 'If you do X, we think it will take you *here*; if you do Y, it might take you *there*.' It's the job of communicators to help their organization's decision makers understand their choices, as well as the impact of the decision that they're making, from the perspective of the publics being addressed."

ON DEALING WITH THE MEDIA

"More and more, media, like many businesses, find themselves operating with smaller staffs, with those employees handling increased workloads. For example, in a print environment, reporters now have the media outlet's website to write for. And they are, as always, trying to write on complicated matters quickly. Communicators need to spend time with the media, providing backgrounders and other material, when the organization is *not* in a crisis situation, so that the media have an understanding of how the organization works *before a crisis hits*. Spending time with the media — setting up lunches for the organization's executives with the media, setting up meetings between the organization's media relations people and the media — is essential. It's bound to help both the media and the organization when crisis hits and response needs to be quick; communicators need to understand what drives the media. It's relationship management: communicators manage relationships with the media — and they need to see it that way.

"I strongly believe that communicators can choose to have their side represented in the reporter's story or not. The news story is going to be written anyway. Participating in it is better than stepping back and waiting to see what will be said, and hoping that the crisis will just go away."

Exercise: A Death in Professional Sports

The news item in Canadian newspapers in April 2005 was a small sidebar carried by news services and used to fill a few column inches: a defensive lineman on the Los Angeles Avengers of the Arena Football League died after making a routine tackle in a game. Al Lucas was healthy, young (26 years old), married and a father of two. A former college all-star who played briefly in the National Football League, he had been playing with the Avengers for two years. During the tackle, a player on the opposing team, blocking for his teammate, inadvertently drove his leg into Lucas's helmet, forcing Lucas's head down and injuring his spinal cord. The lineman was taken to hospital and pronounced dead after attempts to resuscitate him failed.

THINK TANK

Alone or with a partner, take five minutes to analyze this event:

1. What questions might the media ask about Lucas's death?
2. What people will the media want to talk to for information and quotes?

Write down as many ideas as you can come up with and develop three key messages. Then reflect on the situation: if you were representing the Arena Football League, what would you say about the player's death?

Exercise: A Company in Crisis over Its Principles

Who today doesn't know of Wal-Mart? The ubiquitous merchandiser has made a name for itself selling goods at low prices; at the same time, it has attracted criticism from many for paying low wages, being anti-union and driving mom-and-pop stores out of business in the towns where it sets up shop. The company made it onto *Fortune* magazine's Top 500 list in 2005, with 2004 sales of over US$288.8 billion, up 11 per cent from its 2003 revenues.

Wal-Mart's traditional anti-union stance is well known. According to Robert Slater in his book *The Wal-Mart Triumph*, Wal-Mart founder Sam

Walton was adamantly against unions. According to Slater, Walton felt that introducing unions into his stores would only increase his costs and went so far as to say he would rather close a location than accept a union.

The unions clearly had a bone to pick with Wal-Mart. In the fall of 2005, the United Food and Commercial Workers (UFCW) and the Service Employees International Union targeted Wal-Mart with more than 4,000 activities designed to discredit the company. Through their websites Walmartwatch.com and WakeupWalmart.com, they kept track of Wal-Mart's adherence (or lack of) to its stated environmental commitments, such as zero waste and a commitment to selling products that sustain resources and the environment (e.g., recycled materials), and created a Site Fight of the Week, which kept track of where the next North American Wal-Mart was to be built and suggested ways to fight the company's expansion. The organizations also co-released a documentary titled *Wal-Mart: The High Cost of Low Price.*

Wal-Mart responded by establishing its own "war room" in its Bentonville, Arkansas, headquarters to plan strategy to fight the union's accusations of low wages and poor working conditions.

THE ISSUE

In Quebec in early 2005, Wal-Mart came under fire for its plans to shut down a store in Jonquière, in opposition to a move by the UFCW to union-ize that store's employees in February 2005. The UFCW claimed to represent 1.4 million workers in supermarkets and food processing, meatpacking and other industries and was anxious to bring Wal-Mart employees into the fold. Union representatives were angry at the company's response and promised to gird themselves for battle. Some consumers in the town promised to conduct what turned out to be, for most, a short-lived boycott. This came on the heels of a bomb threat against a Wal-Mart in Gatineau, Quebec, and a statement by a Parti Québécois leader that his "advanced social conscience" would never allow him to shop in a Wal-Mart again.

THINK TANK

1. What is the public's attitude toward Wal-Mart?
2. Will the public likely rally behind Wal-Mart?
3. How might this union battle affect public perception of the company?
4. If you were working in corporate communications for Wal-Mart, what key messages would you develop for the company, given the current sentiment toward it?
5. What messages could the company develop if there were a boycott of its stores?
6. Speculate: if the company closed the Jonquière store but was forced to reopen it, what would its key message then be?
7. If you were working for the union, what would your key messages be?

II

Communications Planning:
Coming out on Top

3 Identifying and Monitoring Issues

What is the issues stage of planning, why is it important, and how do we do it? The issues stage of crisis communications is, of all the stages, probably the most worthwhile to study, given its importance to preserving a company's reputation. It is the stage at which a company exerts the most control over problems that could turn into full-blown crises, with all the attendant risks of loss — loss of life, reputation and revenue. In this chapter we consider the following:

- The interests of the essential "publics" that communicators serve as they draft their internal and external communications plan, as well as their policies;
- The possible issues that face the organization. Issues are any potential outcome that could lead to a negative perception of the company that in turn harms its reputation, profile or business. We will study how to identify issues and recognize the difference between an issue and a crisis.
- How leadership affects both the messages communicators deliver and the credibility of their organization;
- How the emotional tone, and the emotion-versus-logic balance communicators establish at the outset of a crisis, affects the organization in the long term.

Looking Out for Trouble:
The Communicator in the Crow's Nest

Before communicators find themselves in a crisis, they need to think about what they know about their organization and its relationship with their publics. They must look ahead, anticipate what *might* happen to their organization and prepare.

Communicators plan for potential crises by looking closely at daily business practices and asking:

- What are things that could go wrong on a daily basis? What are those things that we have control of here, right now, in the organization? It could be in a product or a process. What mistakes could we make in processes that we use to create and deliver our products?
- What could go wrong outside the organization, possibly with a supplier, or because of a natural disaster or a terrorist attack? What would we do in these cases? What backup systems do we have in place?
- What issues are looming on the horizon? What information have we gathered from our sources that tell us something might go wrong?

Communicators must also keep in mind that there are potential crises they will not be able to anticipate. Part of their planning for those cases must focus on having a sound set of business practices and an established vision, mission and values statement. Communicators will find that, when an organization has a strong sense of itself and its philosophy, many decisions and key messages to be made during an unanticipated crisis are more or less already written; the crisis team must not panic and instead look to what the company stands for.

Increasingly, however, communicators are being asked to anticipate the unexpected, and to think of the widest-ranging possibilities in terms of a crisis. Banks and other major corporations, for instance, have a "war room" ready to go to if their headquarters are destroyed in a terrorist attack. They will have information stored at this second secure location, and they will run through possible scenarios involving the loss of their headquarters and their response in those situations.

SUN TZU AND CRISIS

The Chinese general Sun Tzu (*c.* 450–380 BCE) is seen by many historians as a composite of military ideals. Sun Tzu is credited with composing brilliant pieces of military thought, of strategic and tactical insight, gathered in his singular text *The Art of War,* written around 400 BCE.

The image of Sun Tzu is of a general whose battlefield tactics guarantee success, but who also vehemently opposed war. In *The Art of War,* he stated that the first rule was not to make war: do everything you can to avoid it. War costs a government, a society and a country dearly. Despite his reservations about war, Sun Tzu said that war "is a matter of vital importance to the State; the province of life or death; the road to survival or ruin."[1] But if war is the only option, ensure that you enter it with a decisive plan: to win.

It is the same for modern companies and crisis: the last thing they want is a crisis. But communicators have to recognize emerging issues, see how they might turn into a crisis, and have a plan in place. When communicators approach the crisis, they must ensure that they have the interests of their organization in mind. They should come away with a sense of having won, even if the gains appear to be small. Winning in a crisis means winning back the organization's reputation, the confidence of its publics, or its market position. As the seventeenth-century samurai Miyamoto Musashi wrote in *A Book of Five Rings,* sometimes winning a battle is a matter of just surviving — to have come away whole is the goal.[2]

Sun Tzu appraised warfare in terms of five basic factors: moral influence, weather, terrain, command and doctrine. These factors can be easily applied to working with crisis.

- **Moral influence:** For Sun Tzu, this was the ability to persuade people to take the right actions in war. For communicators, this is the human factor in their crisis — *who* the crisis has affected and *how* it affects them, and *why* action needs to be taken. Communicators think about how to influence people to do the right thing, to move with them toward a common goal. They have to be focused on the greater good, thinking about how the crisis has affected people first, then the organization. Communicators' ability to engage in moral influence is reflected in their ability to feel out affected parties, to understand how they can work with others, both inside and outside the organization, and to create a common sense of purpose that will allow them to work together to achieve a greater goal. Communicators may think with their minds, but they lead with their hearts.

- **Weather:** Sun Tzu understood the influence of sun, rain and wind on his battlefield tactics. For communicators, weather can be thought of as the variations in the political, social and market climate that will affect the perceptions of the organization's publics. Looking at weather involves looking at how the recent and ever changing social context within a city, a country or even the world will affect how communicators' messages are received. Weather is also about how publics react, what they are saying both *about* the organization and *to* the organization. As such, crisis communicators too can affect the weather in which their army will fight.

- **Terrain:** Sun Tzu saw a rocky slope or an expanse of water as a challenge to implementing his strategy for winning a war. He knew he had to cross boundaries to meet the enemy and do battle. Modern-day crisis communicators look at their terrain in terms of the contacts they must make and the people they must reach with their message to win support or understanding. At the onset of a crisis, they decide who they need to reach and try to predict how those contacts may react in a crisis. Are some key people, whether journalists, members of regulatory boards or leaders of community groups, open or closed to giving these messages to the wider publics they represent or otherwise have access to? Are the gatekeepers friendly or hostile? Communicators don't necessarily see enemies on the horizon, but they do need to ask themselves, "Who do we need to talk to and what do we need to say?"

- **Command:** For Sun Tzu, it was as simple as being there to take charge, to rally the troops, to deliver messages of inspiration and to lead. Communicators are often called on to provide leadership during a crisis or to help their organization's executives understand all the dimensions of the leadership role those executives are called on to play as they come before the company's publics. Command to a communicator is principally two things: first, the organization of the company's people into strong response units during a crisis; and second, the projection of a strong leader to represent the company with a single face and voice, and who presents the company's actions and messages to its publics. Communicators are always heavily involved in the first command role but are usually the coaches and advisors of someone else in the second capacity.

- **Doctrine:** This is the set of overriding principles governing the development of a strategy that allows the organization to deliver on its goals. Sun Tzu saw doctrine as a set of principles for proper behaviour, an authoritative set of beliefs that would guide his army to victory. Communicators must look to their organization's vision, mission and values to guide them, and at each step ask, "Are we maintaining our commitment to the organization's doctrine as we manage our crisis?"

Of all five of Sun Tzu's factors, moral influence may be the most important for communicators. Communicators' ability to understand and measure the emotional response of their publics during a crisis, find a common ground, and work with them is probably the most important element in strategic thinking. It is by taking people's emotions into account that communicators are able to manage, to a degree, the responses of the various publics affected.

FACTORING IN EMOTIONS

Why emotions? As motivational guru Dale Carnegie once said, "When dealing with people, let us remember we are not dealing with creatures of logic. We are dealing with creatures of emotion, creatures bustling with prejudices and motivated by pride and vanity."[3] When handling a crisis, it's wise to understand that external stakeholders and the public have invested in the organization at an emotional level. Advertising campaigns, for example, appeal entirely to emotions. Companies spend billions of dollars on branding in order to engender and nurture an emotional identification by their publics with a brand. These "creatures of emotion" are filtering the messages communicators draft, along with what they know of the company's behaviour, and deciding whether they fit with their own set of ideas about what is right and what is wrong. If communicators jostle those emotions, people stop buying from the organization if it is a manufacturer or retailer; they stop supporting if it is a not-for-profit; they stop donating if it is a charity.

Communicators recognize that there is a balance to be struck between logic and emotion. They may deal with issues in a logical way, while recognizing that their publics will continue to process their messages and actions emotionally.

A case in point: In October 2005, an earthquake devastated South Asia, hitting parts of Pakistan hard. It was estimated that up to 4 million people were missing. Canada immediately pledged $300,000 for earthquake victims. The federal government increased that amount to $20 million a couple of days later. Still, the government was criticized for reacting slowly; $300,000 compared with $20 million is a small sum, given the dollar volumes that the public is used to hearing about when it comes to government programs. We can open a newspaper or click on the news anytime and see just how much our government can spend, and how well it can justify its expenses. So for the federal government to take the initial amount of $300,000 and then multiply it almost 70 times over, then present it two days later and expect that the public will accept it suggests that the government was at first either scrimping or did not understand the impact of the crisis, or both. The government's response was succinct, with International Cooperation minister Aileen Carroll attempting to balance the pronounced emotional tone of the event with sound logic:

> Carroll rejected criticism that Ottawa had not reacted fast enough to the current crisis. She said it was important to make money available on the ground quickly and then to conduct a needs assessment. "However much we may emotionally react, we have to react effectively. The first thing to do is get an assessment, put the money in with the United Nations and others, and then as [the assessment] comes back to you, then step forward with a large amount, as we did.[4]

Sun Tzu's moral influence has application here, in that the federal government was trying to do the right thing, first by giving money immediately, then raising the contribution soon afterward. But the action — or how it was perceived — fell short with many people. Still, Carroll engaged the Canadian public initially by emphasizing that it is correct behaviour to give assistance to people in time of need. Even though a knee-jerk reaction from her publics might have been, "It isn't enough," Carroll correctly stated that giving, connecting and helping the unfortunate was paramount, and that giving more money was the natural outcome as more information became available. A first-aid specialist helping someone in an accident will offer immediate aid, first checking breathing, then bleeding, then consciousness — in that order — and providing additional care once the initial assessment is done. In the case of the South Asian earthquake, the federal government tried to lead with its heart. Granted, it might have been better to present a statement that the assessment was proceeding at the time of the first pledge, demonstrating that there was some understanding of what was happening instead of waiting for criticism to come and then being in response mode.

THE KEY MESSAGE

The key message (also called core message) is the "sound bite" that delivers the main idea communicators want to get across to their publics. It is straightforward, definitive and action-oriented. It's designed to not leave a lot of room for speculation, and it summarizes the organization's approach to handling the crisis. Key messages are meant to leave the publics with the impression that the organization has done its homework and is working hard to resolve the crisis. Key messages will be developed as communicators work through a crisis, capturing recognition of the matter at hand, its cause and its resolution. They will be found in all the materials communicators create and deliver to their publics.

Key messages during a crisis must be short and clear. They must take into account what may happen in the future. A proactive stance forestalls negative events by dealing with their causes before they happen, and it answers questions that will likely be generated by the company's publics. It manages the "what next?" feeling that publics have during a crisis. Telling people "This is what is happening now and this is what *may* happen" gives them a chance to put the information into context and prepare for the next stage.

Here's an example: A mining company has a cave-in, trapping 20 miners deep underground. Company officials are unsure how many are alive. Contact is made with six of the miners (and the media knows this), but there is still a chance that the other miners died. Company officials, knowing the dangers that exist in mines, are highly unlikely to come out with a statement of unbridled confidence such as, "We're certain we can get them all out alive." Instead, it makes sense that they proceed with cautious optimism: "We are overwhelmingly glad that several of the miners are able to communicate with us. Unfortunately, we do not know the current condition of the other 14 miners, but we are hopeful that they are safe. However, we must be cautious because we have a difficult job ahead to get to all of these miners. Please be assured that we are using all our available resources to get them out safely and back to their families."

> "If you don't have your message ready, and get it out to the public quickly, you're leaving it to somebody else to make their own message. Conversely, if you jump out too quickly in front of the media before you have all the information, sometimes you can precipitate a crisis where none existed. Avoid the knee-jerk reaction."[5]
>
> — Rick Winston, president, Win-Win Communications, Toronto

Identifying Issues: The Start of the Plan

WHAT IS AN ISSUE?

Issues are significant to communicators because through identifying them, they are able to recommend actions that will benefit the company and its publics before a crisis occurs — in fact, their identification will often help communicators head off a crisis before it starts. An issue, for the purposes of this book, is any potential event, procedure, practice, action or statement by a member of the company or any of the company's internal or external stakeholders that might trigger a crisis.

Quality of service or products and good treatment of customers, employees and the public are, of course, ongoing issues, but these really are under the umbrella of marketing factors and forces. They are broken into how a company positions itself in the market, monitors its sales and service, and does research and development. The issues we are considering in this book are those that may manifest themselves in uncontrolled damage to a company, its publics and the company's reputation. These issues are entirely different from those that, if not addressed, lead to a gradual loss of sales.

Issues monitoring is about reputation management. This takes place in the face of possible doubts, accusations or allegations on the part of a company's publics. These concerns may have already been expressed in the past, or they could be looming in the future. Either way, they result from a change in the community or in the market in which the business operates.

Issues can generally be expressed as a question about the organization's practices, people, or products and services. The answer may be positive or negative, depending on the person's point of view. For instance, if a pulp-and-paper company is involved in logging in British Columbia, does it have effective training for foresters working in its clear-cutting operations? Is the company responsible for loss of biodiversity by replacing forests with fields of only the trees useful for pulp and paper? Should the company be allowed to continue this practice? All these questions reflect issues that emerge from, and are implicit in, the operation of a pulp-and-paper business in the twenty-first century. This is considered a moral gap, not a value gap.

> Issues generally exist in the perceived morality gap between a company's conduct and the expectations a company's publics have regarding that conduct.

If a person expects a good cup of coffee for a reasonable price and gets a lousy cup for a high price, that person is not liable to feel victimized, except in the most rhetorical of senses, but there is a gap in the *value* expectation that will lose the company sales. A communicator's business is to constantly assess how much gap there is between the company's *moral* conduct and its publics' expectations. Anything that falls within this gap is worth considering as an issue of the kind we are covering in this book.

For example, a communicator working for Rockstar Games, the makers of Grand Theft Auto: San Andreas doesn't ask, "What are people's attitudes toward our video games?" This kind of analysis is the province of market research, and of value gaps. Instead a communicator asks, "What does this string of phone calls from parents enraged about the violence in our Grand Theft Auto game mean, and what is the potential harm to our publics and to us? What will it mean to our long-term reputation as a games maker?" The issues communicators are focused on tend to turn up in specific, concrete events, especially if they have the potential to become a crisis. They turn up, as in this example, because of a *moral* issue. Good communicators are able to anticipate issues long before angry phone calls, letters, petitions or protests bring them into sharper focus. A good issues approach would have yielded the question, "What if some of our customers are offended by the contents of our game once it hits the shelves?" In some cases, of course, that can be a selling point and shrewd youth-targeting marketers know that anything that Mom and Dad disapprove of can generate dollars for them. It certainly worked for a legion of heavy-metal rockers who bit the heads off animals and knew well the adage "There's no such thing as bad publicity." Still, the tipping point may come when suddenly the swell of anger is so overwhelming that it profoundly affects the company's reputation and it crosses a line. That's what communicators are watching out for.

TWO KINDS OF ISSUES

The difference between the second and third question above is the difference between identification of a *potential* issue and a *concrete* issue, respectively. A potential issue is something ethereal, which could have the potential to become concrete. In the Grand Theft Auto example, the answer to the question "What if some customers are offended by the content in our games?" is a matter of speculation, but it's certainly worth planning for, even before the first complaint is made. Prior to distribution, it is a potential issue and it is at that moment that the most control can be exercised. The irony is that the earlier an issue is tackled, the more power and choice a communicator has in dealing with it. The moment the phone starts to ring with scandalized parents, faith groups and educators, the issue is concrete. A concrete issue is more serious because it must be treated as having the potential to become a crisis. It has gone beyond the realm of mere possibility: there is beyond a doubt danger to the product and to the company. Communicators must act, their options are fewer, and their time is short.

> "I think today we're more disciplined than we were before in having formal processes. The worst-case scenario is getting a phone call from somebody outside who tells you what the crisis is. One of the things that I always stress is that if there is a problem, we are always better off having discovered it ourselves. Whatever it is, it's a heck of a lot better for us to self-identify and then come up with a solution than to have a radio interviewer or a press release or a customer bring it to our attention."[6]
> — Robert E. Waite, senior vice-president, Communications and Stakeholder Relations, Canada Post Corporation, on examining issues[6]

Communicators can deal with issues flagged far in advance and prevent them from becoming real issues with negative feedback that may or may not ignite a crisis. Therefore, the value of issues identification is twofold: first, the company can anticipate the crisis in advance and plan to minimize its harmful effects; and second, the company can observe its own potential issues and plan to dissolve them before real events turn them into concrete issues.

CONCRETE ISSUES VERSUS CRISIS

So, what separates a concrete issue from a crisis? First of all, not all concrete issues, not even those that go unremedied, will become crises. But even an issue that, left unaddressed, would not cause a crisis would likely be detrimental to the organization's reputation. Here's the distinction:

Crisis: A crisis is an event that poses a danger to the organization's stability or progression; it has temporary out-of-control elements that demand immediate action. It can be triggered by issues that have been allowed to develop unchecked or unsolved. Or, in the case of a natural disaster, it has been thrust on the organization. Coping with a crisis requires an amount of the company's resources (in the form of time, money and energy) that is generally out of proportion to the organization's regular day-to-day activities. In a crisis, control is a matter of tackling the crisis as soon as possible.

Concrete issue: A concrete issue is something that can still be controlled. It is any potential issue that has manifested itself as negative attention to the company. This negative feedback may be a forerunner of an imminent crisis, or it may be an indication of a controllable but deteriorating situation with a company's publics. Harm to the company's reputation is a given, and a crisis is likely if a crisis team does not act quickly and effectively. The point at which a concrete issue becomes a crisis cannot be precisely or quantitatively defined outside a specific case. In general, the tipping point from concrete issue to crisis is the point at which a company's publics' negative reactions are energetic or contagious enough that they cannot be diverted, absorbed or otherwise controlled without an extremely expensive and time-consuming reorientation of a company's key personnel, focused specifically at repairing relationships. Smart communicators will attack a concrete issue, once identified, with all the resources they can summon. The reason is that a focused, intense effort at this dangerous but relatively controllable stage along the issue-to-crisis continuum is likely to cost a fraction of the overall cost of a resulting crisis.

Another example: A manufacturer of child car seats receives communication from a federal standards association about a buckle that comes loose on child car seats manufactured by a rival company. This must be treated as a concrete issue, because the potential issue expressed by the question "Is our product as safe as we say it is?" has manifested itself in a specific communication from one of the company's publics. That the company's rival received the communication should not mean that communicators treat their competitor's concrete issue as merely a potential issue for themselves. The models are similar, and due diligence is required. The company should double check the safety of its product and recall its car seats if indeed there is a problem, or take immediate steps to reassure its publics that the company has monitored the situation with the rival seat, and that after a study of its own, found no problem with its product. It just makes sense to communicate with publics — they see a child seat first, then a company name. Their concern is with product safety and the safety of their children first, and then with who made it.

If the company had not done due diligence and if a child was hurt as a result of a similar problem with the seat buckle, the scenario would likely skip the concrete-issue phase, the company vaulted into a full-blown crisis along with its competitor. Media scrutiny and investigation would soon reveal that the company had ignored the warning to its rival — a warning that should have prompted the company's analysis of its similar product — and a communiqué to its publics that the problem was rectified or the concerns unfounded.

ROLLOVERS SPIN OUT OF CONTROL AND INTO A CRISIS: FORD AND BRIDGESTONE

From this point onward, the terms *concrete issue* and *potential issue* are used only when necessary to make a fine distinction; the inclusive term *issue* is used to discuss either a concrete or a potential issue.

An example of an issue that spun out into a crisis was the Bridgestone/Ford tire crisis in 2000, when over 6.5 million tires were recalled because of defects that caused more than 200 deaths and 700 injuries from rollovers in (mainly) Ford Explorer vehicles.

For years, Firestone tires, manufactured by Japanese tire maker Bridgestone Corporation, were installed on Ford Explorer vehicles. But by 2000, U.S. regulatory experts began to notice a problem: Bridgestone's ATX, ATX II, and Wilderness AT tires on Ford Explorers had a high failure rate. Tire blowouts were causing SUV rollovers — when a tire lost pressure, the vehicle would roll. In May 2000, the National Highway Traffic Safety Administration sent a letter to Ford and also to Bridgestone asking for an explanation of the high incidence of tire failure on Explorer vehicles.

Ford distanced itself from the issue, claiming that tire defects caused the rollovers. Indeed, studies showed that rubber was peeling off the tires, and information had been collected since the early 1990s showing a history of defects with the tires. So from Ford's perspective, the problem was with Bridgestone.

Initially, Bridgestone was quiet on the issue; both companies appeared ready to work together to present a common front in handling the situation;

in this case, a recall of tires. The firms worked together — to a point. They agreed on a tire recall to take place in August 2000, which both companies initiated. Yet, when that recall went into effect, both Ford and Bridgestone jumped into denial mode, an example of the avoidance strategy discussed in Chapter 1. They had planned to do a joint conference, but Bridgestone wanted to read a joint statement and not answer questions, while Ford officials felt that a Q&A was necessary. The blame game had begun after the initial recall announcement, each company claiming the other one was at fault.

Bridgestone held a news conference in Japan on August 9, 2000, at which Tadakazu Harada, Bridgestone's vice-president of Overseas Operations, said: "No specific problem was found with the design or production method of our tires." Bridgestone blamed not tires but the conditions under which they were driven, stating that tire pressures were too low and that the design of the Ford Explorer, with its high centre of gravity and poor stability — a common criticism of SUVs — was creating the problem. Harada claimed that most of the accidents occurred in the southern United States and could be attributed to driving in high temperatures at high speeds and with low tire pressure. But many questions, especially about tire specifications, went unanswered. For its part, Ford stated that between 1995 and 1997, rival company Goodyear also supplied tires — almost 500,000 — for Ford Explorers, with no indication of tire failure.

The problem escalated, especially after documentation filed with congressional investigators indicated that Ford had data indicating that Firestone tires may have had little or no margin of safety when installed on Ford Explorers. In other words, Ford may have known for years that it was installing bad tires on its vehicles.

The case was brought before the U.S. Senate for a series of hearings; as a result of the negative publicity, sales of Explorers dropped 6 per cent in August 2000. Bridgestone lost US$750 million in revenue in 2000, its stock price declining as the impact of the crisis was felt. Ford and Bridgestone spent millions on lawyers and research during hearings into the matter; they also faced 300 lawsuits. By the fall of 2001, the first of the lawsuits was settled out of court for US$7.85 million. By this time, the federal government had recorded 203 deaths and 700 injuries in vehicles equipped with Firestone tires. A mandatory recall was issued in the fall of 2001; in May 2002, Ford announced a third, voluntary recall of 13 million tires that were still on company-made vehicles as a precautionary measure to forestall future damage.[7]

But the companies' reputations were already seriously tarnished as they battled each other in the court of public opinion over who would bear the brunt of the crisis. Both companies cast blame on the other right through the issue stage of the crisis, instead of working together while the problem was only a concrete issue.

What should they have done? They should have taken joint responsibility and worked with each other to rectify the problem at the front end when it was discovered, using an attachment strategy. Ford and Bridgestone could have forestalled the crisis by outlining, back when the crisis began to loom large in May 2000, first with each other and then with the public, the issue, the shared responsibilities and the tasks necessary (through better tire development and compensation to victims) to maintain their reputations, rather than facing the challenge of rebuilding them after the crisis broke. They should have answered the questions that were put forth to them. For the public, the crisis helped initiate greater transparency for consumers — easier access to consumer reports on tire durability, strength and traction. But for Ford and Bridgestone, it meant having to regain the confidence of their customers.

WHOSE ISSUE IS IT?

Before dawn one day in early January 2005, two commuter trains in California derail after smashing into a driverless SUV.

The SUV was left on the tracks by a suicidal man who changed his mind about dying at the last moment. The resulting crash killed twelve commuters. Almost 200 rail passengers were injured. In the early morning hours outside of Los Angeles, the scene was one of horror, sadness and helplessness as emergency workers, including 300 firefighters, along with workers from a nearby Costco outlet (drawn to the scene by the sound of the crash) strived to help the survivors; those survivors filled the emergency wards of local hospitals. The crash was a crisis for the operators of the Metrolink commuter rail service, and the most serious rail tragedy since a 1999 Amtrak crash in Illinois killed 11 and injured 100. Metrolink is meant to deliver its customers to their destination in a quiet and uneventful manner; it is a rail system noted for its commitment to safety and efficiency.

But was the crisis isolated to one single rail commuter system on the west coast of the United States? Not at all, for communicators working for a railway company, commuter or otherwise, would identify this as an issue, one requiring careful follow-up within their own organizations. For rail commuter systems such as GO Transit in the Greater Toronto Area and the national VIA Rail system, it would mean answering inevitable questions such as, "What is the likelihood of a tragedy like this happening here in Canada?" "What safeguards are in place to prevent something like this from happening?" "Do you have an emergency plan to handle an emergency like this if it happened here?"

It would mean a careful assessment of the Metrolink tragedy and a study of how the issue is being covered by local, national and international media. A capable communicator would review the facts and create or update a briefing note (a document used to report on issues to senior communicators, discussed below) for senior staff, as well as prepare the organization's spokespeople for the media questions that could follow.

Issues Identification: Methods

As famed Spanish author Cervantes said, "Forewarned [is] forearmed." At the same time, communicators don't want to be fighting windmills, as Cervantes's fictitious character Don Quixote was fond of doing. Communicators begin the process of preparing for potential crises by being aware of their surroundings; as Sun Tzu might have said, taking stock of the terrain and the weather.

They do this by putting into practice a system of issues identification. This includes assigning personnel to scan newspapers, popular magazines, trade publications, stakeholder newsletters and television news programs and clip relevant news stories. Or an external service may be employed to review the news for information dealing with the organization, its industry sector, or legislation relating to it. Such items will be clipped or a transcript prepared (in the case of broadcast media) and the information provided to senior communicators.

Typically, issues identification begins at about 6:00 a.m., with staff in the communications department checking the news, clipping and reviewing the relevant stories, and preparing an issues report. The report is provided to the senior communicator, usually a manager or director, by 7:30 a.m. By 8:30 a.m., the most senior staff has been briefed on them.

Issues identification allows communicators the opportunity to get ahead on an issue — to identify gaps in the publics' knowledge and understanding of the issue. It will help them identify some of the "little whispers" that take place in an industry or sector. By being aware of what is being said and by whom, communicators can gather important information and develop strong key messages that will help reconfirm their organization's position on an issue. Issues identification provides a barometer of the feelings and perceptions of the general public, the actions and stance of competitors, the attitude of members of stakeholder groups, and anyone else who may have an interest in what the organization is doing.

FRAZZ   **BY JEF MALLETT**

© Jef Mallett/Dist. by United Feature Syndicate, Inc.

IDENTIFYING DANGEROUS ISSUES

Discussion with senior communications staff and senior operational personnel from key areas in the organization is necessary to determine just which issues might become crises, and to identify those relatively minor or localized issues that could become more serious. In addition to reviewing the media and publications from external stakeholders and the industry, it's important for communicators to look at their organization and identify trigger points that could precipitate a crisis, such as:

- The firing of top personnel;
- The death of a senior person, such as a CEO or president;
- A scandal involving top officials;
- Plant closures or layoffs;
- The creation of a new company by former employees;
- A company product causing illness or death;
- Natural disasters;
- Terrorist attacks;
- A plant accident causing serious injury or death;
- Disease outbreak;
- Toxic spills;
- Inquiries by government bodies or regulatory commissions;
- Product malfunctions;
- Class-action lawsuits;
- Industry disruptions, such as crises at other companies within the sector.

Communicators will want to look at the broadest range of issues possible to see what areas need to be addressed, plumbing the depths of their organization for feedback on these issues. A good communications department establishes and maintains a regular line of communication with all departments in its organization (this aspect is examined further in Chapter 7). A hospital, for instance, keeps track of information dealing with everything from disease outbreaks in other hospitals to fundraising and government relations. It keeps track of investigations by government agencies into hospital practices. It also is linked to its community. For example, if there is a major manufacturing plant nearby, the hospital's communicators will ask, "What if there is a disaster at the plant? How would the hospital handle the extra load? Who could we turn to if we had to divert patients to other facilities?" This information is gathered from the media, external stakeholders, industry publications and professionals. Communicators also garner information from meetings held with hospital boards and from discussion with practitioners from other hospitals.

Briefing Notes: The Next Step in Issues Management

Once communicators have identified potential issues, if senior communicators require more information (usually because of the possibility that the media or external stakeholders will contact the organization), they will request briefing material. Often, this comes in the form of a briefing note.

A briefing note is a document that lays out the basic information on the issue and the company's planned responses and next steps. It does what its name implies: it briefs senior communicators on an issue, in three ways:

Organizes information. The communicator organizes into logical parts all the key information he or she can access on the issue. A briefing note suggests the basic structure for a crisis communications plan, should it be decided that one is needed, and it also details further information that may be needed as the issue develops. Because the briefing note contains the broad strokes of the essential five Ws (the who, what, when, where and why) of the company's actions and communications, the plan can then be extended and deepened with new tactics, products and contacts as needed to accommodate the organization's evolving response to the issue.

Outlines organization's position. The communicator expresses the organization's official position on the issue succinctly, through key messages with some supporting basic information. But *basic* is the keyword here, for while a briefing note may contain some chronological history and essential messages, it should not go into great detail. Whether the briefing note is used for a simple or complex issue, the focus is on saying, "This is where we stand on this issue."

Outlines planned actions. The document includes likely outcomes of the issue based on the various responses of the organization. It specifies exactly what actions the company will take to control the issue.

A briefing note is a working document that allows an organization to have a record of original assumptions and also adapt to the changing situation. The information it contains enables all members of the communications team to understand how the company is approaching the issue and the direction in which the issue is heading. As such, it works like a memo as well as a road map. Because it contains all the important information and key messages, the briefing note allows anyone in the organization who must take a spokesperson role to be ready to relay the most up-to-date information and the most current key messages.

> A good briefing note allows executives and members of the communications team to cope with a situation in advance.

Typically, the briefing note is no longer than two pages. It is used by internal staff only; it is not given to the media or other people outside the organization. It is written in plain language. It provides the foundation for understanding how the organization will represent itself on an issue, whether its spokespeople are discussing the issue with the media, the public, or external stakeholders.

BRIEFING NOTE TEMPLATE

THE ISSUE: Provides a brief but clear overview of the issue in one to two sentences.

SAMPLING OF QUOTES: Offers senior-level staff a chance to read what has been said about the issue.

SUGGESTED RESPONSE: Provides key messages in a sound-bite format. These concisely establish the organization's position on an issue. They express the actions the company will take, or at least communicate the company's direction — the "This is how we're dealing with the situation." These key messages may be used in media interviews or in discussion with the public or external stakeholders.

BACKGROUND: Positions the issue within the context of the organization's activities. It puts the issue into historical perspective and talks about future directions the organization is taking. It gives staff a chance to quickly review the major points that are not necessarily covered in the key messages.

POSSIBLE OUTCOMES: Gives personnel a heads-up of what might happen if the issue isn't addressed.

CONTACT INFORMATION: This provides the name, title, department, phone number and email address of the communications contact — the person who put the briefing note together.

Case Study: Cougars Threaten Alberta Residents

Sally Ito works in the communications branch of the Department of Natural Resources in Alberta. As part of her duties, she has been reviewing the daily clippings and transcripts and sees that cougar sightings are on the rise. This is normal at certain times of the year, particularly in the early spring and fall, when cougars hunt closer to developed areas in search for food. Ito notes from her research that citizens, fearful of attacks, are calling radio shows and writing letters to local newspapers. She knows that people's concerns are often exaggerated. The wildlife rangers in the department do a good job of patrolling the region; still, it's wise to be prepared in case more questions come to the department.

Ito recommends to her manager that the branch issue a briefing note out-lining the issue. Note that this is an issue only — the situation is still under control. It would become a crisis only if there were attacks and the general public came to feel that officials were not handling the situation. Managing perception is a big part of a communicator's job. How the publics view a situation, whether real or imagined, is just as important as any true threat to those publics.

Ito creates a set of rough notes, to be discussed with her manager before finalizing them into a briefing note. After the notes are reviewed, Ito will organize them using the standardized subheadings so that the briefing note is easy to read; she will also use bullet points — this to help senior staff who want to scan for the most important points. Ito gathers the following:

The date: This is the date the briefing note is finalized and ready for use.

The organization: Department of Natural Resources.

The issue: Cougar sightings in many towns in western Canada are on the increase. Are the department's measures adequate to protect the public? Will public anxiety increase?

Department spokespeople: James Smith, deputy minister; Wendy Loeb, director, Communications. A government department will often have its minister — an elected politician assigned to his or her role by the premier of the province — act as spokesperson. In this case, the deputy minister, who is a civil servant and the head of the day-to-day operations of the ministry, will be spokesperson, given his long-time experience with this issue and the fact that the minister is at a meeting overseas.

While communicators would usually look to the minister to provide commentary, the situation is one of enforcement and patrols, and therefore the handling of inquiries is within the realm of the department's bureaucracy. Wendy Loeb, as head of the communications department, will offer support to the deputy minister and fulfill the role of backup if the deputy minister is unavailable for comment.

The media/public position: Three articles in local newspapers cite "concerned residents" who are afraid to walk their pets in the early morning hours or in the evenings. Two hikers were attacked in the mountains earlier in the year, but they managed to scare the cougar away. Joggers have felt threatened. Cougars have been spotted in backyards on the outskirts of towns, and there is a general anxiety among the local population. It might be expected that people living in close proximity to cougars have narrow escapes or even experience attacks, but the department's concern is that as cougars move closer to human habitation, the anxiety level of the population will increase.

Other stakeholder positions: The local board of education is seeking to have the department increase its Cougar Awareness Program presentations; the program has been touring schools in cougar country for the past three years. Officials lauded the program for helping increase awareness of cougar behaviour among school children. School boards are aware of speculation that the department might cut back on the program.

The position of the department: The department is stepping up patrols by wildlife officers in smaller towns, particularly on the outskirts and in rural areas. Residents are encouraged to call the department if they see a cougar. Because of a downturn in the populations of their standard prey items in their territories, cougars are roaming farther afield in search of food. Albertans are generally familiar with cougars, and the department has taken steps, through schools and open-house sessions, to increase citizens' knowledge of cougars and their habits. The department has produced and widely distributed a booklet containing tips for living in cougar country. Obviously, the department has a strong desire to reduce panic and demonstrate that action is being taken. It has discussed hiring 10 additional wildlife officers in specific areas of concern, such as Banff, though this has not yet been approved. The proposal is, however, known to the public.

Is this a crisis or an issue? The department does not see this as a crisis; rather, it is an emerging issue that needs to be reviewed, addressed and monitored. The safety of citizens is the primary concern; a secondary concern is that the department be seen to be doing its job, by making regular patrols and ensuring regular contact with its publics. Being quoted in a newspaper or broadcast story would allow the department to affirm its proactive stance on the cougar situation.

DRAFTING THE NOTE

Using the information outlined above, Sally Ito drafts a briefing note for the cougar scenario. Sally takes the information and crafts it into a short, pithy piece of writing, focusing on four things: the perception the public will have of the department, the sightings, the possibility of attacks and the department's action. The briefing note takes a people-focused approach. The messaging reflects careful consideration of the effect of department policy on people and on the public's perception of the situation.

Here is the briefing note that Sally Ito wrote. Note the use of plain language and subheadings that clearly present the issue.

```
-----------------------------------------------------------------
               CONFIDENTIAL: FOR INTERNAL USE ONLY

Date:  April 2, 2006

The issue: Local media are reporting that small-town residents
are concerned over an increased presence of cougars. Citizens
are calling the department hotline and flooding radio call-in
shows with complaints.

A sampling of the quotes:
— "I'm afraid to let my children play in the backyard." — call to
  local radio show.
— "I used to go hiking every day. I can't do that any more." —
  letter to local newspaper.
— "When are you people going to do something about the cougars?"
  — call to Department of Natural Resources hotline.
— "Is government soft on cougars? Ministry not actively pursuing
  solution." — newspaper editorial headline.

Possible outcomes:
— Calls for Natural Resources minister's resignation.
— Demands from opposition politicians to step up patrols.
— Demands for increased presence of the cougar awareness program
  in schools.
— Demands from citizens for vigilante squads to patrol neigh-
bourhoods.

Suggested response (key messages):
— The department is aware of the situation and our wildlife offi-
  cers are continuing to provide regular patrols throughout
  neighbourhoods and towns.
— We encourage the public to contact us if a cougar is seen. All
  sightings will be dealt with immediately.
— We know that many citizens are familiar with cougars. Tips and
  advice on dealing with cougars is available in a booklet, pro-
  vided free by the Department of Natural Resources and also
  available at www.natres.ca.
— Discussion on hiring additional wildlife officers is ongoing.
  However, the safety of citizens is not contingent on hiring
```

more officers. We are confident that our wildlife officers are doing a good job of ensuring the safety of our citizens.
— The cougar awareness program for school children will continue.

Background:
— The issue began with three recent articles in local newspapers that have focused on citizens who are afraid to walk their pets in the early morning hours or in the evenings (names of newspapers, dates and copies of articles attached).
— Details included mention of the two hikers attacked in the mountains but who managed to scare the cougar away.
— Those familiar with cougar country know to stay on well-travelled pathways or roads, keep small children and pets close to them, and move slowly away from cougars if confronted.
— Wildlife patrols have been increased in the areas cited. Hiring additional wildlife officers is under review.
— There is a desire to reduce fear in the general public and to encourage the view that cougars are part of our natural heritage. The department will hold additional information sessions for interested parties and will continue to visit local schools.
— The issue should be monitored, particularly if further attacks in neighbourhoods take place or if this becomes a national story.

Contact information: Sally Ito, senior communications officer, Department of Natural Resources, 555-2222, ext. 222; sito@albertanaturalresources.ca

----

The cougar-sightings issue is a good example of the need for communicators to include the view of people outside their organization into their activities. People within the Department of Natural Resources, on hearing concerns of the public, might simply sigh and say, "There's no problem. We know that attacks are bound to happen from time to time." In a sense, communicators might be too close to the issue; they have knowledge that clouds their ability to see the public's concerns clearly. The Natural Resources people are specialists; they understand the cycles of cougar behaviour, and they can put it into the context of the cycles of nature. The public is different. It sees the cougar issue as a crisis waiting to happen. It isn't the public's job to know how a cougar behaves. Therefore, communicators need to educate the public, but they also need to educate their organization's spokespeople so that they too understand the concerns driving the public to contact radio call-in shows and write letters to politicians and the editors of the local newspapers.

Remember, communicators can't control the questions that come to them during a crisis. But they can manage the crisis in such a way that they control the flow of information in their organization and outside it. Communicators can control when they want to speak and what they want to say. They do this best by carefully preparing their approach to the issue, to ensure that it addresses the feelings and concerns of their publics.

PRINCE HARRY: WOULD A BRIEFING NOTE HAVE WORKED?

Sometimes there is no way of knowing when a crisis will happen. This is particularly true of the British royal family. Because they are inextricably tied to symbolism, ritual and history, issues for the royals can become crises overnight. There is often a vast gap between the public's expectations of a symbol and the behaviour of human beings born into the duty of maintaining that symbol.

Granted, many of those crises have been of their own making . . . no surprise there. In *The PR Crisis Bible*, author Robin Cohn says: "Studies show 80 per cent of potential disasters are people-generated and can be prevented. With few exceptions, people-caused problems leave a trail of early warning signals well in advance of the actual crisis."[8] Cohn quotes the Institute for Crisis Management, a Kentucky-based organization that since its creation in 1989 has focused solely on crisis consulting, training and planning, when he notes that "69 per cent of business crises are smoldering and 31 per cent are sudden."[9]

The royals have left a few early-warning signals, and in January 2005, a(nother) crisis occurred. Harry, third in line to the throne and son of Prince Charles and the late Diana, attended a costume party dressed as a Nazi. The Queen was not amused, and when a *Daily Mail* photograph showed the over-refreshed 20 year old in the uniform of Germany's Afrika Korps, the swastika prominently displayed on an armband, the media went to town. Headlines ranged from "Hail Harry: prince goose-steps out of line" to "Royal Nazi," "Prince's sorry mess," "Come out and say sorry," and "Army must sort out Harry" (a reference to his impending though unrelated trip to military school).[10]

The British newspaper the *Guardian* noted that "Prince Harry seems less interested in preparing for a life of royal service than auditioning for the role of village idiot."[11] In the *Daily Telegraph*, columnist Tom Utley nailed the relationship between the royals and the symbolism of their roles: "A constitutional monarchy is above all else about, and justified by, symbolism. Prince Harry could not have engaged in any worse symbolism than with the swastika."[12] One could almost hear the rumble of Sir Winston Churchill stirring in his grave. And yet the media were, for the most part, willing to forgive the young royal, underscoring that the public tends to cut famous people a lot of slack when it comes to misdoings.

One can only imagine the royals' media handlers attempting the delicate task of preparing a briefing note for Her Highness:

THE ISSUE: Prince Harry offends.
SAMPLING OF QUOTES: "Prince's sorry mess," "Royal Nazi."
SUGGESTED RESPONSE FOR HARRY: "I'm sorry. I'm ignorant, and I need to be enlightened as to the history of the world and my place in it."
SUGGESTED RESPONSE FOR HER HIGHNESS: "We are not amused."

It was a situation where appropriate stakeholder interests played a particularly important role. From World War II veterans to Holocaust memorial associations to Jewish organizations to average citizens, everyone had something to say on the subject. In fact, the media wasted no time in contacting Jewish groups for their opinions. Roundly chastised for insensitivity, all Harry could offer was a very weak "I am very sorry if I caused any offence or embarrassment to anyone."

Harry was urged by the Simon Wiesenthal Center to visit the Auschwitz-Birkenau complex or other such sites where Jews died in the millions during the Holocaust. Afterward, Harry was dutifully quiet when not offering apologies in the wake of another public relations disaster for the royal family.

Conclusion

Events in the community at large — the place where the organization "lives" and where it builds relationships — and the marketplace in which a communicator's organization operates, are naturally not all of the same significance. But it is essential that communicators assess all events and issues for their potential to have an impact on the organization's reputation. Events with some crisis potential should enter the next phase of issues monitoring; communicators must reorient themselves to tracking the issue as it progresses and begin preparing a briefing note. Communicators must also begin planning and taking action immediately to exploit the opportunity to head off a crisis.

It is essential that communicators, who, like journalists, often work under the pressure of many deadlines, be empowered to block off the time they need in their schedules to give issues monitoring appropriate attention. It can't be overemphasized that the issues stage, whether an issue is potential or concrete, is a point at which communicators may still exert a great deal of control over the situation. At this stage, communicators can do the most to keep their publics informed and to build a sense of understanding and acceptance for the path the organization will take. It is also the time when the terrain, to use Sun Tzu's term, is most advantageous.

Key Concepts

GAP: The difference between a company's conduct (especially its ethical conduct) and its publics' expectations of its behaviour. A communicator's business is to constantly assess how much gap there is between these two components. If the gap is wide, the company has an issue; if there is absolutely no match-up between what an organization does and what its publics expect, there may be a crisis.

ISSUE: Any event, procedure or practice, action or statement by a member of the company or any of the company's publics that has the potential to trigger a crisis and cause harm to the organization's reputation or business. We see them in terms of potential and concrete issues:

CONCRETE ISSUE: An issue that has manifested itself in a negative way and requires a concerted effort on the part of the communications team to prevent it from becoming a crisis.

POTENTIAL ISSUE: An issue that communicators have control of but which may escalate over time to negatively affect the day-to-day operations of the organization and its reputation.

ISSUES IDENTIFICATION: The process of identifying the events that could go wrong, through identifying potentially uncontrollable factors both within and outside the organization's environment and taking steps to correct them before they grow.

KEY MESSAGES (CORE MESSAGES): The "sound bite" that delivers the message communicators want to reach their publics. The message is concise and action-oriented. It summarizes the organization's approach to handling the crisis.

4 | The Crisis Communications Plan

Communicators who have identified an issue, that dangerous ship on the horizon of a company's operations, know they must gauge its progress as it moves toward them and across their field of vision.

Now, communicators need to think about the crisis itself. They know that a crisis may develop over a period of time — days or even months. Or it can happen, as with the RBC computer glitch (discussed in Chapter 2), in seconds. Most organizations have their day-to-day activities well covered, especially in the area of emerging issues. Remember, the issues that arise are the early warning signs of a crisis — they may or may not grow to become a crisis. Planning for crises requires a more in-depth look at the possible outcomes of an issue. Once the issue is deemed dangerous enough to require a plan, it is the job of communicators to foresee ways the issue might escape their control.

This may require that a company dedicate one or two people to crafting crisis strategies, and that can take weeks — time that is often regarded as better spent having communicators handle the daily tactical grind. Today, many organizations hire planners from outside who can sit down with the communications director and other senior staff, drill into the organization's infrastructure, review past crises (within the organization and in its related industries), and then create effective crisis scenarios. Once the crisis plan is created, the planning process involves a commitment from senior personnel to participate in crisis scenarios, deciding who will make appropriate contacts to media, stakeholders and other external contacts, who will keep the internal stakeholders informed, who will answer questions and who will stage manage the crisis.

In this chapter we focus on:

- Using a formal system for drafting plans;
- Designing a plan with the right strategy, supported by the right tactics;
- Using the plan to ensure that information or understanding gaps of publics can be quickly closed;
- Anticipating the various stages of the evolution of a crisis.

The Purpose of a Crisis Plan

A crisis plan presumes that the organization has lost control of a situation. Either it has failed to exert control of an issue, or it has had to cope with a truly unforeseeable event, perhaps a natural disaster, an accident, or an error, and the crisis arrives on the doorstep, skipping the issues phase. As such, crisis plans don't *prevent* anything; primarily they *anticipate* the path of the crisis, as meteorologists chart the path of a storm, and they help a company prepare for each stage of the crisis by being ready to take appropriate actions to deal with crisis and by establishing a flow of information to its publics.

The plan is organized around the five Ws of journalism (who, what, when, where and why). A crisis communications plan lays out who will represent the organization in the crisis, what he or she will say and when and where it will be said. It will also seek to answer the *why* — often the most important question for the communicator's researchers to answer, in terms of the impact on the plan. If researchers discover that a crisis may happen because of negligence or corruption, the plan must be reworked to address this specific harm to reputation and perhaps even new stakeholders, such as the police.

The plan is the road map for handling the crisis. In addition to providing a series of questions and answers, it spells out decisively what the organization will do. It focuses on action, not just response, and on a step-by-step process of taking charge and righting the imbalance that the crisis has created. It creates a chart for educating people within the organization, not just telling them what they need to know but also putting it in the context of what the public is thinking.

In his book *Managing the Media,* Canadian media expert Ed Shiller writes: "The purpose of a crisis communications plan is not to prevent crises ... it is to prevent crises from becoming disasters."[1] Shiller cites two stages in an effective plan:

> [The first will] ensure that you, the communications specialist, are alerted to any situation within your organization that could escalate into a disaster. The second is to provide you with the necessary information, access to senior management and financial and human resources to take the proper corrective action.[2]

Shiller, in discussing the purpose of plans, makes sound points. The first speaks to the foreknowledge that comes with doing an effective assay of your organization, its industry sector and the community in which it functions. When you see dark clouds in the sky, you reach for an umbrella — even if you don't need to use it, you know you have it just in case it does rain. So knowing what's coming allows you to plan ahead. Shiller's second point addresses the ideal communications planning: having access to the decision makers, having the money to undertake projects that may require outside resources and having human resource power, in terms of sizeable staff numbers, to do a complete planning job. This is the kind of process mechanism that communicators need to set in place well in advance, by building sound relationships within the organization, so that when a crisis hits, they can handle the situation in a seamless fashion.

Laying Out the Crisis Plan

A crisis plan should be laid out as follows:

1. **A statement of the issue.** One or two lines describing what the crisis is about.
2. **The goals of the plan.** Simply stated, the goal will tell how a communicator wants the organization to be seen in light of the crisis. Goals for the crisis plan are linked closely with the organization's goals and address the crisis as a temporary obstacle to fulfilling those goals. As such, the communicator should take a good look at how the organization wants to see itself. This must be a focus when establishing the goals for weathering the crisis.
3. **Details of the crisis team.** Provide names, titles, departments, email addresses, and phone (including cell phone) numbers. Each crisis team member must also have a backup person in place, ready to go. Include staff who will work on these components: the plan itself, the crisis information log, key messages, stakeholders, speeches and news releases, briefing notes. Detail each person's role.
4. **A determination of the severity of the crisis.** Is the crisis minor or major? A minor crisis is one that can be handled by a company spokesperson, perhaps

a media relations officer; a major one requires the presence of the company vice-president or president. This important strategic consideration allows communicators to think about the resources they have to put into handling the crisis. Do they need to arrange full-scale meetings with senior executives, or does copying them on emails or hard-copy communications materials suffice?

© United Feature Syndicate, Inc.

THE CRISIS INFORMATION LOG

It is important for communicators to outline and maintain a log of who has been notified during the crisis, and when and what information was provided. The contact name, title, organization, and phone and email information should be included, as well as entries for calls to within the company. The follow-up column lists a contact name for the communicator who made or received the call and a general description of what action that communicator took. This log is used for all external publics, including government organizations (these may have a regulatory role to play in the organization's operations), stakeholder groups, and the media.

CRISIS INFORMATION LOG TEMPLATE			
DATE	CONTACT	SUBJECT MATTER	FOLLOW-UP
	NAME: TITLE: ORGANIZATION: PHONE: FAX: EMAIL:		BY: ACTION TAKEN:

Using the Log

Here's an example of how a communicator might fill in the log. Salmon River Flying School offers a course in flying gliders — the engineless planes that can soar for hours. The build-and-fly company has operated out of a small town in central Nova Scotia for 20 years without incident. It builds glider planes from kits provided by major manufacturers, modifies existing crafts and provides flying lessons, all out of one location. The company employs 20 workers and draws both locals and tourists to its site.

The crisis: Several suggestions are being bandied about concerning the cause of a crash that killed an experienced glider pilot two days ago; among them are pilot error and a defect on a wing assembly. While it's rare for glider pilots to crash — and deaths from crashes are even rarer — they do happen. The crash came on the heels of two recent though unrelated crashes: one at a flying school in southern Alberta just two weeks previously and another three months earlier at a flying centre in British Columbia.

Yolanda Hawkins, a freelance communications specialist who has worked in the aviation industry, has been called in to deal with the situation. Yolanda does an assessment and creates a communications crisis plan, key messages and a crisis log. The company has set up a spot for her in the front office; she has worked through the previous day, sitting down with company president Ernesto Ferreira, an experienced commercial and glider pilot, and with company engineers to develop key messages, and she is handling calls from the media. Here is how her log might look:

DATE	CONTACT	SUBJECT MATTER	FOLLOW-UP
August 29	NAME: Jack Loper TITLE: Technology reporter ORGANIZATION: *Halifax Chronicle Herald* PHONE: 902-555-4321 FAX: 902-555-0960 EMAIL: loper@chronicle.com	1. Needs to know how aerodynamically safe gliders are. 2. What led to the crash? 3. What precautions are usually taken with gliders, e.g., training for pilots, equipment checks?	BY: Yolanda Hawkins ACTION TAKEN: key messages and national safety statistics on glider flights. Set up interview with Ernesto Ferreira. Interview to take place today at 10 a.m.
August 29	NAME: Andrea Tsang TITLE: Reporter ORGANIZATION: CBC Halifax PHONE: 902-555-3434 FAX: 902-555-3433 EMAIL: tsang@CBChalifax.com	1. How did the crash happen? 2. What federal regulation is the company required to meet? 3. Where did the pilot who died live? Was he a local?	BY : Yolanda Hawkins Chief engineer Sam Persaud to provide details on federal regulations. Interview set up for 2 p.m. on site with Persaud and Ferreira.
August 29	NAME: Jerry Langkowski TITLE: Writer ORGANIZATION: *Wings* (national aviation magazine) PHONE: 519-555-1900 FAX: 519-555-4445 EMAIL: Jlang@wings.com	Needs basic information on the crash and also the technical specifications for the glider.	BY: Yolanda Hawkins Provided overview; spoke with Sam Persaud and faxed specifications to reporter.
August 30	NAME: Martha Salvador TITLE: Investigator ORGANIZATION: Government of Canada, Transportation Safety Board, Ottawa PHONE: 613-555-3569 FAX: 613-555-8547 EMAIL: MSalv@gc.ca	Requested background information on crash, as well as information on glider pilot and basics on Salmon River Flying School.	BY : Yolanda Hawkins, Ernesto Ferreira Telephone interview set up for 11 a.m. for Ferreira.

5. **Details of key spokespeople.** Communicators need to decide in advance who in their organization will convey messages during a crisis. Does the crisis warrant a need for a technical spokesperson? In the past, it was seen as absolute that a company have only one crisis spokesperson. That notion has changed, for in a world where media and stakeholders value specialized training and subjects, and where complex technology (especially in computers) is a major issue, it may be essential to have a technical spokesperson on board in addition to the main spokesperson. For example, in many organizations, the president or CEO will handle the broad-based messages governing the direction the company is taking, while the vice-president or the chief information officer handles technical questions. An organization may have several spokespeople, all capable of handling the same messages or passing a question to another spokesperson with specific knowledge in that area.

Crises of a lesser nature — a minor spill, an accident at a local level with no loss of life and no immediate threat — can be handled by communications experts lower on the authority chain. But a significant event, one with a loss of life or injuries, or which damages the company's credibility (such as a computer glitch that affects a wide range of clientele), demands that the organization have the top people on hand to speak for it.

6. **The breaking of the crisis into stages to ensure tactics address each stage.** Establish a clear understanding of the crisis as it is likely to develop and as it may change. Six main stages characterize any crisis.

The initial stage. A crisis emerges that unbalances the organization. This stage is characterized by a scramble of the communicators to get in position and get ready. Plan or no plan, the crisis team is just forming, and few communicators are ready to take action. One or two senior communicators manage the teams, ensure roles are assigned and understood, and mobilize company resources. The communicators prepare to plug into action mode and review their plans, along with any mock scenarios they may have run in the past that bear resemblance to the current crisis. Depending on the severity of the crisis, crisis team members and other staff may be anxious. If there have been incoming calls and pressure from publics, many communicators may be tempted to move into a reactive posture. To move easily to the next stage, they need to resist this impulse, especially senior communicators. This stage is best completed by activating everyone in their respective roles and action units, letting everyone know what the internal information flow will be, taking questions and then directing the relatively smaller number of people on the crisis strategy team to prepare for the next stage and update all materials, including the crisis plan.

The strategic stage. Communicators and executives work to establish a game plan for the crisis. A communicator will make needed revisions to the plan and collaborate with senior communicators to anticipate as many contingencies as possible for the next phase. The strategic stage includes efforts to work the overall approach and the tactics to be used into the loose stages listed here. To a degree, events and pressures of a crisis must cluster into stages. For example, the particular aggravation of a crisis caused by outrage at a company's poorly thought-out key messages cannot happen before the tactical stage in which the key messages are presented.

Communicators must always be thinking of how to maintain, and in some cases rebuild, a positive rapport with a public that increasingly distrusts corporate organizations. According to a 2002 Gallup poll, 80 per cent of Americans believe corruption is endemic in corporations. Public opinion researcher and psychology professor Daniel Yankelovich has said that organizations must move away from "jealously managing corporate image or spinning the truth to influence public opinion and instead practice open and honest dialogue to build 'trust equity' with the public."[3]

The information stage. Communicators scramble to prepare information for press releases, Q&As, backgrounders and other information vehicles. The organization's publics will create opinions about the organization as the crisis unfolds: providing the action-oriented information needed will effectively answer questions about what the company is doing and will serve to underscore the positive steps it is taking to resolve the crisis.

The tactical stage. Communicators engage publics using the prescribed channels for delivering information to each public. The company takes necessary action to contain a crisis (including working with research results as they come in), taking control of operations that represent danger to publics, such as recalling products or suspending operations. This stage is the real test of the plan's effectiveness and execution as information is poured onto the flames of the crisis, so to speak. This stage represents the first delivery of information, context and explanation to publics in an effort to close information gaps. The dangers inherent in this stage are failure to include all contacts into the information flow, failure to follow up with contacts and failure to attend carefully enough to the tactics used to close the identified information gaps.

The adjustment stage. Either the information flow to the organization's publics has sufficiently addressed concerns and closed the gaps, or it hasn't. Sometimes these publics are especially demanding or they are being carried far on a tide of emotion. A company's messages may not have been perfectly targeted or drafted, and a gap remains. Alternately, a new gap may form simply as a result of new information coming to light — for instance, a whistleblower turns up late in the crisis to criticize the company, and the crisis takes a new turn irrespective of the communicators' solid work. After the tactical stage, when information has been presented along with key messages, communicators will receive feedback that will tell them whether the situation is coming under control. If the situation is not under control, they must go back to the crisis plan and add new strategy and tactics.

The end stage. The company does a post-mortem on its handling of the crisis, evaluating its successes and failures and learning from the experience.

7. **Key messages.** Communicators must draft three or four key messages that encompass the direction the organization is taking on the crisis.
8. **Target publics.** Whom do the communicators need to contact? This list includes stakeholder groups, government and internal personnel, along with a complete listing of media.
9. **Strategies.** What steps will the organization take to get its messages out? Strategies must directly relate to the overall objective. They will include tactics — the tools communicators use to get the message out.
10. **Follow-up and evaluation.** What steps will communicators take to see that their messages were received? How will they evaluate the success of these steps?

Crisis Plans as Working Documents

"At the end of the day, I would say that it is good to do planning and a solid thought-out communications plan (or plans) can get you reasonably far down the road in a crisis. But there is always the unforeseen and the unknowable. And for that you need to keep your wits about you, and you need to have the ability to be flexible. You cannot let the plan be a straitjacket: circumstances may dictate new tactics and sometimes a different strategy."[4]
 — Robert E. Waite, senior vice-president, Communications and Stakeholder Relations, Canada Post Corporation, on flexibility and planning

Changes happen and, as a crisis unfolds and more elements are added to it, the crisis plan must be flexible enough to accommodate them. For instance, if a facility has a fire, initially communicators will impart messages that focus on ensuring the safety of workers and putting out the fire. But what if several workers die as a result of the mishap, or the fire results in an explosion that sprays poisonous chemicals into the atmosphere? In these cases, the crisis plan *as a template* remains the same, indicating that the company is investigating the matter, working with authorities and taking action to ensure cleanup of the site. What changes within the plan are the minute-by-minute messages, which must acknowledge any new crisis element. The communications plan must note these changes in subsequent versions of the original plan.

For instance, the unexpected death of a plant worker requires acknowledgment, sympathy for the family and a demonstrated commitment to investigate the matter, as well as, in some cases, assurances that safety improvements will be implemented in the workplace (this is an area of the plan that may also need legal review, as a communicator does not want to commit his or her organization to accepting blame, or imply corporate guilt, in a situation where the worker was at fault or negligent). The discharge of chemicals into the environment demands acknowledgment, a commitment to work with authorities such as the fire department on cleanup and assurances that the company will improve its safety guidelines, working in conjunction with the environment department and local authorities. The point of a crisis plan is that it is flexible: its structure must allow for information, messages and tactics to be added as the crisis moves toward its conclusion.

Case Study:
Saskatchewan Chemical's Industrial Spill Crisis Plan

CORPORATE GLANCE: SASKATCHEWAN CHEMICAL COMPANY
(A fictional but realistic example of a manufacturer)

Saskatchewan Chemical is a wholly Canadian-owned and -operated small manufacturer of paints, caulking and adhesives. The company is located just outside Regina, Saskatchewan, and employs 500 people: 400 in the plant, 75 in the front office, and 25 in research and development. In its 21st year of operation, Saskatchewan Chemical is located in an industrial park, along with about 20 other manufacturing firms. Although the company has clients worldwide, most are in Canada and the United States. Its manufacturing facility includes high-tech computerized production equipment and three reactor units that are used to combine chemicals in a high-heat process.

Safety: The company stringently follows federal and provincial guidelines for the use of chemicals in the factory, is ISO certified for manufacturing and safety standards, and ensures that its employees are fully trained in safety procedures, especially for hazardous materials. The company's safety record is strong, and days lost to accidents are at a minimum. Saskatchewan Chemical is a member of several federal and provincial industry associations. Safety associations have lauded it for its achievements in this area.

This safety record is in keeping with the company's other positive aspects: a superior product and a progressive workplace that is guided by the principles of "excellence, product quality and service to customers," principles captured in the company's vision, mission and values.

BACKGROUND

Devon Laramie has been hired to oversee all internal and external communications. In addition to generating news releases when the company has an "announceable," such as a plant expansion or charitable fundraiser, he handles a small internal newsletter, media calls, and stakeholder and government relations. He has a communications officer handling news monitoring and news release writing, and an administrative assistant.

The company president is J.S. Singh, who is guided in his decision making by vice-president Harry Smith (to whom Devon reports directly) and R&D chief Simon Chung. Singh has an open-door policy on any issues Devon wishes to discuss, though Smith has requested that Devon copy him on correspondence to the president.

Because Devon is new to the job, he decides to give the company a full crisis review, looking at its preparedness for crisis. He discovers binders full of correspondence on some minor issues but little else. He works on a long list of possible issues for the company, drawing ideas from the binder. He finds no concrete issues other than one: an article clipped from an American newspaper about a plant in Kentucky that had a reactor core explosion six months ago, resulting in millions of dollars in damage and two deaths. The company makes exactly the same products, using the same processes and machinery, as Saskatchewan Chemical. Articles attached to this news story relate that other facilities in the United States have had chemical spills and leaks, and while not as serious as the Kentucky incident, they resulted in questions about safety. In Kentucky, the incident created negative attention from community groups and local media. As well, it created very negative media attention for that company. Business was lost, and the company had to lay off workers.

In a meeting with Singh and Smith, Devon gets approval to devote the time needed to draft a crisis plan.

SASKATCHEWAN CHEMICAL: PLANNING

Later that day, Devon sits down with Larry Mohamed, the communications officer, and Lily Nguyen, his administrative assistant, to map out the plan. Lily is given the task of determining who in the plant is in charge of workplace safety — the reporting system if there is a mishap; she will also make calls to appropriate work areas to determine who backs up whom in the event of an absence. Larry takes on the task of reviewing archive material to develop a set of key messages for the plan. Devon will ensure that backup positions are in place should a member of the team be unavailable.

Devon develops a set of key messages, working with his staff, that will focus on a "people first" scenario — he wants to assure the company's publics that people are the most important part of what they do. Larry has recruited the key personnel from the plant to take part, and Devon has recruited professional writers to play the role of reporters who will drill the company within two weeks of the crisis plan being completed. Devon has a commitment from Singh to run a test crisis — the president has committed to a half day to work through the potential scenario.

Here is the plan Devon creates:

Crisis communications plan:
Reactor core mishap, Saskatchewan Chemical Company

Crisis issue statement: An explosion in Reactor One at Saskatchewan Chemical, with non life-threatening injuries to staff. Chemicals and gases released into general work area.

The goal of this plan:
1. To ensure the safety of all Saskatchewan Chemical personnel and the safety of people in the area.
2. To provide assurances to the public, the media, and our clients that we are taking action to find the cause of the reactor mishap and to correct it.
3. To ensure a comfort level with our publics that Saskatchewan Chemical adheres to strict safety guidelines.
4. To let our clients know that business will not be disrupted.

The crisis team (phone numbers and email addresses to be provided):
Devon Laramie, director, Communications; Larry Mohamed, communications officer, Communications; Lily Nguyen, administrative assistant
J.S. Singh, president; backup: Harry Smith, vice-president
Harry Smith, vice-president; backup, Liliane Coté, CIO
Simon Chung, chief, Research and Development; backup: Carmen Jones, senior researcher
Paula Langford, director, Manufacturing; backup: Chance Everton, senior manager, Manufacturing

Hour by hour

Immediately after the crisis is announced: Contact police and fire department.

Hour one: Establish crisis command centre: Communications Department boardroom. Bring together crisis team. President and vice-president to be available on call for updates where appropriate. Gather information on casualties, damage to plant and safety of facility.

Hour two: Larry Mohamed to draft media release. Release to outline following messages: there were no life-threatening injuries; injured workers taken to hospital; fire and police departments contacted; provincial labour ministry and environment ministry contacted; damage to plant assessed; immediate community in no danger. Release to be vetted by Devon Laramie and J.S. Singh. Send to all media, community business association and mayor's office. Larry Mohamed to contact media to advise of press conference on site, to be held next hour.

Hour three: Hold press conference. J.S. Singh to speak to media. Establish schedule for media updates. Updates to take place at 11 a.m. each day.

Hour four: Contact hospital to check on status of injured workers. Gather report from fire department. Devon Laramie to contact community business association to offer assurances that there is no damage to the surrounding community.

Crisis Information Log

Lily Nguyen to create and update crisis information log: all calls (media, stakeholders, government agencies, and others) and times of the calls. Also noted is information the company provided to these contacts.

Key Spokespeople

J.S. Singh: all news conferences, handling questions from general media, business media, stakeholders.
Simon Chung: technical questions, technology reporters.
Devon Laramie: general media, business media. Will also handle all general questions when J.S. Singh or backup unavailable.

Key Messages

1. The health message. Despite damage to our reactor core, there were no deaths and no life-threatening injuries. Injured workers were taken to hospital with breathing difficulties. Workers also suffered minor bruising after slipping on material. It is expected that these workers will be discharged from hospital within a day. All other workers were examined by

a doctor and given a clean bill of health. If there is a death: the message changes to offer sympathy to the bereaved and a commitment to a thorough investigation of the mishap.

2. The reactor core message. The damage to the reactor core has been contained and there is no threat to the community. Our record for workplace safety is very strong and this mishap is certainly not typical for our operations. However, we are going to find the source of the problem and correct it.

3. The cleanup message. The area has been contained and our hazardous materials (HAZMAT) team is working closely with fire department officials to clean up the resulting spill.

4. The follow-through message. Our research team is working to determine the cause of the mishap. We don't wish to speculate, and we will have an answer within 48 hours. Message will be consistent with determination of cause (human error, equipment problems).

Target Audiences

Local media
Local police and fire departments
Stakeholder and industry groups
Saskatchewan Chemical employees

Note: Key messages, while taking into consideration the publics being addressed, are not exclusive to a particular audience; rather they deliver the essential information that the company needs to get across, based on investigation and analysis. In other words, they are all-encompassing and can be delivered to all publics.

Strategy

Our overall approach is as follows:

- Ensure that all plant workers are safe and anyone requiring medical attention is promptly taken to hospital. Notify police, the fire department and the mayor's office.
- Release our initial statement and key messages to all publics to be followed as soon as possible via our report on the cause of the reactor spill. Obtain corroboration of our union steward in charge of safety (with whom our relations have been good — in fact, we recently worked with union stewards on an agreement to phase out current safety equipment for new models in our next fiscal) and with the provincial Labour department. Coordinate with these partners to ensure that publics will know when and where the corroborating report is available.

Tactics

Day One:
1. A news conference attended by senior personnel and representatives of the local police and fire departments. Police and fire department personnel will corroborate company position on safety within the plant.
2. A news release sent out at the time of the news conference. Establish company responsibility, possibility of human error and the company's determination to find the cause of the mishap.
3. Media availability of crisis team personnel at all times.
4. Establishment of daily 11 a.m. briefing to media, in the plant.

Day Two:
1. Second news release sent out to all local media with update. Stick to 48-hour timetable for releasing "cause" information.
2. Once cause is determined, create and distribute third media release concurrent with 11 a.m. briefing.

Day Three:
1. Media tour after successful cleanup with president and crisis team personnel.
2. Message to media and publics: "We are taking the necessary steps to ensure the complete safety of our personnel and will ensure that every step is taken to maintain plant safety."

Follow-up and evaluation:
Media "hits" — how many media outlets covered the mishap on a daily basis?
Media messages — were our key messages relayed through the media? What was said?
Perception — how was our organization perceived?
Industry — what has been said in industry or workplace safety newsletters about the situation?
Crisis plan — review and update crisis plan.
Community outreach — is there more that should be done in the community to ensure that our publics are aware of what we do? (This can include job creation at the company, community service, charitable work.)

Crisis Ignites: Taking Action

> "Clearly, the quicker you can get your message out, the more definitively you do it, and the more credible your spokesperson is, the better off you are. What you don't want to do is make a blanket promise that says 'at 3 o'clock tomorrow afternoon the problem will be solved.' Because then, who apologizes next? You may not want to start off by making a guarantee."[5]
> — Robert E. Waite, senior vice-president, Communications and Stakeholder Relations, Canada Post Corporation, on the first stage of a crisis

The spirit of Sun Tzu's strategic thinking, discussed in Chapter 3, applies to aspects of tactics and innovation that communicators must call on once a crisis arises. It is for this reason that the key concepts of Sun Tzu's military framework are valuable in organizing the principles for action in the face of crisis. These are the fallback principles that communicators must rely on when they are working fast under fire — when they're working intuitively or instinctively — and no longer have the luxury of time to think critically.

LEADERSHIP UNDER FIRE — COMMAND

Pulling together the crisis team. Communicators in senior roles may be tempted to do peremptory thinking, communicating or planning on their own rather than immediately assembling their team. They must resist this inclination and assemble the team at the communications command centre. The first four hours are crucial for assessing the situation, disseminating information within the organization, establishing key messages and creating the crisis scenario timeline, and these activities cannot be done alone. During most crises, the team should meet face to face once or twice a day and stay connected by email and BlackBerry the rest of the time. For the crisis team, there is no downtime until the crisis is over.

Establishing a timetable. A timetable for briefing the media (usually a regular briefing every day and often in the late morning, in keeping with media deadlines) is important. Communicators need to create such a timetable, and then *stick to that timetable*. A timetable gives a sense of consistency and continuity for the company's publics, and this creates an important comfort level during the crisis.

Updating materials. Communicators need to ensure that materials being distributed, whether externally or internally, are current, with all the proper approvals in place. These materials then must be distributed to the proper personnel: everyone who is part of the crisis management team must be singing from the same song sheet, with no exceptions. The crisis plan must be updated to include all the specifics of the actual crisis as opposed to the one that communicators anticipated.

Identifying key spokespeople on the crisis team. Ensuring that key spokespeople on the crisis team are ready to deliver the key messages is another part of the communicator's job — ensuring that they are always ready to speak with the media and keeping track of who speaks to the media when, and what was said. As Carole Howard and Wilma Mathews note in *On Deadline: Managing Media Relations,* "Continually remind yourself and your spokesperson to be sensitive to the needs of audiences as they discuss an accident or other disaster. Business people tend to be concerned with money, facts, figures, and the reality of a situation: reporters and their readers or viewers are normally more interested in the emotional, dramatic, human aspects of the case."[6]

CONTEXT OF THE CRISIS — WEATHER

Conducting research. This is essential in crisis communications. Communicators may already have a template for research, but this must be checked against new, incoming information. Research is necessary because it helps communicators frame their own evolving set of responses to the crisis against what has happened before and what is happening now. It allows them to anticipate questions and keeps the plan they develop as current as possible.

Research takes the form of discovering what is currently happening within the organization. In the case of a computer malfunction, for instance, communicators will ask the company's IT professionals for background, then link this to the context of the company's direction; find out if this has happened before and, if so, how it was handled; and develop an understanding of what the company can do to fix the problem. Research also means looking at every available source of information that is related to the company's activities and the current state of affairs in the sector in which it operates. It means staying current with the news (did that computer glitch happen as an isolated incident in the company or was it a network problem?) and conducting research, perhaps via the Internet, on similar crises in other places. What happened and how did the participants handle the crisis? What was the outcome? This information will assist communicators in developing the approach of their own organization. All available information, including the current crisis communications plan, issues or briefing notes, and the organization's vision or mission statement, policies and practices should be brought to the table. Remember that the goal in the crisis must be linked to the organization's business plan and overall direction.

ORGANIZATIONS' WILL AND RESOLVE DURING A THREAT — DOCTRINE

Briefing internal stakeholders. It is up to the communicator to inform employees of what has happened and what they can expect, and to ensure that they understand that all media calls are to be handled by the communications department. Communicators need to teach others how to handle media calls — no speculation, no discussion with media — and to route those calls to the communications team. "Blast" emails distributed internally to all staff during the crisis are useful for giving regular updates.

Distributing briefing materials. Senior managers and directors need to provide an overview to staff within the organization, and it is the communicator's responsibility to see that this has been done. Employees often feel anxious during a crisis and will want the same comfort the company is providing to external publics. While all of the organization's staff will not be privy to every element or aspect of a crisis, heightened employee confidence will reduce the likelihood of leaks from disgruntled or frightened people within the organization, particularly in cases where health is involved. The 2003 SARS crisis in Toronto is an example of where people within an organization, such as nurses, hospital cafeteria workers and caretakers, needed to be as well informed as the doctors and senior executives. Keeping employees satisfied and in the loop is as much a goal of good crisis communications as is ensuring that the president and vice-president are well briefed on the issues. Chapter 6 discusses in more detail the need to keep employees informed.

Maintaining vigilance. During a crisis, communicators need to beware of focusing in too tightly on just the crisis. The business of communications is ongoing, and issues identification and management must continue. They need to be especially aware of arising issues that may have a further impact on the crisis.

REACHING OUT TO BUILD SUPPORT — TERRAIN

Deciding on the approach. The crisis team must decide whether it will contact the media or wait until the media contacts it once a crisis has arisen. If there is sensitive or legal information, communicators may want to wait until the media contacts them, and then provide a series of statements to position the company in light of its crisis activities. Most organizations find it beneficial, once initial contact has been made, to keep the flow of information moving.

Reviewing and updating contacts list. Communicators must be sure that they have current contact information for those with whom they communicate. While this activity is part of the Crisis Preparation short list that appears earlier in the chapter, it applies during the crisis as well.

Establishing a communications link with the organization's publics. Deciding on the best way to approach a public representative — by phone, email, or a face-to-face meeting? — is yet another important task of communicators. Once the link is established, they need to maintain that link on a regular basis. If a communicator promises to call a reporter back within three hours, he or she needs to follow through on that promise.

Answering all media inquiries. This is crucial, even if there is nothing new to report. Communicators should monitor and record all media clips and the company's responses to its publics' inquiries.

Establishing key messages and delivering the first message. Communicators need to prepare their senior spokespeople to deliver an initial message to the company's publics, even if that message is only, "We have a situation that is causing some difficulties for our organization. We are determining its cause and we are working hard to rectify the situation. We will be providing regular updates as we work toward a solution." This initial message tells the company's publics that the company is aware of the situation and has taken control. It also creates an expectation that communicators can meet — with information that comes directly from their organization.

Creating tactical materials. Such materials include news releases, question-and-answer sheets (Q&A), backgrounders and speeches. The content may change over the course of the crisis, but some messages communicators will want to repeat and reinforce.

Evaluating. The crisis is winding down — the media calls have stopped and the stakeholder concerns subsided. This is the time for communicators to begin evaluating the success of their crisis plan, updating the plan for the future and using it to identify gaps in their crisis communications approach.

RESEARCH AND RESPONSE TIMES IN A CRISIS

As *Maclean's* writer John Intini noted: "Those of us who've grown up in the Internet age, have — at least in our own minds — reinterpreted the meaning of intelligence. We've largely replaced our parents' traditional knowledge-based book smarts with resourcefulness — the ability to navigate through reams of information quickly and effectively, and isolate what's important."[7]

In today's world, where information networks are loaded with facts (not all of them useful), it's vital that communicators pull their facts together quickly and effectively. Today, the clock starts ticking as soon as the crisis lands on the communicator's desk. And woe to those who miss the 11 a.m. media update!

Crisis Plans as Living Documents: Revising under Fire

A plan is only as good as the people who use it. It should be recognized as a guideline, a set of steps that are used to help people work through the crisis. It's not cast in stone; rather, it simply says, "Here is the situation, here is the goal, here's what we need to do, here's what we need to say and here are the steps we're taking on the path to our goal."

TEAMS AND PEOPLE

The plan is intended to be used in a way that allows communicators to maintain contact with specific people within the organization and outside it. Some organizations work without a plan: they may be small organizations with a handful of people or, if they are larger, the thinking may be restricted to one or two individuals who oversee the crisis. But most organizations will need to work to a plan. Why? It allows an organization to work cohesively to create and distribute information. Furthermore, a plan includes backup people for every role, and so if people are absent, communicators instantly know whom to contact. A plan gives communicators solid ground from which to work. It is a document that needs to be updated on the go — "ownership" of it should be limited to one communicator (with one backup), but the revised plan needs to be shared with all members of the crisis communications team.

NEW MESSAGES

The messages communicators create must be reflective of the company's mission statement and express clear actions. Bear in mind, too, that unless it's absolutely clear that the crisis is going to be over quickly (and frankly, almost no one can be certain of that), communicators *need* to plan. Ad hoc messages or information that is not consistent often create more problems for the organization because they may contradict something that was said or done earlier in the crisis. They can also affect the desired outcome. The communications plan is the starting point for messages, action, reputation building and direction.

The messages must be fluid and must be able to be changed as communic-tors see fit. If changes occur during the crisis — if things go off schedule or something out of the ordinary happens — the plan must be updated to reflect these changes. The communicator works with contacts in the organization to update the plan and revise the messages accordingly while continuing to han-dle the situation. The messages may change during the crisis, but there will always be a record of what was said at the front end of the crisis, what was said as it moved toward conclusion and, finally, what was said at the end.

© Scott Adams/Dist. by United Feature Syndicate, Inc.

DEVIATING FROM THE PLAN

So what happens if a senior person or spokesperson goes off-message? What is the outcome if a plan is not followed? Few companies will improvise when it comes to handling a crisis. Results in these situations vary, depending on what the spokesperson says. The challenge for the communicator is in capturing what was said by the spokesperson and ensuring one of three things:

1. This new twist, introduced by one of the organization's own members, is understood and contextualized against the existing communications plan. Communicators may have to incorporate this new messaging into their existing plan.
2. The information is explained as being an opinion and not representative of the organization's direction (this can be dangerous, though, as the next log-ical question your publics will ask is "Then why did he or she say that?").

3. The statement is ignored and the company continues to stick to its key messages. Essentially, the company lets publics interpret such a misstep as a foible and not indicative of the organization's stance.

If a senior person in the organization decides to go against the direction and key messages outlined in the communications plan, the organization may face lawsuits and problems created as a result of speculation of publics, and its reputation may be harmed if the publics do not accept that the divergence was a hiccup in otherwise fair dealing.

Case Study: Canada's Flag Flap

It's not often that one sees a self-created crisis. As mentioned earlier, most crises are accidents of nature or the result of human error. Much of the time, as communicators, we are *responding* to a crisis: identifying the key elements, recognizing the perception of our publics and responding to it. But Newfoundland and Labrador premier Danny Williams *created* a crisis that reached international proportions in late 2004 when, in a dispute with the federal government, he decided to take down the Canadian flag from provincial government buildings.

THE FLAG FLAP: KEY MESSAGES

NEWFOUNDLAND AND LABRADOR PREMIER DANNY WILLIAMS: "The federal government's offer of allowing the province to keep only part of the royalties from oil is outrageous and unfair to Newfoundlanders. It will not be tolerated."

PRIME MINISTER PAUL MARTIN: "The Canadian flag is a symbol of unity and it should not be used as a lever in federal-provincial negotiations."

On December 22, 2004, Williams said that talks with the then federal Finance minister, Ralph Goodale, over offshore revenue were "fruitless" and that he, Williams, had "no intention" of bargaining. On December 23, Williams told reporters that "when you come into this room for press conferences in the future, that [Canadian] flag won't be there." He added that his province could lose $1 billion over eight years under the federal deal. By removing the flags on December 23, 2004, he was protesting against what he saw as the federal government's failure to make good on a pledge to allow the province to keep 100 per cent of its oil royalties from offshore development; under a federal equalization program, Newfoundland and Labrador would see a portion of those royalties clawed back.

The flags stayed down until January 10, 2005. In the intervening two and a half weeks, Williams got the attention he wanted, though not all of it came in the form of support. In a crisis that was played out in full view of the media — and through the media — Williams used the court of public opinion to voice his concerns. Williams was attempting to shame the Canadian government for its policies toward his province; in doing so, he sought to create a crisis to which the federal government would have to respond.

Why *create* a crisis? Williams had several compelling reasons. He wanted to focus public attention on his issue. He wanted to force the government back to the bargaining table. He wanted to use the political view of his province as effective leverage to get his point across. As the seventeenth-century Spanish philosopher Baltasar Gracián y Morales said, "Never contend with a man who has nothing to lose." And in Williams's view, there was indeed nothing to lose from the province's perspective.

Over the course of 18 days, the crisis polarized the media and the general public. The federal government, however, appeared to bide its time; then prime minister Paul Martin responded, also through the media, more than a week after the flag flap started, criticizing Williams for using the Canadian flag to further his own political agenda.

CBC *Newsworld*, DECEMBER 22, 2004: "Premier Danny Williams said offshore revenue talks with the federal government have failed to produce a deal."

CBC *Newsworld*, DECEMBER 23, 2004: "Newfoundland and Labrador's premier ordered the removal of all Canadian flags from provincial government buildings Thursday. Danny Williams made the order in retaliation for an offer from the federal government on offshore royalties he calls a 'slap in the face.'"

Globe and Mail, JANUARY 6, 2005:
THE HEADLINE: "Martin blasts Williams on flags."
THE LEAD: "Paul Martin upbraided Newfoundland and Labrador Premier Danny Williams yesterday for using the Canadian flag for political purposes, as Ottawa increased public pressure on Mr. Williams over his decision to walk away from talks on offshore oil royalties."

Globe and Mail columnist Margaret Wente, in a January 6, 2005, column titled "Oh Danny Boy, pipe down," had little sympathy for Williams's cause. Certainly, Wente acknowledged the popularity of the charismatic Williams: "Angry [Newfoundland and Labrador] citizens are flooding open-line shows and threatening that, unless they get what's owed to them by Canada, Newfoundland should go it alone." But she also weighed in with criticism of Newfoundland and Labrador following the trend in Canadian history that has "turned Canada into a permanently aggrieved nation, in which every region of the country is convinced that it's being brutally ripped off by every other region. No one is better at this blame game than the Newfs, egged on by generations of politicians."[8]

WILLIAMS'S STRATEGY

Williams wasn't worried about the view of "outsiders" like Wente. He knew he could garner support from an internal stakeholder audience (the Newfoundland populace) by drawing attention to an issue that soon became a crisis. His key message of "deep disappointment in Ottawa" was underscored by his dramatic and symbolic act of defiance, an act that drew a line in the sand and attracted media coverage to his issue.

Williams did his planning well. He knew his internal audience and knew that they would side with him. Constituents rarely go against a politician who will promise them more money, especially in what had for a long time been a have-not province under Confederation. Williams was less concerned about the view of the rest of Canada or the media that delivered the messages to Canadians outside his province; he knew that his goal — to bring the federal government back to the bargaining table — could be achieved through a single dramatic act. Would outsiders view it as a cheap publicity stunt? Perhaps, but their opinion was not a factor in Williams outlining and pursuing his goal.

Yet, it was a crisis that served Williams's end in focusing attention on a particular issue, because Williams knew the target audience, knew what his stakeholders expected of him and, most important, was in a position of having little to lose. There was a risk involved, that of appearing ineffectual and of being ignored, but the province was already in a losing situation. Williams risked his national reputation as a politician against the stakes — oil revenues, prosperity for his province — and enhanced his reputation as a significant politician in Newfoundland and Labrador. A win would mean more money for the province and, for Williams, a place in Newfoundland and Labrador history. A loss (no additional revenue for Newfoundland and Labrador) would mean the status quo and back to square one in discussions with the federal government. So for Williams, the risk was negligible.

As risk management expert Peter Sandman said in an October 2005 column on his website (www.psandman.com):

> Trying to arouse concern about anything is pushing a rock uphill. But if you're lucky, the rock gets to the top of the hill and starts rolling down the other side. As it gains mass as well as momentum, it converts to a snowball. Of course there's more than one hill; your rock/snowball is likely to need more pushing before long.[9]

Williams was pushing the rock uphill, betting that he could force attention from the federal government, put pressure on the feds through the media, gain the support of the people of Newfoundland and Labrador and allow the crisis to gain momentum on the downhill slope. Sticking to his key message and with a powerful image (a flagless flagpole) to underscore it, Williams scored again and again with national media, his message reverberating for weeks. He knew, too, that other provinces, all with their own sets of financial grievances with the federal government, would watch with interest to see the outcome. Williams was the proverbial David against Goliath, and as a general rule people love the image of the "little guy" not only challenging the seemingly undefeatable monster but subduing him in single combat. This drama was compelling to many publics both within and outside Newfoundland and Labrador.

THE OUTCOME

The public, in responding to the flap, was split on the issue. Those on radio and television call-in shows alternated between support and criticism. Many from Newfoundland (or those who had been born and raised in that province but had subsequently moved) hailed Williams's efforts; others, largely from outside Newfoundland and Labrador, called for him to be removed from office.

THE FLAG FLAP: ENDPOINT MEDIA COVERAGE

TORONTO STAR, JANUARY 10, 2005:
THE HEADLINE: "Nfld. Calls truce in flag flap."
THE LEAD: "Newfoundland Premier Danny Williams is ready to climb down the flagpole and let the Maple Leaf fly again."

TORONTO STAR, JANUARY 11, 2005:
THE HEADLINE: "Maple Leaf raised in Nfld . . . Williams ends 3-week protest."
THE LEAD: "With the Canadian flag flying once again in Newfoundland, Prime Minister Paul Martin is sending a letter today to Premier Danny Williams, urging him to rejoin the talks he broke off shortly before Christmas."

By January 10, 2005, Williams had reached his goal of generating interest on the part of Canadians and forcing the federal government to pay attention and give his province a better deal. He announced to the media that he was putting the Canadian flags back up. A January 11 *Toronto Star* editorial, titled "Back to you, Mr. Martin," said that "[b]y removing the flag for two weeks, Premier Danny Williams got what he wanted: the attention of Canadians, if not their sympathy."

Indeed, Williams had garnered enough attention and sympathy to ensure that his province would get a better deal. By the end of January, the federal government signed a deal with the province ensuring that 100 per cent of oil revenues would go to Newfoundland and Labrador, creating an extra $2 billion over eight years in revenue. Other provinces (while not resorting to a flag flap) were inspired to negotiate their own deals as a result of the general feeling that the federal government was taking financial advantage of them.

POST-MORTEM OF THE STRATEGY AND PLANNING

What are some of the issues that this crisis focused on? Let's look at it from both sides, and how those issues served both Williams and Martin. Remember, in a democracy, a politician's policy can be just about anything, so long as he or she has the backing of the electorate. So, did the federal government have the right to take the proceeds of a revenue-generating industry from the province? According to Williams, the answer was clearly no — and his means of forcing the hand of the federal government could be seen as a fair and reasonable way of handling the situation, appealing to his own electorate for support and influence. Williams got what he wanted and so did his province.

Williams was able to use a powerful symbol of patriotism to drive home a point and draw attention to an issue. Using the platform of the little guy against the powerful nation-state, the crisis resulted in support for Williams from his constituents; support was also felt outside the province, from the media and members of the public Canada-wide. While the support was not total, it did not matter: Williams drew the attention of the federal government and managed to win back Newfoundland and Labrador's royalties.

Clearly, Williams demonstrated that he was aware of how this crisis would affect the Martin government.

Other issues of crisis planning need to be addressed, however. Did Williams plan for the long-term consequences of using such a strategy — causing a crisis? His ploy resulted in some anti-Newfoundland sentiment. He also found his reputation tarnished by what was seen as grandstanding, resulting in lowered credibility. His ploy was a strong card to play, but how often can such a card be played? Such a dramatic gesture could not be repeated with the same effectiveness. A dramatic gesture like this, used more than once, becomes comedic or worse. Arguably, this tactic purchased a victory today at the expense of credibility tomorrow.

Communicators must remember that publics have a longer memory than they are often credited for. While they may not remember details, they will remember how they felt about a company. When a company's actions during a crisis get the company clear of one or more crises at the expense of its long-term reputation, the strategy is questionable. Cigarette companies for years hid behind expert testimony that addictiveness and cancer risks associated with smoking could not be proved. The public has followed the issue up to the present day, and is well aware of a recent court finding that cigarette companies deliberately deceived their customers about the health issues of smoking. It is unlikely that the industry will be seen as honest in our lifetime, whatever it may do to repair its image.

THINK TANK

1. Did Newfoundland and Labrador premier Danny Williams have a plan? Did he think about the possible outcomes before he made his dramatic announcement of removing the flags?
2. The federal government did not appear to be in a hurry to respond to the crisis, despite protests from Canadians nationwide. Did the government have a rationale in waiting for a week to pass before having the prime minister comment? If yes, what was it?
3. How do you think Williams assessed the success of his venture? How did the federal government assess it?

Conclusion

A critical component of crisis communications is the crisis plan — a plan that is prepared and on hand *before* a crisis arises. Before crisis hits, communicators must carefully examine what they know about their organization and their relationships with their publics. They must look ahead to see how emerging issues may affect the organization: planning for crises requires an in-depth look at the possible outcomes of an issue. The crisis plan establishes a goal of how the organization wants to be perceived, the roles of people in the organization, the key messages to be delivered and a strategy for how communicators will deliver those messages.

Proper crisis communications planning must consider:
- Internal and external publics and how they view the organization;
- The company's leadership, recognizing that it affects key messages and credibility;
- The emotional tone communicators set at the beginning of a crisis, as this can affect the success or failure of the organization.

Communicators cannot control the questions that come to them during a crisis, and they cannot control the media. However, they *can* control the flow of information throughout the organization and outside it. They also can control when they want to speak and what they want to say, as well as the venue where the messages are delivered.

Communicators should not overlook the importance of the plan's review component. Evaluating how the situation was handled once it has subsided allows communicators to measure the success of the crisis management and adjust their crisis plan accordingly.

Part II: Interview and Exercises

Robert E. Waite,
Senior Vice-President, Communications and Stakeholder Relations, Canada Post Corporation

Born in the United States and holding dual Canadian citizenship, Robert Waite started his communications career in newspapers in Massachusetts. A newspaper journalist by training, he recommends that communicators get a solid background in subjects such as history, political science and economics and then hone their journalistic skills with practice.

Waite worked at various jobs in politics, including as press secretary to American senator and 1996 presidential candidate Bob Dole, before moving to the corporate world with Ford and later IBM.

He came to Canada in 1986 and worked for CIBC from 2000 to 2005 as senior vice-president, Communications and Public Affairs. Since 2005 he has served as senior vice-president, Communications and Stakeholder Relations, for Canada Post. With CIBC, Waite handled communications during the 2003 power outage that affected most of southern Ontario and the U.S. eastern seaboard, as well as during the 2003 SARS (Severe Acute Respiratory Syndrome) crisis in Toronto, and he played a lead role in the bank's handling of various regulatory issues.

ON PLANNING

"In an organization of any size and scope, communications planning is important. It is especially critical that roles and responsibilities be clearly defined and that mechanisms, such as call trees, be in place to ensure that the organization can respond to a crisis in a timely fashion. Can a communications department wing it? Of course it can — but why would it want to? It seems to me that the more communicators can work from a pre-arranged and pre-discussed plan (which has management onside), the more effective they will be in rolling out their messaging."

ON TEAMS

"With experienced communicators as the foundation, at CIBC I established a business continuity management team to handle crisis situations. Team members represent every major business unit in CIBC, from legal and human resources to information technology, world markets, communications and specific business areas, such as personal banking and loans.

"The team uses a crisis room at its Toronto headquarters, and the bank also has an emergency crisis management unit at an undisclosed location. The unit is fully serviced and ready to go at a moment's notice. It's hard-wired to be used if necessary during a full-blown crisis."

ON ADVANCE PREPARATION

"The key to dealing successfully with a situation is proactive management through the course of the emergency, from emergency response to assessment and disaster declaration, right through to normalization and return. CIBC runs practice sessions for a typical crisis; the team doesn't know in advance what the crisis will be. Afterward we did a post-game analysis of our response. We used that to continue to build up our crisis response capabilities. We had real-world scenarios and practice scenarios — our team was well practised: all the members knew what to do when they went to their battle stations.

"In some crises, leaving messages on people's voice mail [within the organization] is an effective means of getting out an emergency message. If you have already planned for this, it can be accomplished in less than an hour — as I found at IBM and CIBC on two occasions. But if you are starting from scratch to set up such a communications mechanism, it can take days to figure out. The key is to identify voice mail nodes that service employee groups. At CIBC, 22 nodes serviced almost 40,000 employees. By leaving 22 identical one-minute messages, we could reach virtually all our employees."

A PLAN THAT WORKED, AND ONE THAT DIDN'T

"At CIBC we had a robust communications plan that was ready to implement when 9/11 happened. We had foreseen and planned for the loss of a facility as part of our business recovery plan. We had a team in place that had experience in real estate, technology, facilities management and so on. We also had a plan and mechanism in place to contact employees not only at work but at home. So when we lost One World Financial Center, adjacent to ground zero [in New York City], we could move fairly quickly to contact our 2,000 people — accounting for all 2,000 by the Sunday morning following the disaster (eight were injured but no one was killed) — and to transfer our data and technology activities to other sites, in New Jersey and Ontario. We were also able to have our trading floor up and running at an alternative site on Lexington Avenue when the New York Stock Exchange reopened. This required a good deal of both internal and external communications, as our workforce needed to know where to report and our customers needed to know where to find us. So this case, while spectacular, was very close to what we had all practised and simulated. Planning was a big help. And we learned lessons from the 9/11 crisis that allowed us to add to and refine the plan.

"A case where we might have done more and better planning, had we anticipated the scenario, was the SARS outbreak. In this case, buildings were not the issue — concentrations of people were. One fortunate and critical piece of planning at CIBC was to have the company's staff physician, Dr. David Brown, trained as a spokesperson in addition to his role on the business continuity team. This allowed us to move far quicker than we might otherwise have been able to, to provide employees with reliable, trustworthy information and guidance very swiftly. As part of our overall planning process, Dr. Brown had established strong relations with Toronto, provincial, and national health authorities; those relationships were of great value and led to us ordering a shutdown of business travel into and out of Toronto well ahead of other businesses doing so."

ON ASKING FOR HELP

"I have never been afraid to ask my counterparts at competitive firms (while at CIBC, people like David Moorcroft, senior vice-president of corporate communications at the Royal Bank, for example) what they think and what their plans call for. There is an informal, 55-year-old association called the Public Relations Seminar that is made up of the top 150 communications people from around the world. It has no paid staff — it's all volunteer. We hold an annual conference, and this year, one of the exercises was a pandemic simulation. But more important, we have an unwritten rule that if one seminarian calls another seeking information or advice, that person must take the time to provide it. And while those folks are probably pretty good at winging it when they have to, my experience is that virtually all have communications plans in place and are constantly adding to their understanding of how to use them."

Exercise: A Religious Holidays Debacle

Review the background information on Saskatchewan Chemical presented in Chapter 4. Below are details about another contentious issue. Your task is to plan for this issue: decide how to handle it and prepare appropriate communications materials.

THE CRISIS

Saskatchewan Chemical has good relations with its local union, to which the majority of its plant workers belong. However, there have been some questions from staff about religious holidays. Recently, a member of the Wiccan Church, Martin Trask, asked for Wiccan religious days off. He has offered to work on traditional holidays during the year, such as Christmas, to compensate for the time off. Trask, a supervisor in the manufacturing area, is an employee of 12 years. Unnamed sources alerted the media of Trask's request, and it has created a stir in the local media, which expressed opinions both for and against it. Initially, the company said no to the holiday request but, under pressure from union officials, relented.

A columnist in a local conservative newspaper wrote a story stating that Saskatchewan Chemical was promoting devil worship. You know from your research that this is erroneous — that Wicca does not involve devil worship. Conversely, a television talk show in Regina called for compassion, understanding and acceptance, and suggested that preventing Trask from worshipping would be akin to denying him his rights under the Canadian Charter of Rights and Freedoms. On top of all this, an unidentified worker has left a picture of a devil at Trask's workstation, and a small group of fundamentalist Christians in the workplace is threatening to walk off the job if the company continues to employ Trask. By this time, the matter is starting to draw the attention of national media.

THINK TANK

In reviewing the issue, ask yourself these questions:

1. What is Trask's work record like? Are there issues about absences, outside his religious observances?
2. Is the situation creating a disruption in terms of productivity?
3. Is the situation creating resentment or fear among other staff members?
4. What does the company need to do for its internal stakeholders to help them understand Trask's choice of religion and worship?

5. What should the company say to its external stakeholders?
6. Is the company president, J.S. Singh, prepared to handle media inquiries? What materials does he need to ready him?
7. What initiative can be taken to address the column about devil worship that appeared in the local paper?

YOUR TASK

Prepare a briefing note and Q&A for the company president, outlining the company's position on the Wiccan Church and on Martin Trask.

III | Publics

5 Publics I:
Communicating with External Stakeholders during a Crisis

> Men honor what lies within the sphere of their knowledge, but do not realize how dependent they are on what lies beyond it.
>
> —CHUANG TZU

When airline carrier Jetsgo Corporation abruptly went out of business on the eve of March Break 2005, it left a lot of people in the lurch. More than 17,000 external stakeholders — Jetsgo's customers — were stranded across North America, and many more lost money on travel reservations. The company's 1,300 internal stakeholders — its employees — lost their jobs. Newspaper headlines ranged from "Airline fiasco: 17,000 stranded; 1,350 lose jobs" and "Workers enraged, tearful" to "Flighting mad," "Clipped wings" and "Jetsgo passengers seek flights, refunds."

If you were handling corporate communications for Jetsgo at that time, what would you have recommended the company do?

Now imagine you worked for a competing airline. What key messages would you have created for your stakeholders in the wake of the Jetsgo bankruptcy?

As daunting as these questions may seem, they're exactly the types of questions communicators need to be prepared to answer if a crisis hits their organization — or even their industry. In addition, these questions illustrate the importance of taking stakeholder concerns into account when developing a crisis communications plan: it's essential to recognize that just because a crisis falls in someone else's lap, it doesn't mean the communicator's own company won't be affected. This chapter focuses on thinking through how issues impact stakeholders, with emphasis on external stakeholder groups, by examining these problems:

- How do communicators identify their company's various stakeholder groups?
- How do communicators cultivate a better understanding of their stakeholders' information needs and interests, and how do they integrate those interests into their crisis planning and issues monitoring?
- How can communicators work with external stakeholders to resolve a crisis?

In this chapter we explore these and other stakeholder issues — because, as we're about to see, stakeholders can make or break a company's success, especially during a crisis.

Who Are the Stakeholders? Why Are They Important?

Stakeholders, often called "key publics," are groups of people that can be affected by the actions of the organization. They can also have a profound effect on the organization's direction. Consequently, they have a particular interest in the decisions the organization makes. These key publics include internal stakeholders, the organization's employees — the topic of the next chapter — and a wide variety of external stakeholders.

THE FOUR CORNERS OF THE STAKEHOLDER MATRIX

During a crisis, four groups of people will be most involved in disseminating a company's message, receiving it or shaping it. In other words, they will most heavily influence how the organization is perceived in the marketplace. And since that perception is an organization's lifeblood, the communicator's job is to get these groups onside as quickly as possible, reaching out to them on a regular basis as the communicator works to resolve the issues at hand. The four groups are —

- *Internal stakeholders.* As we've discussed, employees are a key part of an organization, its culture, and its values. They are often also the spokespeople and ambassadors for the organization to its external stakeholders and publics.
- *External stakeholders.* They may be most affected by what's happening in the company — whether it's a change in the organization's policies or procedures, or something more significant.
- *The community at large.* Although the community in which a company is located is effectively one of the external stakeholder groups, it deserves special consideration during a crisis. Strong community relations are essential because a highly contentious issue or crisis can have a profound effect on the community.
- *The media.* The media is discussed in Chapter 7. For now, suffice it to say that a crisis always makes good fodder for news, so the communicator must expect the media to scrutinize every move his or her company makes as it responds to the issue. And remember: the reporting will reflect how quickly, effectively and sensitively — or how slowly, poorly and callously — the media believe the company handled its problem from a human and community perspective.

External stakeholders, the focus of this chapter, may include:
- Customers and potential customers
- Neighbours (both businesses and residents)
- Business partners
- Suppliers
- Investors
- Distributors
- Government
- Lobby groups and activists
- Regulatory bodies

There are many more possible external stakeholder groups; who they are depends on the company and the industry in which it operates.

Stakeholders play a crucial role in building a business's profile. Customers, for example, don't just buy a product, use it and then throw it away. They talk about the product and company to family, friends and other current or potential stakeholders, thereby sharing their criticism or support. In other words, they are a mirror of how the company is seen "out there," just as the company's employees provide a much-needed window on how things are going "in here."

PERCEPTION IS KEY

This leads us to one of the most important foundations of successful stakeholder relations. When dealing with stakeholders, what a communicator *knows* about his or her organization isn't necessarily as important as understanding how the organization is *perceived* in the marketplace. Communicators simply *must* be able to see the company the way others see it, otherwise the outcome can be disastrous.

For example, a CEO who works for a worldwide bottler of soft drinks may seldom if ever think beyond the sales of the company's product. Communicators need to see things differently. It can't be emphasized enough that public perception is the company's lifeblood. Communicators need to be aware not only of what people think of their company's product but of what they think about the company's practices as a whole — how it treats its employees and the environment, whether it's involved in unethical business practices, and what charities and causes it supports. Failure to be keenly aware of how people see the company can result in a tarnished reputation, fewer jobs and lost revenue.

Developing, growing and nurturing brand loyalty is a major goal of organizations and is often considered marketing's ultimate goal. According to Richard L. Oliver, marketing professor in the Owen Graduate School of Management at Vanderbilt University, in *Whence Customer Loyalty,* true brand loyalty implies that customers who possess it will forego their own desires for the sake of the brand.[1] Fans of brands will do what they can to demonstrate they are brand savvy — we see examples of this every day with labels and logos on clothing, oversized vehicles and overpriced coffee — but whether they will forego their own comfort might be a debatable point.

Pepsi-Cola, for example, builds brand loyalty by allowing fans to buy products with Pepsi Points, through a mass distribution of billions of points on cups and packages that are redeemable for merchandise.

People can become enamoured with a brand to the point where it usually doesn't matter how the product was created or where (in other words, any perceived moral comfort is not involved; often consumers don't really care if sweatshop workers were paid a penny a day to produce a product for which the consumer pays $200) — what matters is the positive emotion the brand creates.

What does this mean to a company? If it builds brand loyalty, it means that people are making an investment in the company. They identify with the company, with the product, with the good emotional feelings the product creates for them. Brand loyalty is good for a company's business. But if something goes wrong, even something simple, brand loyalty can be affected; a 2005 study conducted on behalf of the frozen food industry found that dented or even slightly damaged frozen-food packaging could have a severe effect on brand loyalty — customers won't trust a food product that looks like it might be unsafe. And tinkering with a brand's perception, through actions such as massive product price cuts, can also affect loyalty, as consumers associate value of the product with the amount of money they pay.

Over the past decade, American and Canadian makers of athletic shoes, leisure wear and other products found that offshore production can affect brand loyalty, particularly if they juxtaposed a "Made in USA" or "Made in Canada" *promotional feel* against the reality that the company's products were made in Southeast Asia by workers who could never afford to buy them. In some cases, this created disenchantment with the brand. Large multinational companies countered the negative effects — media accounts of densely packed sweatshops where workers were paid a few cents a day, with a resulting drop in sales as once-loyal customers stopped buying — by pouring more money into promotional campaigns, supporting more community causes and redefining the company's marketing image by explaining how and why the company was doing business in that particular way — usually with a promise that things were changing.

Corporate communications deals with an organization's image and reputation; that image goes beyond the counter sales of soft drinks, running shoes or leisure wear. No matter what a company produces and markets, communicators are in the business of building links, polishing reputations and demonstrating that the organization is committed to, and plays an active role in, its community. An important component in that community is the stakeholder. Napoleon Bonaparte once said: "Four hostile newspapers are more feared than a thousand bayonets." When it comes to stakeholder relations, one might even venture to say that a mere handful of hostile stakeholders may be more feared than those hostile newspapers.

Why? Because although crises may rise and fall, stakeholders stick around. They'll keep their collective eye on the company long after the reporter has filed the story, turned off the computer and clicked off the video camera. And, in an Internet-connected world, a company's stakeholders will set the tone for how others see it.

ACCOUNTABILITY IN THE MARKETPLACE

The power and importance of stakeholders cannot be overstated. Clearly, companies are accountable to them. In the documentary *The Corporation*, Robert Keyes, president and CEO of the Canadian Council for International Business, discusses an organization's responsibility to its stakeholders and the possible side effects of either fulfilling or not fulfilling that responsibility: "Does there need to be some measure of accountability? Yes. If companies don't do what they should be doing, they're going to be punished in the marketplace. And that's not what any company wants."[2]

Think for a minute about accountability. How many people are you directly accountable to in your day? How many people matter to you, in terms of how they view your work? How significant is their input on what you do and say? Most communicators view stakeholders as partners in the communications process — in building a company's profile, delivering messages to the community, protecting the environment and creating stronger business links. Stakeholders, like the media, are also the watchful eyes that keep track of what communicators do. However, communicators often have a closer relationship with stakeholders than with the media. While communicators work to build their media contacts, they may find that they are meeting with stakeholders as often as necessary to keep them apprised of what they are doing. Communicators owe them transparency, within reason, and if they want stakeholders' support, they will actively demonstrate that they are living up to the standards they have set for themselves through their organization's vision, mission and values.

In a crisis, stakeholders can be communicators' worst critics or their top supporters. Communicators ignore them at their peril, but if they treat them well, stakeholders can provide effective support for the crisis management team — not necessarily as participants but as third-party endorsers who will back up the organization's position, often with something positive to say about the action it is taking.

THE BIG DOG

If you're a stakeholder, a crisis is like a big dog facing you in the middle of the street. The street is wide and the dog is close; there's nowhere to run for cover; you have nothing with which to protect yourself. So you ask yourself what you really, really need to know about that dog: "Will it bite me?"

That's exactly what stakeholders want to know about a crisis: Am I going to get hurt? And they need to know the answer fast — just like you, if you were facing that dog.

Forget about the specifics of the breed, its coat, its intelligence, how good a companion it makes. The only question is whether it's going to hurt you.

That's the same question communicators have to ask themselves from the perspective of their stakeholders during a crisis situation: Will our stakeholders be hurt by what happens during the crisis? Will they be hurt in the wake of it? What do we need to tell them about the big dog? And, after the crisis is over, how will they feel about it?

Identifying Stakeholders

Because stakeholders are crucial to the success of an organization, it's important for communicators to think as broadly as possible when setting out to identify them. The research to identify stakeholders, as well as the work in building links to them, should begin long before a crisis hits.

When identifying stakeholders, look carefully at:

- Customers who buy the company's product or service and the consumer groups that take an interest in the product or service;
- Groups that actively watch the company and that comment on the organization's or industry's initiatives, whether for or against them;
- Government regulators that set the standards for how the company and/or industry conducts itself;
- Industry or business organizations the company belongs to.

For example, a bank's stakeholders include employees, management and the board of directors; current and potential clients; other banks; the Canadian Bankers Association, to which all major chartered banks belong; organizations such as the Canadian Federation of Independent Business, which looks to banks to provide good service to its members; and regulatory bodies such as the Bank of Canada, the Ontario Securities Commission, and, at the grassroots level, local chambers of commerce.

For a government body such as the Ontario Ministry of Transportation, stakeholders include employees; organizations such as the Canadian Automobile Association, Mothers Against Drunk Driving, and the Ontario Trucking Association; various policing organizations, such as the Ontario Provincial Police; grassroots road-safety organizations, such as the Ontario Cycling Association and the Ontario Safety League; and the general public, which uses the province's roads every day.

Knowing the organization's stakeholders is essential, but it's only the first step. Communicators must understand their stakeholders' needs and expectations, and their relationship with the organization. This leads us to our next topic of discussion: stakeholder analysis.

© Stephan Pastis/Dist. by United Feature Syndicate, Inc.

Stakeholder Analysis

In terms of business history, the twentieth century was defined by the rise of the corporation; according to the Joseph L. Rotman School of Management at the University of Toronto, in its publication *Principles of Stakeholder Management,* the corporation was "uniquely effective in mobilizing resources and knowledge; increasing productivity; and creating new technologies, products and services. Corporations have proliferated and grown because they meet the needs of various members of society: customers, workers and communities, as well as investors."[3]

With that rise came the stakeholder, the individual or group that is affected by the corporation's operation. In the twenty-first century, the increased speed of information, especially via the Internet, has contributed significantly to the impact that the stakeholder can have on a corporation's profile, operation and success. Stakeholders can find like-minded stakeholders through chat groups, blogs, email networks and other sources — they can share information and opinions much faster than in the past and can receive, analyze and disseminate information more quickly than ever before. Stakeholders who have a problem with a particular organization can share their views and rest easy in the knowledge that they are not alone in their opinions. And, with every shared communication, they and other disgruntled stakeholders will be eroding the reputation of the organization that offended them. Conversely, if stakeholders are sharing positive attitudes about an organization, they can be helping to put a shine on the organization's reputation through collective endorsement and support. Since the advent of the Internet, organizations are facing a highly independent media channel within which opinions are being forged around the clock, seven days a week.

To use Sun Tzu's concept, this change in the media terrain has spurred companies to create positions that deal *exclusively* with stakeholder analysis and relations. Many corporate communications departments employ people who scan stakeholder information. They carry out research through accessing, reviewing and gathering information from publications and reports created by like-minded organizations or groups. They also conduct focus groups, polls and direct meetings and engage in stakeholder analysis — parsing the stakeholders' positions on the organization's activities and creating plans that respond to the concerns raised.

Stakeholder analysis requires that communicators take a look at stakeholders' influence and power on the organization, as well as their stake — their interest or concern — in the particular activity or decision under scrutiny.

DIFFERENT STAKEHOLDERS; DIFFERENT STRATEGIES

Stakeholder groups need to be linked to the communicator's everyday activities. They need to be recipients of regular newsletters, advisory emails and phone calls where appropriate — any information that is geared to a general audience should be provided also to stakeholders. Here is a way of looking at how communicators can build and maintain relationships with common stakeholder groups.

Stakeholder Group	What They Need Day to Day	What They Need in a Crisis	How We Communicate with Them	Gaining Their Support
Customers	Newsletters Product information Updates on new products and services	Information on product recalls — sent via email Direction to website for product information Information phone numbers and email addresses to express concerns over product or issues during a crisis	Email Newsletter Website Customer service office Blogs	High-quality products and product information Excellent customer service
Investors	Updates on company progress through: Regular meetings Phone calls Newsletters	Daily updates to apprise them of progress being made during the crisis Stakeholder meetings to seek their advice, opinion and support Briefings to provide information on company's next steps	Email Phone calls Personal contact with executives News releases sent directly to investor	Proven track record of the company Demonstration that the company is progressive and proactive in seeking ways to protect the investor's interests

SUPPLIERS	Regular meetings to ensure continuity and a satisfactory business relationship	Daily updates on the crisis as company progresses toward resolution Briefings on steps being taken during the crisis	Email Phone calls; contact with in-house business consultants News releases	Continuity of business; satisfactory performance and ability to fulfill contractual obligations
GOVERNMENT AND REGULATORY BODIES (ALL LEVELS)	Regular meetings to ensure strong relationship and to maintain awareness of government issues and programs (e.g., marketing, international business programs)	Where appropriate, daily updates on crisis resolution Meetings to brief representatives of government bodies on actions taken to end the crisis Meetings to garner support for company's actions during the crisis	Email Phone calls Regular contact from company representative News releases	Compliance with government regulations
LOBBY GROUPS AND ACTIVISTS	Newsletters Provision of email updates as well as occasional meetings (where appropriate) to ensure that groups are aware of new developments at the company	Blast email distribution to keep groups updated Meetings/briefings to give groups a chance to ask questions about the organization's actions during the crisis Provision of news releases to keep groups updated on company's actions	Email Meetings and briefings Blogs Regular contact with company's stakeholder relations representative	Compliance with government regulations Demonstrated respect for human rights Demonstrated commitment to environmental values Compliance of products to established codes Community action: participation in local activities and support for charities and civic events

PLAYING FAVOURITES

Though it's true that communicators will likely have more contact with certain stakeholders — generally those linked most closely to the business — they would be remiss to put themselves in the position of favouring one stakeholder group over another. Even a marginal stakeholder group can be important. Banks, for example, monitor their customer base most closely, but they do not ignore the Canadian Bankers Association, regulatory agencies or international business associations.

Assume, for example, that a metal fabrication company's primary stakeholders are customers, industry associations and regulatory agencies. An engineering council located far away — seemingly insignificant, with a small membership, and with whom the company usually has little contact — discovers an alleged defect in a piece of equipment the company makes. If the council is right, the defect could endanger lives. But the company's engineers say it's not a problem and so the company decides to ignore the warning. Then one morning the newspaper runs a story in which representatives of the association are interviewed about the possible defect in the equipment — and the company's share prices fall dramatically. Suddenly, that obscure council is not so insignificant. Instead, the communicators have been placed in a reactive situation, trying to recover from accusations and tainted perceptions about what their company stands for. Unfortunately, the game of "stakeholder favourites" has resulted in a public crisis of confidence in their company and its products. Here, the issue stage of the crisis was missed entirely because of disdain for a stakeholder.

A REAL-LIFE EXAMPLE OF "WHAT WERE THEY THINKING?"

As we've seen in the fictional example of the metal fabricator, disconnects between an organization and its stakeholders can lead to serious problems with a company's perception in the marketplace, if not full-blown crises. If there's an information gap between an organization and its stakeholders — such that they don't understand what the organization is doing, when it's doing it or why — communicators need to bridge that gap. Otherwise, stakeholders will feel their interests are being ignored, and that could have negative repercussions not only on how the company is perceived in the marketplace but on its bottom line.

Let's consider a real-life example of the damage that can result if communicators ignore a stakeholder group's interests.

"The Little People" versus Coca-Cola

A shopkeeper in Mexico City, Raquel Chávez, won a case against the Coca-Cola Company, which had tried to prevent her from selling another brand of soft drink in her tiny store in a poor neighbourhood. In a classic David-versus-Goliath battle, the shopkeeper, a single mother with three kids, fought back.

The result? The company faced US$68 million in anti-monopoly fines. Even if the full fine is not imposed following an appeal by Coca-Cola, at the time of writing, the company was facing a bigger gap in its credibility.

With its 70 per cent share of the Mexican soft drink market, why on earth did Coca-Cola try to crack down on an independent shopkeeper who was simply trying to make a living? The company had lost sight of its stakeholders — the government agencies that regulate business (the legal decision came down from the Government of Mexico, penalizing Coca-Cola and several dozen other bottlers and distributors), the shopkeepers who sell the product, the customers who buy it and the media who reported on the proceedings. It would have been better for Coca-Cola to have left the matter alone and stand by the business credo of supporting an open market. As Coca-Cola says on its website, its manifesto includes doing the right things for the marketplace, environment and communities in the 200-plus countries where it does business. Yet, it was seen as trying to strengthen its grip on what was already deemed by many to be close to a total market monopoly.

This example illustrates the importance of perception in the marketplace. Did Coca-Cola actually intend to prevent a single mother from making a living so she could feed her children? Of course not. But that's how these events were perceived in the marketplace, and the marketplace reacted accordingly.

This example also shows the importance of stakeholder analysis. Communicators — as the people who research and write key messages for their organization — must know who their stakeholders are and how they feel about the company. In addition, they must carefully consider whether any of the company's actions, decisions or communications could be perceived negatively in the marketplace.

The How-To of Successful Stakeholder Relations

As we've already established, effective corporate communications — and, by extension, good crisis management — depends on sound relationships with the stakeholder base. But how can communicators ensure strong stakeholder relations during a crisis? The answer is clear: they can't. They need to start building those relationships, as well as their understanding of stakeholders' needs and expectations, long before a crisis hits. They need to —

- Understand stakeholders' needs in relation to the organization's stated goals, vision, mission and values;
- Ensure regular reports on stakeholder activity are circulated through the communications department and, if necessary, at the executive level;
- Keep track of the correspondence that comes in. Letters and email help an organization identify its stakeholder groups and the key issues that may be emerging.

BUILDING AND MAINTAINING RELATIONSHIPS

As with any successful relationship, effective stakeholder relations are built on open, honest, frequent communications that flow back and forth between the various stakeholder groups and the company.

In his book *Excellence in Public Relations and Communication Management,* James E. Grunig calls this back-and-forth flow of information a "two-way symmetrical model." Internally, there should be an open flow of communication between employees and management; externally, the "flow" should move between associations, customers and the organization itself. This two-way symmetrical model of communication is the foundation of relationship maintenance, ensuring a steady stream of understanding between an organization and its stakeholders.[4]

While the theory behind Grunig's model is easy to understand, what does it look like in practice?

In working with external stakeholders, it's important for communicators to identify the appropriate people to talk to in each stakeholder group. Communicators must be sure that those people are empowered to pass the information up their own chain of command. Once communicators have identified these people, they begin building their relationship with them through open, honest, frequent communications. These communications can take the form of meetings, emails, newsletters, phone calls and invitations to corporate events. Whatever the method, the organization should have communications staff whose job, at least 25 per cent of the time, is focused on helping to build good stakeholder relations.

Keeping track of when representatives from the company have met with stakeholders, always ensuring that someone takes notes on the issues discussed and the outcomes and expectations that resulted, is an important task. In doing so, communicators are building a strong and continuous business relationship and an unbroken flow of communication that will lead to a better understanding of the organization's direction.

To further explore the range of information communicators might collect from their stakeholder meetings, let's use an example from the Ontario Ministry of Economic Development and Trade (MEDT), a government ministry responsible for building links to business and boosting the province's business profile to its primary publics: the Ontario business community (its primary stakeholder), as well as business communities in other provinces, representatives at the federal level and the international business community. MEDT's common practice is to pay regular visits to stakeholder groups, including local chambers of commerce, to determine their positions on the ministry's various programs and services. Sometimes these are simple round-table sessions — a meet-and-greet to get to know people in the stakeholder group. Other meetings are on specific topics, such as the ministry's loans programs for small business. The results of these meetings are presented in reports with charts like the example below, outlining the stakeholders' positions on the ministry's activities:

STAKEHOLDER ORGANIZATION	SUBJECT	REACTION	KEY ISSUES	PROPOSED MEDT STRATEGY
Lakelands Chamber of Commerce	Government's Small Business Loans Program	Positive — organization felt MEDT responded effectively to chamber's request to provide more service to this region	Questions regarding why there is only one MEDT business representative in the local office	Weekly phone calls to MEDT local business rep; quarterly meetings with chamber staff. Outreach involving regular meetings. Requires regular updates on chamber's position on serving small business.

According to John McHugh, senior vice-president and partner, Avant Strategic Communications, it's essential to track issues in the stakeholder community. Sometimes an issue becomes contentious, potentially even a crisis, because sufficient attention was not paid to stakeholder concerns. A direct link to stakeholders will give communicators a better sense of the pulse of the community around them.

Often, says McHugh, an issue can fester in the stakeholder community long before it becomes public: "If you do a good job of identifying, monitoring, managing and resolving emerging issues, you are likely to be more effective in heading off most highly contentious issues, or potential crises, which may affect your organization."[5]

The need to listen to stakeholders, as communicators work to plan and deliver communications initiatives, especially crisis plans, cannot be overstated. In his book *Seven Cardinal Rules of Risk Communication,* Vincent Covello, Ph.D., of the Center for Risk Communication in New York, says stakeholders are essential players: "Key publics are accepted and involved as legitimate participants ... [P]eople and communities have a right to participate in decisions that affect their lives, their property, and the things they value. Demonstrate respect for stakeholders and company sincerity by involving the community early, before important decisions have already been made."[6]

But it should also be clear that communicators don't invite stakeholders into their war room to sit down and kick around thoughts on how they are going to approach handling the crisis. Communicators meet with stakeholders elsewhere — they may seek stakeholders' advice, but the planning and execution is left to them as communicators. What is important is that they listen to, acknowledge and respond to stakeholder needs.

Let's take a look at what can happen when, in McHugh's words, a company ignores the pulse of its community.

TIM HORTONS AND THE ENVIRONMENTAL STAKEHOLDERS

In quaint St. Andrews, New Brunswick, a tourist town popular with summer visitors, a Tim Hortons that opened in 2004 became the focus of environmentalists. People were drinking their coffee and then tossing the empty cups on the roadsides, creating a serious litter problem.

According to regional news stories, a local man, Larry Lack, collected more than 500 empty cups during daily jaunts with his dog and eventually complained that the company should implement a deposit-return system on all its paper coffee cups. Speaking from the head offices of Tim Hortons in Oakville, Ontario, a spokesperson replied that the company already recycled many of its cups from its outlets in Moncton, New Brunswick, and had no plans to implement a deposit-return system in St. Andrews, calling such a system a tax. The spokesperson said the company preferred to educate people about picking up litter.

The media responded to the issue, playing on the one-man-against-a-big-corporation theme. Canadian Press covered the story, as did newspapers in the Atlantic region. The *Halifax Daily News* quoted Larry Lack as saying: "Tim Hortons is a Canadian icon for good reasons, but in many places we go, people are talking about how Tim's cups make up a big percentage of the waste. This company is in a position to change the landscape of Canada."[7]

Media sought out respected organizations such as the New Brunswick

Solid Waste Association. The Sierra Club of Canada (an 11,000-member organization that began in 1963 and is affiliated with its American namesake, an environmental organization founded in 1892) cited a study sponsored by the Nova Scotia government that noted that 22 per cent of the litter in Nova Scotia ditches was in the form of Tim Hortons coffee cups, followed by McDonald's containers at 10 per cent. Soon the Conservation Council of New Brunswick and Pitch-In Canada (a national non-profit organization with more than 1.5 million volunteers Canada-wide — its stated goal is to improve communities and the environment) joined in on the side of those calling for Tim Hortons to take action in the form of a deposit system rather than an education program.

Tim Hortons stuck to its guns, implementing an anti-litter education campaign in July 2005. The campaign, specific to Atlantic Canada, worked from the key message that education, not taxation, was the way to combat the litter problem. Not surprisingly, the initiative didn't go over well with environmental groups, which pointed out in the media that a deposit system would have brought in money to effectively combat littering. Indeed, a portion of the proceeds could have gone to industry to cover recycling costs, and another portion to the government's environmental trust fund. In this way, they argued, both the company and the environment could have benefited.

Tim Hortons may have erred in refusing to listen to and involve its stakeholders. What should the company have done? It should have held meetings with the various stakeholder groups to develop a solution *in partnership* with them. Perhaps it could have organized a pilot project for a deposit-return system or engaged local school boards to encourage school children to pick up cups and return them for a few cents per cup; the children, in turn, could donate a portion of the money they received from turning in the cups to school projects. By actively engaging stakeholders in finding a solution rather than speaking from the distant corporate head office, the company would have demonstrated its ability to work with people at the local level. Instead, the confrontation was played out in — and played up by — the media. In the court of public opinion, which almost always favours the little guy and defers to environmental groups, Tim Hortons lost, regardless of money made or the company's market position.[8]

When the Crisis Hits

By now, it should be clear that the success of a crisis communications plan depends, at least in part, on the success of stakeholder communications. It should also be clear that the best time to start preparing for a crisis is long before its shadow emerges on the horizon. Build contacts before the crisis, demonstrate a leadership role in the acquisition and sharing of knowledge and in the actions taken, and then deliver on that mandate during a crisis. Former New York City mayor Rudolph Giuliani, generally disliked by constituents before the events of September 11, 2001, but who shot to fame following the crashing of two jets into the twin towers of the World Trade Center, knew the value of connecting with stakeholders. As he says in his autobiography, *Leadership*: "Over time, honest and forthright leaders build faith with investors and constituents, which is valuable when one eventually does require the public's confidence in the face of bad news."[9]

Fine. But what do communicators do when the crisis hits? Effectively handling a crisis demands that they be direct, determined and proactive: gather information, bring together the crisis management team, create the key messages, *target them to stakeholders* and then tackle the crisis head-on. In other words, they need to remember these four Ps: people, product, process and perception:

- **People.** The crisis management approach must consider the people affected — internal and external — and the people who will deliver the company's message.
- **Product.** Communicators must ensure they have all the appropriate information and materials they will need to address the concerns of the various stakeholders, including an updated website, news releases, backgrounders, and, for the company's spokespeople, speaking notes (based on the key messages) and a Q&A to help them address any questions they may be asked.
- **Process.** A game plan for distributing information to stakeholders must be developed — and then stuck to. A company's publics want to know that when it promises to deliver information, *it will deliver.*

- *Perception.* The fourth P is perception. While the principal mandate as communicators is to ensure the company is perceived by its stakeholders to be doing the right thing at all times, this is never more true than during a time of crisis, when all eyes will be trained on its every move. Accordingly, the first three Ps — people, product and process — should be managed to serve the most important P of all: perception.

The bottom line is responsiveness, says John McHugh. "Organizations can encounter difficulty when they're not responsive. Confront an issue and start working to fix the problem as quickly as you can," he says. "Stakeholders look for fairly quick action, and that's critical. An organization that's attuned, open, and sensitive to its stakeholders and publics is likely to be successful in managing through difficult times."

Because stakeholders' support or criticism can be far-reaching, McHugh stresses the importance of keeping them informed and involved during a high-profile issue or crisis: "On some issues, you may have stakeholder groups that are supportive and who believe that your organization is doing the right thing or has been unfairly criticized. This kind of third-party validation is very important."

At the same time, however, a crisis can breathe life into rumours, so communicators must be quick in addressing or dispelling them. "Otherwise," says McHugh, "they can mutate in a way that ... can create difficulty or cause harm to your organization going forward."[10]

Through phone calls and emails, communicators should invite stakeholders to visit the company website for specific information and updates. They may even want to set up informal, face-to-face briefing sessions for the most important stakeholders. Whether a face-to-face meeting or a phone update, the messages used must always be approved ones. Speaking off the cuff or speculating about the crisis or the outcome is to be avoided; rather, communicators should work from the briefing notes, speaking points, and key messages developed to help them navigate the crisis.

RAGE AGAINST THE MACHINE: STEMMING THE TIDE OF STAKEHOLDER ANGER

Once a crisis has hit an organization, one of the communicator's important roles will be to stem the tide of stakeholder anger that usually results. A crisis occurs because something has fallen off the rails, and in most cases that something will negatively affect stakeholders. How can stakeholders' support be regained? How can their trust and loyalty be regained? Before communicators can address these questions in any meaningful way, they have to be sure they understand the source of that anger, to determine how they are going to lay it to rest.

Although specifics depend on the exact nature of a particular crisis, there are a number of universal truths about stakeholder anger. Stakeholders often get upset because they feel devalued — they do not see themselves as being involved. Government actions are a perfect example of this. Citizens get mad because they see government as a large, amorphous construct that is impenetrable, unresponsive and unmoving. They're keenly aware of the energy they put into their government (what taxpayer isn't?) but what they want to see is results. They want to feel they have a measure of control over what is taking place or, at the very least, to be informed so they can take action themselves.

Two mistakes communicators can make that may aggravate this anger are failing to get the key messages right, and failing to ensure that those messages reflect the emotional tone of the crisis. In other words, organizations often fail in not seeing the crisis the way their stakeholders do, not recognizing the impact of the crisis on the community and not living up to public expectations.

Case Study: Carnage Alley

A case in point is the crisis of the so-called Carnage Alley. In 1999, the then minister of transportation for Ontario, David Turnbull, heaped a self-made crisis on top of an existing one. Crisis One occurred in the aftermath of a series of fatal vehicle collisions on Highway 401 in southwestern Ontario, between the cities of London and Chatham.

The fatalities, a high number in a relatively short time, had raised concern among police services, the local community and the general public. It had been a bad summer for traffic fatalities in that part of the province, where they were normally below the provincial average. But concern had been building: a serious accident occurred in late June, another on the August long weekend and then a major pile-up in early September. The situation in southwestern Ontario had reached a threshold point, and stakeholders wanted answers. Why was this happening?

In June of that year, the Ministry of Transportation had undertaken the development of a $20-million action plan to deal with the situation. The minister made a public commitment to take action — and the ministry did, though it took some time to get the action plan in place. In late July, weeks after the June accident and just days before the next one, Turnbull travelled to the area to connect with the community and to show concern for the families of the victims and deliver the proactive message that the deaths would be investigated and the highway conditions reviewed as part of the overall plan. The crux of the problem? The plan wouldn't be ready for unveiling until late September, the collisions continued to take place and the minister didn't have clear answers to questions about what he planned to do.

Crisis Two, the crisis-on-top-of-the-crisis, happened when a member of the media, in late August, asked the minister his thoughts about the highway, which by this time had been given the unfortunate-but-catchy nickname "Carnage Alley" by the media. The minister answered, "I found it a rather pleasant drive." Unfortunately, although it could be argued that the minister answered a simple question with an honest answer about his personal experience, he had failed to see the question in the greater context of the issue itself.

CARNAGE ALLEY: THE HEADLINES

"Carnage Alley: Is it the highway or the drivers?" — *TORONTO STAR*, August 8, 1999
"CAA wants bad section of 401 widened with paved shoulders" — *SARNIA OBSERVER*, August 16, 1999
"Killer highway closed after crash" — *NORTH BAY NUGGET*, August 19, 1999
"Killer road described as pleasant" — *TIMMINS DAILY PRESS*, August 31, 1999
"Disaster on an Ontario highway" — *MACLEAN'S*, September 13, 1999

"It was a lesson in not letting your guard down," says Derek Deazeley, now a senior manager at the ministry but at the time serving as the minister's communications assistant. "The minister wasn't prepared with the kinds of messages that would have helped establish a course of action. If you are going to put the leader there, at the scene, in a crisis situation, you have to make sure he has something strong to say."[12]

Two problems plagued the minister: the off-the-cuff comment and being unprepared to comment on an action plan that was still being developed and wouldn't be ready for announcement until late September.

The "pleasant drive" comment was particularly damning when juxtaposed in the media with a comment from a little girl whose father had died in an accident along that stretch of highway: "If it's such a pleasant drive, why isn't Daddy coming home?"[13] Reporters had a proverbial field day with the quote. Yet, the minister had made the comment when he had taken a test drive with engineers and felt that the upgrades being put into place were going to improve the drive. But to reporters it appeared that not only did the minister have no plan, but that he didn't care a whit about the victims of the collisions. Clearly, he had failed miserably in establishing an emotional link to the victims.

The September crash was particularly devastating. As *Maclean's* magazine reported in its September 13, 1999, issue: "At least seven people died in a chain-reaction series of fiery accidents on Ontario's 401 highway, 20 km from the U.S. border crossing at Windsor. The disaster, which occurred during a thick fog, involved 62 vehicles and sent 34 people to hospital. Horrified witnesses reported that one girl, trapped and unreachable behind searing flames, cried out repeatedly, 'I'm only 14,' before she died."

And between June and September, a major stakeholder, the Ontario branch of the Canadian Automobile Association (a federation of nine automotive clubs that serves almost 5 million members through 130 offices Canada-wide) issued a report calling for new initiatives that included more public education, a review of design standards to be incorporated into every new section of highway, highway lane improvements such as paved shoulders and the dedication of a portion of gas-tax revenue to investigating highway crashes. Faced with a barrage of angry denouncements of inaction, the ministry persevered. By September, the minister and his staff had developed a communications plan that incorporated strong key messages. In response to the crisis, the ministry would implement highway improvements, including the addition of paved shoulders and rumble strips (the corrugated asphalt strips that warn drivers when they are about to go off the road); establish an action group on safe driving, which would promote educational programs; and hire more officers to patrol the highway. The ministry even pre-screened the plan to safety-oriented stakeholder groups such as the Canadian Automobile Association and the Ontario Safety League — a smart move, given that these stakeholders would be expected to work with ministry officials to implement portions of the plan. In late September, Turnbull travelled to the Chatham area to announce the plan.

Says Deazeley about the minister's visit:

We went to the centre of Carnage Alley to speak to the community directly and give the community the message that we listened and here is our action plan. When the minister came into the room, he received a round of applause from local community groups. He effectively answered all of the questions and didn't waver. He gave assurances that the government was on top of things. I knew we were successful when, a few weeks later, there was another fatality in the area and the question wasn't, "What is the government doing about it?" The message came out in the media that there was an action plan and the minister of transportation was *already* doing something about it.[14]

Risk and Outrage

The sense of outrage felt in the communities across southwestern Ontario over what was deemed, initially, to be dithering by the provincial government over life-and-death issues can be analysed in terms of the research and theory of risk management experts such as Dr. Peter Sandman, one of North America's pre-eminent risk communications consultants.

According to Sandman, who created the Risk = Hazard + Outrage formula, most companies evaluate risk by assessing the probability and magnitude of damage. But, he says, that's only one component of risk, something he calls the "hazard." The other component of risk is "outrage," which is in part a group's predictable response when it feels it's not being dealt with squarely, when there is a gap between reasonable expectation and what actually happens. Sandman determines the seriousness of outrage by how many people it upsets, and how badly it upsets them. According to Sandman's formula, an accurate assessment of risk includes not only an evaluation of the hazard but also of the outrage over the hazard (and the way it is handled) that could potentially be instilled in the public. In other words, risk is equal to the hazard plus the backlash from publics for the harm that they suffer. For instance, a train plummets off a bridge, hurtling toward a village at the bottom of a valley. The total risk is equal not only to the hazard (the loss of lives on the train and in the village, damage to homes and property) but to the hazard *plus* the outrage felt by people — not only those who suffer but those who are observing the suffering and asking: "Why did this happen? What went wrong? What did the train company do wrong? How could they have let this happen? Why didn't people know there was a problem with the railway tracks beforehand?"[15]

As Sandman notes on his website (www.psandman.com), when corporate clients approach him for help in dealing with crisis communications, they tend to believe their stakeholders are upset mostly because of media sensationalism, or activist distortions or their own ignorance. To help them figure out how to reduce the outrage, he must first help them understand its dynamics. "If people are outraged because they do not understand the hazard, educate them about the hazard," Sandman said in a 1993 class at the Hanford Nuclear Reservation. "If they are outraged and *do* understand the hazard, you must address the outrage. 'Educating the public' is not sufficient to deal with public outrage."[16]

Sandman's concept of outrage specifically addresses stakeholders' response not only as it applies to a crisis but also to how it is being handled. In the case of Carnage Alley, people continued to see the dangerous stretch of highway as a hazard, and they were outraged by what seemed to be a lack of government action. This added up to a feeling on the part of stakeholders of high risk over the issue.

© Thaves/Dist. by Newspaper Enterprise Association, Inc.

GEORGE BUSH AND HURRICANE KATRINA

Consider American president George W. Bush and the events both before and after Hurricane Katrina tore through New Orleans and other southern U.S. cities in the summer of 2005. The Category 5 hurricane killed more than 1,300 people, left more than 6,000 missing, displaced 1 million people, and caused an estimated US$130 billion in damage.

It's clear from his words and actions immediately following the hurricane that Bush didn't understand the extent of people's outrage. The day after

Hurricane Katrina hit the U.S. Gulf Coast on August 29, 2005, Bush delivered a speech that was big on the war in Iraq and light on the devastation of Katrina. On August 30, he returned to Washington, D.C., from a Texas vacation and, within a news context of the squalor and hopelessness of the people of New Orleans, told interviewers on the nightly news: "I'm confident that, with time, you can get your life back in order, new communities will flourish, the great city of New Orleans will be back on its feet, and America will be a stronger place for it." This was not the time for "pick yourself up by the boot-straps" messages. It was time for caring and empathy — and Bush failed to take advantage of the chance to offer the right message. He failed to see the crisis the way his stakeholders did. He failed to get his key messages right. And he failed to address the emotional tone of the outrage in his initial communications to stakeholders. Bush's attitude was lambasted by media. A September 1 editorial in the *New York Times* said: "George W. Bush gave one of the worst speeches of his life yesterday, especially given the level of national distress and the need for words of consolation and wisdom."

Bush continued to stumble through the ensuing days, piling one inappropriate message on top of another. This was in the face of increasing evidence that the Bush administration had failed to respond to requests for assistance from both Mississippi and Louisiana three days before the hurricane hit. Instead, Bush continued to stay on vacation until it became clear that he had no choice but to get back to work. On September 2, five days after the hurricane hit the coast, the president visited New Orleans, but he apparently still couldn't "get" the significance of the devastation. Although he had some of his messages right in his media interviews — "We've got a lot of rebuilding to do. First we're going to save lives and stabilize the situation …" — he couldn't help making comments that were inappropriate given the seriousness of the situation: "Out of the rubble of Trent Lott's house [Lott is a U.S. Republican senator from Mississippi] … there's going to be a fantastic house. And I'm looking forward to sitting on the porch."[17]

Meanwhile, the problems — and public outrage — mounted. There was looting; New Orleans police officers quitting amid the chaos; the inability of authorities to move residents to safer ground; problems with the management of the Federal Emergency Management Agency (FEMA), which responds to disasters; and allegations of racism being behind the lack of action on behalf of the mostly African-American citizenry of New Orleans who were still in the area.

It took until September 13, two weeks after the disaster, for Bush to take full responsibility for the government's inadequate response to the hurricane. Not surprisingly, the damage to his reputation was severe.

According to Sandman, Bush's primary error in dealing with stakeholder outrage after Katrina was not connecting to the public's universal sense that there had to be more the federal government could have done. "It was horrible to watch people waiting on rooftops for help that never came," he says. "What the White House needed to say, early and often, was how horrible it was to watch people waiting on rooftops for help that never came." Sandman suggests that the president's key messages should have been along these lines:

> Even though we followed procedure, and on the books we did a good job, we saw the TV pictures too. We have the same feeling everyone does that there must have been more we could have done. We're not sure what that means for next time. Maybe it means we need new procedures. Maybe it means we need the initiative (and the right) to throw the procedures out the window in a major catastrophe and improvise effectively. Because that's the paradox: By and large, we did what we were supposed to do. And we feel horribly guilty that we didn't do enough. We have a list here of dozens of mistakes we made, but they're surprisingly minor. The big truth is that what the procedures said we should do wasn't anywhere close to what the people of the Gulf Coast needed.[18]

As Sandman points out, "defensiveness and scapegoating generated more and more criticism. Self-criticism might have generated a more balanced picture of what actually happened."[19]

What should practitioners do when they have a leader who "just doesn't get it"? They should show them the results of situations where the crisis was handled well, such as with former New York mayor Rudolph Giuliani's performance in the days and weeks after the 9/11 terrorist attacks, and where it was handled poorly, as with George Bush and Hurricane Katrina, or the Ontario Transportation minister and southwestern Ontario's Carnage Alley.

Siege and Denial Mentalities

In examining the Bush administration's initial response to Hurricane Katrina, we've started to address the rules of "what not to do" during a crisis. Let's continue by taking a closer look.

As we saw in the Katrina example, it's important to remember that an organization *may or may not* be at fault in a crisis. What matters to stakeholders is how quickly that organization can keep them updated on what it is doing to resolve the crisis. What won't work with them is backing away, blaming others, playing the victim or pretending the crisis doesn't exist. Taking responsibility — and being perceived to be doing so by stakeholders — will have far greater mileage.

Unfortunately, many top executives develop a siege mentality in the face of a crisis. Because they tend to be shielded from the buzz that takes place at the ground level, in the form of blogs, complaints to the customer service department and media stories, they may feel that if they don't look, or don't react, then perhaps everything will simply right itself. Accordingly, they attempt to hide away and wait until things blow over — or they deny that there's a problem at all. These are the worst possible reactions.

In his book *In the Chamber of Risks: Understanding Risk Controversies*, William Leiss, a risk management expert and professor at the University of Ottawa and Queen's University, points out that denial is an instinct that tends to run through an organization's management structure: from denial of the issue's significance, to denial of the level of expertise in outside persons discussing risk factors, to denial that the public really needs to be part of the process.[20]

MAD COW DISEASE AND THE "NO-RISK" MESSAGE

William Leiss, along with co-authors Douglas Powell and Amanda Whitfield, stress the danger of risk denial and of the failure to recognize the publics' ability to cope with risk. He addresses these dangers in a chapter of the book called "Mad Cows and Mother's Milk," which examines the crisis that unfolded with bovine spongiform encephalopathy (BSE), or mad cow disease:

> [T]here is a terrible risk in seeking to comfort the public with "no-risk" messages. For almost a decade the British government and its leading scientific advisors insisted there was no risk — or that the risk was so infinitesimally small that it could be said there was no risk — of BSE leading to a similar malady in humans, CJD [or Creutzfeldt-Jakob disease, a neurodegenerative disease that is both rare and fatal], even in the face of contradictory evidence. The no-risk message contributed to devastating economic and social effects for Britons ... to the mass slaughter of British cattle, and to a decrease in global consumption of beef, all at a cost of billions of dollars.[21]

Organizations are always worried about spreading unnecessary panic, and BSE provided a good example of this. The old jokes about Nero fiddling while Rome burned or the captain of the Titanic rearranging the deck chairs as the ship ploughed into the iceberg certainly apply here as well. As occurred in those situations, the government's "no need to panic" message became a benchmark of deceitful behaviour in the face of a looming catastrophe. An angry public had every right to ask "Why weren't we informed?"

In the case of BSE, a better approach would have been to respect the fact that people can cope with information — sometimes seemingly terrifying information — if it will help them take action to protect themselves. In the case of BSE, the government should have educated the public about the disease and the steps necessary to curb the risk of contracting it, as well as how to reduce the impact on the beef industry. It should have also prevented the development of false hopes, which were dashed when the beef industry was faced with the daunting reality of lost dollars and a devastated livelihood.

AVIAN FLU VIRUS

More recently, the Canadian government demonstrated a much more effective approach to managing the concerns about avian flu, also known as the bird flu. Not only did it educate the public about the disease through a straightforward information website on avian flu at SafeCanada.ca, it served to quell potential fears by arming its public with information. The website included information in the form of online brochures such as "A Quick Guide to Protecting Yourself and Your Family from Bird (Pandemic) Flu," "Avian Flu Facts," and "Flu Watch Report." Instead of being criticized for stirring up fears, the federal government met the potential information gap by providing the public with a consistent amount of information. Its honest risk message was straightforward: "Be ready in the event that avian flu arrives." That message was balanced by a positive message: "Let's be prepared." By the time the bad news arrived, if it did, it would no longer be bad news. The public would understand what to do until the issue ran its course. In light of what the British government did wrong in the case of mad cow disease, let's consider what the Canadian government did right. (How do we know the Canadian government did the right thing? One measure is in the lack of criticism from media, which did not take the government to task for allegedly currying fear. Clearly, there were lessons learned from SARS that were applied to this situation.)

It may seem ironic, but the first thing the Canadian government did right was raise alarm bells long before a crisis hit. The focus was on preparing people for what was to come.

Beginning in late 2004, health agencies began issuing warnings of an impending crisis with the avian flu. By early 2005, the media carried news stories such as the one written by the Canadian Press on February 23, with the headline: "Experts: bird flu outbreak poses grave danger, but there's time to control it." The lead paragraph read: "The deadly outbreak of avian flu in Asia poses a grave danger of becoming a global pandemic that could threaten the lives of millions, United Nations officials warned … [b]ut international health and animal experts said there is still time to control the disease's spread if quick actions are taken to stem the virus at its source — in animals."

In the wake of the SARS crisis (discussed in Chapter 6), which killed almost 800 people in 2003, and with the World Health Organization (WHO) warning that "the world is now in the gravest possible danger of a pandemic," it made sense to let people know the potential fallout: the WHO estimated that the pandemic could kill 2 to 7 million people worldwide and send tens of millions to hospital for medical treatment.

After the announcement, health officers from 17 Canadian cities gathered in Edmonton to develop a plan to handle the anticipated pandemic. In the February 2005 budget, the Canadian government also announced a $34 million outlay to begin developing a vaccine.

The federal plan provided guidelines for distributing antiviral drugs and vaccines and steps for opening up communication lines between hospitals and the public. On February 26, 2005, the *Toronto Star* wrote:

> The federal plan spells out who should get antiviral drugs and vaccines if they are in limited supply, guidelines for controlling it in hospitals, how health officials will communicate with each other and the public, and exactly who will be in charge of each area. Since local health authorities will likely be the first to detect an influenza outbreak, "[i]t is essential that the lines of communication within the community and up the line to the provincial and federal levels are clear and established in advance of a pandemic," [the report] says.

Far from triggering panic in the streets, Canada's handling of the anticipated pandemic demonstrated a clear and consistent approach to creating links to stakeholders during a crisis long before the crisis hits. The federal government demonstrated an understanding of where the public *might go* (panic and uncertainty) and sought to balance this potential reaction with education and with messages encouraging people to be prepared. In this way, the government was able to foster a climate where information could be calmly dispensed to waiting stakeholders in an ordered fashion.

Clearly, using Sandman's formula, it's not enough that the experts knew what was coming and how to deal with it. To prevent outrage among the North American population, they had to talk about the risks and what they would mean to stakeholders at large, and then spell out the steps that would be taken to ensure a consistent approach to the crisis, if and when the crisis hit.

Conclusion

In this chapter, we have discussed stakeholders and how important they are to an organization — the critical role they play in helping communicators build and maintain a positive profile. External stakeholders (customers, special interest groups, business associations, community groups and the media) have specific needs during a crisis and communicators must develop effective means to communicate information to them, and work to keep them informed on a regular basis. Communicators need to effectively identify their stakeholders, analyze their needs and develop strategies that will address their concerns during a crisis. They are legitimate participants in the way communicators approach and resolve their organization's crisis and, where appropriate, communicators need to prepare them in the eventuality of a crisis.

Key Concepts

RESPONSIBILITY: During a crisis, communicators and their organizations must not develop a siege mentality and try to hide or deny responsibility. Backing away, blaming others or pretending the crisis doesn't exist are not options for them. Instead, they must focus on taking responsibility and demonstrate a proactive approach to stakeholders.

SPOKESPEOPLE: Senior spokespeople must be on hand during a crisis to deliver key messages to both internal and external stakeholders.

STAKEHOLDERS: People, both inside and outside an organization, who have a particular interest in the decisions the organization makes. Communicators need to keep track of stakeholders by maintaining a record of meetings and correspondence, and preparing reports of stakeholder activity as it relates to the organization.

UPDATES: Regular contact with stakeholders through phone calls and news releases, and regular updates as events unfold, are essential. The organization's public website also needs to be kept updated.

6

Publics II
Communicating with Internal Stakeholders during a Crisis

It's not surprising that in a time of crisis, employees often feel the stress of the organization most keenly. They want to know what's happening and how it will affect their careers — even their lives. Not long ago, for instance, when the Canadian airline carrier Jetsgo abruptly announced it was ceasing operations, Jetsgo employees were widely quoted in the media as saying they felt betrayed when the company closed down, because there had been no warning whatsoever. The crisis made for compelling and dramatic media coverage, but for a company that might have still hoped to have an opportunity to continue in business, it painted a picture of confusion, missteps and anger.

Clearly, employees have the ability to improve or worsen a crisis; they are therefore a key public to address in a crisis. But beyond the ethical dimension of looking after members of this essential stakeholder group for their own sakes, there is at least as much to gain for a company in ensuring this group is kept calm and handled effectively. Why? Because employees, in addition to having — and vocalizing — their concerns about the organization's operations, play an important role in representing the company to all other publics during a crisis. The employees as a whole will have at least as much contact with other stakeholders as the official spokesperson, and it's crucial that this role be an effective one.

This chapter focuses on three main tasks of dealing with internal stakeholders during a crisis:

- Arriving at the information needs of various employee publics;
- Integrating employees into crisis communications plans;
- Building strong support and understanding between employees and high-level managers.

Different Employees, Different Stakes

Employees form the most important stakeholder group of all, because their relationship with their organization is arguably affected by more factors during a crisis than that of any other stakeholder group. Furthermore, any organization will have employees with very different roles, each of which has a distinct potential to aid or harm a company's reputation during a crisis. A company may have technicians or scientists, mid-level administrators, or tradespeople and labourers, or a mix of the three, with each feeling as though they have a very different stake in their company. Employees who feel their skills are highly in demand are likely to feel differently from those who do not. Some may also feel that they are more in the know than others and have the privilege of access to information that gives them a better sense of the company's direction. Some employees may have benefits packages, stock options or shares in the company, all of which will affect their interest in the firm. Lastly, employees who work in different divisions of a company will each have their own perspective when a crisis hits. Communicators need to prepare each employee and ensure that they understand what is happening in a crisis, what needs to be said and what needs to remain confidential.

Let's look at an example of how an issue can affect different employees in different ways. During early 2006, Toronto Transit Commission (TTC) bus drivers likely felt strongly about a strike looming over safety issues; the potential strike was a result of incidents of assaults against drivers, and the drivers had more at issue than, say, the TTC's marketing people. The drivers certainly had more to say about the subject; after all, those drivers were on the front line, dealing with the public day in, day out. When employees are likely to be most highly affected by a crisis, they will be the most vocal; it makes sense that the most vocal are likely to have a greater impact on an organization's external publics than those who stay quiet or who are unaffected.

Not only will stakeholders have different feelings about and knowledge of an unfolding crisis, they will have different needs for information and reassurance. Of key importance is appreciating that all internal stakeholders potentially have great power to represent their company to its other publics and, depending on the crisis, those who seem to be the lowest status employees may in fact have the loudest voice.

In a theme park, where whales and dolphins entertain visitors, and where, for example, animal rights groups are protesting and calling on the park owners to stop using the animals as a form of entertainment, the animal trainers and veterinarians will have a greater knowledge of an animal's behaviour and its requirements for well-being than the grounds worker who empties the trash cans and cleans the washrooms. By contrast, the park's marketers and administrators may have little knowledge of animal behaviour, but they will be keenly aware of how long the theme park can stay in business if attendance declines dramatically as a result of an animal rights protest.

To a media person getting reactions from park employees, a grounds worker's words may be more dramatic than a marketer's or an animal trainer's because she will be the working-class face that many news watchers will identify with. "How long do you think this protest will go on? How will you feel if the park closes?" a reporter might ask a grounds worker. "What will happen to your job? And by the way, how do you really feel about the treatment of the park's whales and dolphins?"

If the grounds worker is uncomfortable with the treatment of the whales and says so, she might seem to be a victim herself, having to work for an employer that upsets her conscience (a likely story hook). If, on the other hand, management speaks with her before the media arrives and the grounds worker understands (and has been given assurances by the park's animal trainers) that the animal's well-being is its first concern, the grounds worker might still have misgivings, but she is better informed and will also have a sense that her own feelings are significant to the other employees and to park management. Overall, her message to the media is more likely to be positive and may include important information about the park's concerns for the animals. The grounds worker is included as part of a team that helps maintain the park's positive image and reputation.

Naturally, analysis of internal stakeholder groups is much more complicated than noting simple divisions of employees into high level and low level, highly skilled and low skilled, executives and "everyone else." Developing an understanding of the different needs for information that each of several kinds of employee has is essential for effective communications during a crisis. These needs will depend on numerous factors, such as the resilience of morale, ability to be flexible under pressure, and the amount of stake and risk in a crisis. Even once communicators learn how to analyze broad groups in abstract, they must still learn how a group (human resources, marketing, customer service, maintenance, management) differs from the abstract type, and how each group's corporate culture is unique. A customer service representative at Wal-Mart is not the same as a customer service representative at an independently owned adventure outfitter such as Mountain Equipment Co-op, or a representative at an artisan brewery.

EMPLOYEES AS SPOKESPEOPLE

Informing employees has benefits beyond putting them at ease for their own sakes; being plugged into the communicator's key messages will help them respond to questions from outside the organization as well. In many ways, employees are the communicator's link to the outside world. They communicate not only with other employees within the organization but with the world "out there." Internal stakeholders are all potential spokespeople. Armed with the appropriate information, they can help contain a crisis and can be as essential as any well-briefed CEO preparing to go in front of the microphones. They, too, can help in making an organization accountable to its external stakeholders.

> "Your employees, as representatives of the company, are an important first line of defence with customers. A well thought-out and executed communication plan helps convey the notion that a company in crisis is not necessarily in a death spiral."[1]   — Michael J. Epstein, *Communicating with Stakeholders in a Crisis*

Unfortunately, however, the essential role that employees play is often overlooked by organizations in crisis. According to Susan Thomas of Ketchum Thomas, a California-based public relations firm, who is quoted by Jerry Lazar in *Foot-in-Mouth Disease,* "[Employees are] probably the most critical audience to get to first. [They] have a lot of contacts every day. They are the keepers of the brand, and the first five minutes of every phone call they make will be people asking: 'What's going on over there?'"[2]

THE HIGH COST OF IGNORING RELATIONS
WITH INTERNAL STAKEHOLDERS

Employees need to know what direction the company is taking and why. They need to be linked into the key messages communicators have developed so they can relax in the knowledge that the crisis is being managed. The alternative is to say nothing, let the rumour mill fill in the blanks (and it always does — usually with falsehoods, suspicions or speculation that wreak havoc on employee morale) and stand by as the company's productivity numbers plummet. There is always a chance, too, that employees will take it upon themselves to contact the media, either in a direct way or anonymously. Some will feel that they should be protected by whistleblower legislation — indeed in some cases they are — but most will act out of motives that are in line with how they have felt about the job and the workplace for a long time.

It's not a surprise that workers who feel out of the loop at work during the best of times — they never received the kind of information they felt they needed to do their job well, or they felt isolated, threatened or uncertain — are the kind of employees whose comments make for great media fodder, because in a crisis, when things at the company appear to be out of control, their remarks add to the element of human drama in a news story. Employees who hold a grudge or who feel that the organization owes them something can do a lot of damage to a company's reputation. Granted, the middle of the crisis is not the place for employees to air their grievances (though they certainly might), nor is it an appropriate time for a company to be working with morale issues. This work has to happen long before the crisis hits. But well-informed employees going into a crisis are those who understand that they have an important role to play, whether their daily job is crunching numbers, filing reports or taking care of the facilities.

Information Needs of Different Employees

Naturally, assessments of the information needs of employees depend for the most part on the nature of the crisis. That said, it is important to understand how the functions and roles of employees within various departments (human resources, marketing, customer service) and within various classes (full time with benefits, part time, contract, freelance, management, executive) will affect their needs to receive and provide information during a crisis if they are to help bring it to a close. In general, employees' information needs break down into three main categories.

First, employees need information for their own protection or to make informed choices about how to ensure their own well-being and that of their dependants. This includes information about emergency measures during a fire or spill or disaster, or information about possible layoffs, to give only two examples.

Second, employees need added information to do their jobs effectively during a crisis. For instance, police officers in charge of ensuring a protest remains peaceful need to know about the political sensitivities at play and about the particularly vocal or extremist members of the community who are sure to be present. Police officers need, among many other types of information that will help them act with discretion, a briefing on the history of police relations with the community members demonstrating.

Third, employees must be given information to present to the company's publics during a crisis, with careful consideration given to each employee's main and secondary points of contact with other publics. For example, customer service reps need to be able to speak intelligently and often comprehensibly about details of a product recall. CEOs need far more information to present to a meeting of shareholders.

MAJOR DIVISIONS OF THE ORGANIZATION

Human Resources. Human Resources (HR) circulates many messages to employees throughout the company, on subjects ranging from disciplinary issues to notifications of personnel changes, raises, labour relations issues, workplace changes and hours of work. HR also often has a role in increasing morale within the company, organizing events, the company's involvement with charities and, perhaps, publishing newsletters. It is often closely involved in matters of discipline, wrongdoing or layoffs at a company and, along with IT departments, may have a watchdog function. As such, HR's many functions within a company often make members of this group feel unusually privy to information and thereby entitled to more of it than other groups. At various times, information about company key messages that flow from issues analysis may be circulated through the HR department, with messages sometimes vetted by an HR executive.

Let's say, for example, that a police department in a mid-sized town begins to receive complaints about racial profiling. The police department is under fire for incidents in which the mostly white police force is stopping and detaining non-white drivers — and the complaints are backed up by media stories. As a result, a directive is issued by the police chief: the force, in addition to holding mandatory cultural sensitivity classes for all police officers and administrative staff, will hire more non-whites to reflect the increasingly diverse population it serves. A crisis plan or even briefing note to address this situation needs to involve all departments, including the HR department, which will play a critical role in delivering the message of cultural sensitivity training and advising staff of the new hiring practices.

HR officials would need to be briefed on the particulars of the plan and perhaps charged with the responsibility of hiring the trainer who will conduct the sensitivity sessions for staff well in advance of any action being taken. As well, HR staff may be the ones who will relay the new hiring practices to staff and to the police union — and they need to be prepared for union criticism if the hiring practices are dismissed as an affirmative action (i.e., hiring on the basis of colour rather than job skills) program. It would be an added crisis if a police department HR officer were quoted, anonymously or not, in the media as saying that the new policies will never work, as the police force's work culture won't treat it favourably and will resist it at all costs. Therefore, it's essential to keep the HR people in the loop.

Marketing. The marketing department is responsible for creating and delivering the image of the organization to its external publics. It has a role in crafting the information it obtains from various sources and then packaging this information through campaigns that will last for a specific period. As such, marketers have to be tuned in to the overall direction of the organization; they have to be provided with the most up-to-date information so that they are able to respond to executive-level decisions about products quickly.

Here's a real-life example of a misstep involving marketers who were caught flat-footed. On August 4, 2006, the *Toronto Star,* in an article titled "Toronto's official map of misinformation," reported that Tourism Toronto workers were handing out a two-year-old map in front of Toronto's City Hall. While the street routes hadn't really changed, the map advertised plays, musicals and other attractions that were long gone from the city. In the article, Tourism Toronto vice-president Andrew Weir was quoted as saying that he was unfamiliar with the map and directed media to the city's tourism department. The question was tossed over to Tourism Development director Judy Morgan, who made a promise to have the old maps destroyed. She followed up with the *Star* and was quoted in the same story as saying that no more old guides would be distributed to the public. The marketers were quickly apprised of the situation and took action, with minimal disruption to service and reduced impact on the organization's public profile. However, a better informed and more empowered marketing staff would likely have flagged the issue long before it came out in the media.

Customer Service. The public face of an organization, the customer service department provides public messaging. Customer service representatives are the first point of contact for clients; they provide the recall phone numbers, details of products and basic information about an organization. In a crisis, they have to be prepared with the most up-to-date information. Messaging that comes directly from the communications department and is vetted by senior staff must be provided to customer service staff, with the proviso that only those messages approved for distribution to the public can be used.

A common example is of a bank computer glitch: customer service staff are provided with the essential information on the reason for the glitch, as well as steps customers can take if they have further difficulties getting service or a resolution to their problems. Reps are provided with information to direct clients to specific websites for information and are able to answer questions in an informed and professional way.

Manufacturing. The nuts and bolts of the company, the manufacturing part of the organization generates the products that create revenues. Workers in the manufacturing department are as attuned to changes in the company's production approach as they are to any change in a product or component. If there is a reduction in hours, a cut in shifts, labour grievances, a product recall, workers in the manufacturing department need to know. They can't be left to second-guess the actions of senior management. Blast emails, worker-manager meetings, website information: all can help manufacturing personnel understand and appreciate management's actions in a crisis.

Legal. The legal department more than any other may be privy to decisions by a company's executive level and may need to be kept apprised of all developments during a crisis that might have legal implications: a product recall, a death in the manufacturing area, a plant expansion or acquisition. For instance, a food product that causes a customer to become ill would spark a need for the legal department to review and vet all outgoing communications. Internally, the legal team needs to know each step that is being taken by the company and should be kept on the crisis team's list of email recipients.

STATUS AND LEVELS WITHIN THE ORGANIZATION

Full Time with Benefits. These are often lifetime employees within a company's workforce: they are in it for the long haul and have a great deal of influence within and without the organization. These employees can range from specialist and technical staff to administrators and janitorial workers. They discuss issues with an elevated degree of interest and are often seen as being in the know, whether or not they are close to the crisis situation. Yet, they are the ones who will often feel the most threatened during a crisis that could lead to a company shutdown or closure, as their livelihoods are on the line: they could be out of a job.

Many news stories begin by interviewing company staffers who have been with the organization for 20 or more years; their experience and the description of their concern over the crisis adds emphasis to a news story, as media look to them as the old hands who know the company best. These staff members need to be kept apprised of all developments since they have a vested interest in what happens to the organization. Newsletters, staff meetings, and emails are all essentials in keeping them informed. They may need to be provided with key messages in some cases, especially if there is a chance that they may be blindsided by media outside the organization's walls. They should be kept informed with approved, public-ready key messages — the same ones used in the company's news release about the issue — that can be posted on the company's website and made available in a blast email to staff; this is especially useful if they are asked by members of the public about the situation. The information they are provided with empowers them to have knowledge of the situation, while also emphasizing an understanding that they are not the company's spokespeople. And this point cannot be overemphasized: non-communications staff members should be briefed about the situation, but they should also know and understand that they are to refer all in-coming media communication, whether in-person, over the phone or via email, to the communications branch for handling.

Part Time. Part-timers are those whose connection with the company is casual and uncommitted, but many will toe the company line on policies and initiatives because they want to keep a foot in the door should a full-time position become available. However, if they feel they are underpaid or over-worked or, in the case of long-time contract workers, working without paid benefits, they may vent frustration or speak unfavourably about their employer to media during a crisis. To prevent this, part-timers must be allowed to share in information and be given an outlet for their concerns and an opportunity to air their grievances long before a crisis hits.

Freelancers/advisors/consultants/contractors. These casual staff members, if they are working in a communications (i.e., writing) or administrative position, are often brought in to help with the overflow of work related to a crisis. However, their interest in speaking to media and external publics is usually minimal. They can be provided with basic information but do not necessarily need to be prepared with key messages; this is dependent wholly on whether or not they are representing the company to media and to stakeholders during the crisis. The decision is made based on their involvement: If they are communications experts, they will be privy to all the information being developed and approved. If they are not, they may just have a minor involvement, and so information-sharing with them can be held to a minimum. Naturally, the company employing these casual staff members should explain the parameters of the job to them before it begins.

Middle or Line Managers. These managers are a crucial interface between executives and employees in non-management roles: they are the conduit for information between the executive level and the front-line worker. Staffers look to them for direction and messaging on what caused the crisis and where the organization is going. Line managers must be prepared with key messages to deliver to staff, and they must be prepared to meet with staff on a regular basis during the crisis. They are vital in stemming the growth of rumours and can defuse situations where anxiety can often get out of control. Their role is to deliver email to staff and hold meetings, including town hall-type meetings where large groups of employees can meet to air their concerns and question senior staff.

These managers are also essential in the development and delivery of a "telephone tree" of messaging, a system by which short, concise information on the crisis can be relayed to people throughout an organization to keep all staff informed. In a telephone tree, all the people on the tree have a list of contacts to relay information to; in this way, information is dispersed throughout the organization evenly and the message is consistent. It also reduces the challenge of one person having to make dozens of calls. People can ensure that the message is delivered while needing to worry only about being personally responsible for making about six to seven calls each; it allows them to get this particular job done and then refocus on other duties. The same system can be used with email as well, though most organizations will send an approved crisis update by blast email, sending the message to all intended recipients at once. A crisis communications telephone tree might look like this:

Communications Director calls:
President
Vice-presidents
Communications manager calls:
Company directors
Each company director calls his or her division's:
Line managers
Each line manager calls his or her unit's:
Supervisors
Each supervisor calls his or her staff

In addition to managing their role in the telephone tree, middle managers will always be in touch with their own staff directly to provide information as the crisis moves toward its conclusion.

The Organization's Leaders. A small number of people from the internal stakeholder group — the company's team leaders — will formally deliver the key messages to employees, other stakeholders, and the media. From business experts to scientific spokespeople to the company's CEO or president, these leaders are the natural voices of an organization. The media and stakeholders will look to them for direction. And this makes sense: if they don't have the answers and the ability to stream this information through the organization and into the outside world, who does?

Getting leaders trained and ready for a crisis before it happens is essential because once it hits, an organization will have to work with precision to answer all the questions that are bound to arise from a wide range of sources. Leaders need the support of communicators to develop effective messages and to guide them through the process of handling the media. They may even need public-speaking tips or media training. In many cases, communicators won't be able to develop a complete set of messages until after a crisis has unfolded, but they *can* train the leaders in public speaking and media relations beforehand. And they would be wise to do so. During a crisis, when the company's reputation — perhaps its very existence — could be on the line, time will be far too scarce and pressure far too high to be engaged in even basic media training.

Case Study: Splash Rafting

Employees within an organization may all be faced with the same challenge: understanding a crisis. But they may all have a different role to play. Let's look at a hypothetical example. A whitewater rafting company, Splash Rafting, has been operating on a whitewater river in British Columbia for the past 15 years. It has an excellent track record: no deaths since operations began and only four injuries — two broken wrists, a broken ankle and a sprain — during its history. Rafting participants sign a detailed waiver absolving the company of blame if there is an accident.

The company is run by husband and wife co-founders Ruby and Jack deWitt; they've lived in the area for 25 years and actively participate in the local chamber of commerce as well as in several environmental groups. Splash Rafting has four full-time employees and hires summer students for the May-to-October season, who work as guides, front office staff and service workers in the kitchen and on the grounds. All students are at the university or college level, and all go through a government-approved whitewater training program. They also are required to possess Royal Life Saving certification and St. John Ambulance training. Of the students, 20 are guides (including four team leaders who also act as guides: each team leader is responsible for a team of four other guides) and two are office staff. Guides spend time in the front office, answering inquiries by telephone and email, and also book rafting trips. The corporate culture is folksy, friendly and relaxed, with an emphasis on fun while underscoring safety on the river. The company is also strongly tourist-oriented: it belongs to tourism associations, buys space in local and national newspapers and relies heavily on personal recommendations.

THE CRISIS

During a recent trip, a rafting participant died on a particularly dangerous set of rapids. The 52-year-old man drowned after the raft he was in flipped; he was knocked unconscious after being battered against rocks, and attempts by the raft guide to revive him failed. Others in the raft suffered minor bruises and cuts. An autopsy later showed the man, despite having signed a waiver stating his health was good, did in fact have several health problems that might have been a factor in his death. The death was the first of its kind on the river — no other rafting companies had suffered the death of a client — and the local media ran several stories over the course of three days about the incident. Those stories included a call for an inquiry into the overall safety of rafting companies and an editorial in a national newspaper calling for the suspension of operations at Splash Rafting. The mood at Splash Rafting was serious and sombre, with speculation swirling that the company's founders were closing it down.

COMMUNICATING WITH INTERNAL STAKEHOLDERS

How did the company deal with its internal stakeholders in the aftermath of the accident? The co-founders thoroughly briefed all staffers about what had happened. The briefing included discussion of what the co-founders would say to the media, though responsibility for media was restricted to the co-founders and, in some cases, the team leaders. An important key message they would deliver was that no blame must be laid at anyone's feet.

Despite rumours that the company was going to be closed permanently, the co-founders worked to dispel the rumours. The company was closed for one week to allow for a full police investigation and then reopened. External clients were sent emails outlining the known details of the accident and given assurances that the company followed safety procedures strictly. The co-founders stepped up into a leadership role, took responsibility and promised to ensure that safety would continue to be paramount at Splash Rafting. The co-founders also started an internal blog, which works like a constantly updateable newsletter that staff can contribute to on a regular basis on the company's intranet. Staffers were able to contribute to it over the course of the crisis, and it offered them a chance to vent their feelings and share their thoughts about what happened. As well, employees were provided with a daily email update on the status of the investigation and media coverage.

All staffers were offered three days off with pay if requested. The guide on the raft involved in the accident was given two weeks off with pay. All were offered the services of a professional counsellor and several guides took that option. Providing grief counselling is essential in workplaces where injuries or loss of life has occurred, especially in high-pressure environments in which any kind of personal risk or decision making about safety under pressure is a normal part of the workday. Guiding novices through fast-moving, potentially dangerous rapids is an example of such a workplace. In that kind of environment, workers must be able to do their job with confidence.

TEAM LEADERS

Team leaders met for several days with their guide teams, outlining the key messages being delivered to external stakeholders and the media and providing support as the company worked through the crisis. As mentioned, each team leader oversaw a team of four other guides. Each small group — team leader and guides — met regularly to talk about the situation at hand. At these meetings, the team leaders also explained what was being said to external publics. "This is what we're telling the media," the team leaders said. "We're being honest and open and talking about how we're working to make this situation better." The importance of talking as a group, with line management staff — the team leaders — giving a sense of support and direction, cannot be underestimated because it allows front-line staff — the guides — to air their concerns in an atmosphere of support that encourages team building. Team leaders were also provided with the key messages developed to handle the crisis, should media contact them, but with the knowledge that they could talk to the media *only* if given the go-ahead by the company's owners.

TRAINING

All employees were taken through additional training sessions, and a professional national-level coach was brought in to provide emotional support during the training. The addition of a third-party expert was seen as important by the co-founders, who felt that the coach could speak in broad terms about teamwork and the need to continually strive for excellence in the workplace.

THE AFTERMATH

After three weeks, media coverage was significantly reduced and Splash Rafting resumed full operation. There was no significant drop in client numbers, and staff continued to deliver their services in a confident, positive way. No guides quit and the co-founders were pleased to have been able to move through the crisis and find a positive resolution to it.

If the company had not gone to the lengths it did to ensure that its staff members were taken care of, emotionally and physically, they might have had a situation of increasing anxiety among staff, leaks to the media, possible allegations of other problems, real or imagined, at the company, lawsuits from stressed employees or a severe drop in business: all potentially hazardous if happening one at a time, and disastrous if in a combination.

Two-Way Communication between Management and Employees

In keeping with James E. Grunig's two-way symmetrical model (discussed in Chapter 5), there should be an open flow of communication between employees and management. Information from senior executives should circulate throughout the organization via a wide range of channels, including newsletters, emails, voice mails and meetings. But sharing information with employees isn't enough. No matter how far removed they are from head office — either in terms of geography or seniority — employees must feel empowered to share information with executives as well, particularly when it relates to stakeholder relations. Take, for example, the "what if" scenario from Chapter 5, in which a metal fabricator ignored the warnings of a small engineering council about a possibly defective product. Now imagine that an employee in a far-flung branch of the company had heard grumblings from the council about the product in question, but wasn't empowered to pass this information up the chain. Had Grunig's two-way symmetrical model been in place, the company could have likely avoided the crisis that unfolded.

Employees — the people on the front lines and closest to the company's sales, marketing, and service areas — *must* be given the mechanisms to be heard, either through regular corporate meetings or regularly monitored feedback systems where employees can voice their ideas and concerns. One such method is the information-gathering/information sharing session, often called a "cluster meeting," which serves to bring internal stakeholder issues to the table. These meetings are attended by staff members who work on the front lines — these can be communications officers, business consultants, planners, manufacturing and marketing staff. At the meetings, they share the information they have with other staffers, and line managers are provided with reports about their stakeholders, focusing largely on what they are saying and their most pressing concerns. The issues that are identified in cluster meetings can be brought up the line in brief reports, shared with senior managers and directors as well as communications staff. As intelligence-gathering exercises, these meetings help communicators know and understand the organization's internal stakeholders — what they think and, especially, their expectations of the organization. This information can then be used to shape communications messages and plans.

Integrating Employees into Crisis Plans

Here are key elements communicators need to keep in mind to make internal stakeholders, the company's employees, part of a crisis communications plan.

Provide an outline. Give employees a sense of the context of what has happened, the current status of the crisis and the company's most immediate next steps. Often the simplest approach is by using numbered lists.

Deliver messages from the top. Ensure that a senior spokesperson is on hand to deliver key messages to employees *in person* and to let them know specifically how the crisis will affect them. The power of face-to-face communications cannot be underestimated during times of crisis.

Let middle managers be a bridge. Middle managers should be empowered to disseminate appropriate, approved communications to their own departments, and encouraged to tailor the communications to make the news as relevant as possible. For example, all employees should understand the company's key messages, but how will those messages affect this particular group of employees and the way they do business? This brings up two important points about successful employee communications. First, employee surveys conducted in both the private and public sectors consistently show that most employees want to hear company news from their immediate supervisors in face-to-face meetings. Second, key messages are often more effective when they are tailored to meet the needs and expectations of various employee segments. People in different roles have different concerns and agendas, so managers should have the tools and training to target key messages to their audiences. It is essential that managers receive that training before the crisis hits. Bart Mindszenthy and Gail Roberts, partners in the niche communications firm Mindszenthy & Roberts Communications Counsel, agree that corporate "big messages" should be balanced and interpreted to make them more relevant to the different teams in the company. "Management needs to keep team leaders informed so that they can better decide how and when to share information with their teams," they point out in the article "Team Leaders and the Communications Loop."[3]

Update employees regularly. Keep information flowing to employees about the status of the crisis as it evolves. This can be accomplished through face-to-face meetings with their managers, a well-maintained intranet site and email. Email is a good follow-up to face-to-face meetings because it allows communicators to revisit crucial areas that were covered in meetings, offering a chance to revise, modify, clarify or build on items covered in the meeting. It can provide a comfort level for employees, helping to build a sense of confidence in the organization. The last thing employees want to feel in a crisis is that they've been left out in the cold and do not understand the events taking place — events that could have a big impact on their lives.

Deal with rumours immediately. Respond quickly to rumours through the communications vehicles already in place. Rumours among internal stakeholders are born of "what if" scenarios — they are a result of a lack of information rather than of having enough or too much information. Communicators can address each rumour through emails to all staff, outlining the appropriate information and ensuring that staff members are not misinformed.

Give employees full access to all public information, including news releases. Be sure that all external messages — what's reported through the news media, to financial analysts, to regulatory bodies — are consistent with messages being delivered to employees. Communicators should not sugar-coat or spin information in a particular way for employees, either to protect them from certain realities, for instance, impending layoffs, or making a negative situation sound better than it is. Employees should be offered information, direction and outcomes — and made to feel that they are part of the process.

Prepare employees to represent the company well. Ensure that employees know what to do or say when approached with questions by other stakeholders. If they are contacted by the media, for example, should they refer journalists to a particular individual or department? Are there key messages communicators could provide them with to deliver to customers and business contacts? Where should employees refer customers who have questions they can't answer? For example, during its computer glitch in 2004 (discussed in Chapter 2), the Royal Bank provided staff at their information centres with branch-approved answers to help them address the many questions they were fielding from stakeholders and clients.

Case Study:
Internal Stakeholders and the SARS Crisis at Toronto's Sunnybrook and the Women's College Health Sciences Centre

In late February 2003, SARS swept into Toronto on a tide of fear, anxiety and uncertainty, blindsiding a health care system that wasn't ready to handle it and creating panic in the streets.

CORPORATE GLANCE:
SUNNYBROOK HEALTH SCIENCES CENTRE AND WOMEN'S COLLEGE HOSPITAL

Sunnybrook Health Sciences Centre and Women's College Hospital merged in June 1998 under the banner of Sunnybrook and Women's College Health Sciences Centre. They were de-amalgamated in April 2006.

Sunnybrook is a major research hospital for the University of Toronto, one of Toronto's two major trauma centres, and a long-term care centre for war veterans. Services include neurosciences, heart and cancer centres, and orthopaedic and arthritic care. The hospital has over 12,000 workers: staff, physicians, volunteers and medical students.

Women's College Hospital is a teaching hospital (a hospital that provides training to medical students and residents) affiliated with the University of Toronto. It functions as an independent ambulatory care hospital and is known for housing the first ambulatory care SARS clinic in Canada.[4]

When an elderly couple travelling home to Toronto from Hong Kong fell ill with flu-like symptoms, Sunnybrook and Women's College Health Sciences Centre (SWC) was among the first to admit the couple's family members for observation in early March. The fallout from the situation was fast and serious: within a month of the couple's return from Hong Kong, the World Health Organization (WHO) issued a travel advisory warning travellers away from Toronto and the province of Ontario declared a hospital state of emergency.

THE ORGANIZATION: Sunnybrook and Women's College Health Sciences Centre (SWC)

THE CRISIS: The outbreak of SARS in 2003.

THE DISEASE: Severe Acute Respiratory Syndrome (SARS) was a serious lung infection that began with flu-like symptoms. It was caused by a form of a coronavirus (an upper respiratory tract virus infecting mammals and birds) that likely mutated inside domesticated animals, probably chickens. The illness became an epidemic once it spread to humans.

THE TIMELINES:

NOVEMBER 16, 2002: Guangdong province in China reports the first case of an atypical pneumonia.

FEBRUARY 28, 2003: The World Health Organization (WHO) reports on an unknown form of pneumonia in an American business in Vietnam. Around the same time, visitors and Canadians returning from China report flu-like symptoms.

MARCH 10–11, 2003: The WHO's Dr. Carlo Urbani notes outbreaks in hospitals in Southeast Asia, China and Canada and gives the illness a name: Severe Acute Respiratory Syndrome, or SARS.

MARCH 15, 2003: A global health alert is issued by the WHO as more SARS cases are reported in China, Vietnam, Singapore and Canada. Emergency travel advisories are issued.

MARCH 29, 2003: Carlo Urbani dies as a result of SARS.

APRIL 12, 2003: Canadian researcher who identified the first cases of SARS and completed the first successful sequencing of the genome of the SARS-causing coronavirus dies as a result of the disease. Researchers later suggest naming the agent that causes the disease after the infectious-disease expert.

APRIL 23, 2003: The WHO adds Toronto, Beijing and China's Shanxi province as regions for travellers to avoid. Toronto is recognized as the epicentre of the Canadian outbreak of SARS. The advisory is in place for three weeks.

JUNE 2003: Last outbreak of SARS reported.

MAY 2005: SARS is declared eradicated by the WHO, which reported that 8,098 people worldwide became sick with SARS; 774 died, including 44 in Ontario.

THE STAKEHOLDERS: Concerned employees who were putting their lives on the line simply by walking through the hospital doors to go to work.[5]

For SWC, SARS created a challenge on two fronts: handling external communications and ensuring that its internal stakeholders, the employees, were kept informed as the crisis progressed.

SWC recognized that it was essential to be open and direct with nurses — they were putting themselves at risk in caring for patients. There were hundreds of other staff whose needs for information also had to be met: administrators, maintenance staff, cleaners, cafeteria workers, technicians and grounds workers. In fact, over the course of five months, 180 hospital employees would undergo a 10-day quarantine, and 11 of those would be hospitalized with the disease.

In a thesis titled "Effective Internal Crisis Communications," SWC's Craig DuHamel, then chief of Public Affairs and Community Relations (now chief, Communications and Stakeholder Relations at Sunnybrook Health Sciences Centre), discusses the change of communications focus the crisis demanded:

> Typically, about 70 per cent of the communications activity in a Toronto hospital PR department is external such as media relations and lobbying the provincial government. Whatever resources remain are usually allocated to internal communications. For a number of reasons, this paradigm was turned completely around at Sunnybrook & Women's during the SARS crisis. Hospital staff and their families were becoming increasingly nervous about SARS and as a result, hospitals were faced with staff who were questioning the safety of their work environment and were witnessing a frightening disease that was in some cases making their colleagues fatally ill ... The main question hospital communications professionals in Toronto began trying to answer was how can they keep staff calm and informed so that can continue to be productive and provide care for patients.[6]

THE INFORMATION CASCADE: TOP TO BOTTOM COMMUNICATIONS

Although the organization had a complete emergency response plan for external stakeholders, it wasn't as well prepared to handle internal crisis communications.

However, DuHamel and his communications staff quickly applied the tenets of Grunig's two-way symmetrical model of communications to create an organization-wide messaging system that would ensure messages were delivered from the top down throughout the hospital (manager to staff, and staff to staff), all while "maintaining the original integrity or theme of the corporate message," DuHamel says.[7]

This created a "cascade of information." Front-line managers used the broadcast communications message distributed to the entire organization and delivered it, personally, to their own staff. This "sameness of messaging" was effective: it allowed for consistency in the key messages being delivered and reduced confusion in the face of media reports that often differed wildly. In other words, it created one trustworthy story for the employees to rely on.

"The broadcast communication was generated from a central source, the 'war room,'" adds DuHamel:

> This was literally a meeting room that became the nerve centre of the crisis where a team of leaders from across the organization, representing various professions and job functions in the hospital, would meet daily for about an hour or two to discuss and resolve issues. Leaders from this team would then hold meetings with their supervisors or managers to discuss whatever was new that day and then this information would be [transmitted] to front-line staff. Later in the day, similar information was reinforced by broadcast communication from either the President and CEO or the Public Affairs Department.[8]

ENABLING TWO-WAY COMMUNICATIONS

SWC's communications staff also sought active feedback from employees, ensuring they had an opportunity to provide input to the crisis management team via several methods:

- A dedicated intranet site;
- A telephone line with daily recorded messages and a voice mailbox;
- Email alerts sent to all staff, with the option of sending in questions and comments;

- Q&A sessions with all staff in large group meetings with the CEO and crisis management team (staff forums), and also in smaller department meetings with supervisors and managers. Questions were answered by communications staff through broadcast communications, such as email updates, so that everyone could benefit from the information.

Through these initiatives, "Sunnybrook & Women's seemed to be able to provide reassurance for its internal publics," DuHamel says. "The hospital … ensured a two-way flow of information. Judging by the feedback from managers and staff, the hospital listened to its audiences and modified its crisis strategy to accommodate concerns [with the result that] the hospital was able to provide reassurance to its internal publics during the crisis."[9] The sensitivity of senior staff to their workers' concerns allowed them to create an environment of confidence and trust. Those concerns ranged from what measures the hospital was taking to control the outbreak to the treatment being given to those employees whose health had been affected by SARS, and the steps being taken to ensure that healthy hospital workers remained healthy.

CONTROLLING THE MESSAGE

Throughout the crisis, SWC's communications work was anchored in one of the cornerstones of corporate communications: *an organization always has control of the messages it develops.* True to this fact, the hospital never lost control of its ability to develop coherent messages, even in the face of the conflicting, hysteria-driven information that was being delivered by numerous parties.

"During SARS, internal messaging competed not only with media reports, but also with information coming from normally credible sources, such as the Ontario Ministry of Health, professional colleges [the schools that train nurses] and unions," DuHamel says. "But it appeared the information the hospital provided was better than what they were seeing in the news."[10] The reason? The hospital's information was clear and concise. It was free of the speculation that sometimes occurs when media and other agencies filter the data. In the case of media reports in particular, the information delivered was often influenced by reporters asking for opinions from non-expert sources far from the crisis. This tended to produce stories that skewed the reality of the situation. The information from SWC, on the other hand, was straight from the source.

The crisis brought to the table a host of top-level spokespeople. This was, in part, a measure of luck: the hospital is the home of some of the world's foremost disease experts, who were in turn advising the WHO on the crisis. The hospital's expert panel was confident, professional and stakeholder-focused. Working with the hospital's communicators, the panel was able to educate stakeholders about the crisis. Even as the crisis wore on and the media cranked up the level of hysteria, SWC continued to present clear messages to its stakeholders.

Although DuHamel admits there was an advantage in having experts on hand at the hospital, he says, "Even in areas where expertise wasn't required, there was a corporate commitment to communications that people appreciated, even when there was nothing to say."[11] Managers always reported back to their staff after attending an update meeting, even if the only thing to report was that there was nothing to report. As result, the confidence level was high, and hospital administrators were confident that staff could talk to outsiders without delivering the wrong message. Just about everybody became a spokesperson.

EMPLOYEES AS SPOKESPEOPLE

"We also shattered the 'single spokesperson' myth," says DuHamel. "In SARS, because it affected nearly an entire population, we mirrored the population in our messaging. We tried to pair the essence of our message to the receiver, asking ourselves, 'What will the person at home want to know?' We had a cross section of staff [from nurses and doctors to janitors, administrators to cafeteria employees], working in different areas of the hospital, talking to reporters, talking about their experiences — and this to me was one of the most powerful things that we did."[12]

The hospital treated the largest number of SARS patients outside Asia. It would also succeed where other organizations failed in ensuring consistent, two-way communications with its publics — all because SWC followed the principles of effective crisis communications: know your publics and understand their needs and concerns, keep them informed and involved, get your key messages right, capture the emotional tone of the crisis in your communications and communicate quickly and often, even when there's nothing to communicate. Ultimately, the hospital succeeded because it was able to view the crisis through the eyes of its stakeholders, appreciating their concerns and addressing them. This, in turn, helped communications staff contain an already ugly situation that had the potential of growing into a state of uncontrolled panic and hysteria. Most important, it enabled the hospital to be perceived to be doing the right thing by its stakeholders.[13]

Conclusion

We've seen in this chapter just how important it is to keep employees tuned in to the company's actions during a crisis. Internal stakeholders are essential but too often ignored components of the overall crisis communications approach. They feel the stress of the organization as it moves through the crisis most keenly; the outcome of the crisis may affect their careers. By involving employees at the front end, keeping them informed and offering them options to understand and respond to the crisis, crisis resolution will be easier and more efficient.

In a crisis, communicators must —

- See employees as a first line of defence in a crisis, especially when dealing with customers;
- Understand and determine the information needs of different internal stakeholders, often based on their job or seniority within a company;
- Integrate employees into the crisis communications plan;
- Build strong support and understanding between employees and high-level managers;
- Work to build a strong sense of teamwork and support for front-line workers through meetings, emails and sharing of information.

7

Publics III
Media Relations during a Crisis

> All men can see these tactics whereby I conquer, but what none
> can see is the strategy out of which victory is evolved.
>
> —SUN TZU

Sun Tzu knew his adversaries could easily see his soldiers sweeping across an open plain and could watch from a hilltop as they drew their swords, charging into the fray or were deftly manoeuvred and guided by the motion of flags and the beating of drums into a smart tactical position to inflict damage on the enemy's troops. But what the enemy did not know was how those manoeuvres fit into the general's overall plans. Not until the battle was won could the enemy army's general hope to link those tactics together, backtracking as they fell like puzzle pieces into a sequence that would provide a clear view of Sun Tzu's strategy as a whole.

Communicators also use tactics to manage crises: news releases, Q&As, news conferences, website updates. And their critics, members of their various stakeholder groups, the media, and the general public, can easily see those tactics. But like Sun Tzu, communicators are working to a plan, one that their external stakeholders are *not* privy to. They put their own troop of leaders, experts, additional spokespeople and supporters (such as stakeholders and company employees) on the field of public opinion, manoeuvring them appropriately to win a measure of *balance* as they seek to regain the high ground and position their organization's actions in a positive light.

The media's role in all of this is to ask the questions, and sometimes they take an interest in not only the information surrounding a crisis but also the strategy of the organization's communicators. The media want to know the organization's tactics and plans. They know that the terrain may change, and communicators have to be able to adapt to the shift in terrain. Media people are savvy, and they know that many communicators and companies may respond in less than professional ways during a crisis, focusing on highly scripted, tightly controlled tactics and sound bites instead of on getting the media the information they need to write a story. It is incumbent on journalists to make such posturing a factor in their reporting, especially if the pressure and stakes of a crisis lead an organization's people to cover up information, distort the truth or outright lie.

If communicators — if all the tactics and strategy, the aim of which is to provide the needed information but carefully organized to present the organization in the best possible light — are made part of the story, including when they delay in order to develop effective messages and brief their spokespeople, this is not a credit to the company. Ironically, it is *precisely when* the media sense that the posturing of the communicators overwhelms the communicators' concern for discovering and promptly presenting all the facts that media become interested in the organization's tactics and planning. The story shifts from one about a crisis (and how the organization is dealing with it) to one about the presentation or spin of a crisis. This is a nightmare for communicators: the story has become one of "how the organization messed up."

Thus, the work of a good communicator in dealing with the media is largely invisible; the media are informed in a prompt fashion, and the story never touches the careful planning and writing that happens behind the scenes to ensure the organization's publics are well informed. The reporters deal with the facts presented to them.

Communicators must remember that media serve the public — their external stakeholders — and so are a major conduit for information to the public. This chapter examines the significant role of media in crisis management and the relationship that exists between the media and communicators. It explores:

- Preoccupations of the media, and the implications of them for crisis communications;
- Dynamics of the media representative-communicator relationship during crisis;
- Tactics for media relations that create the best communications outcomes.

The Ubiquitous Media

The fact that the media reach millions of people every day alone makes them a powerful force in society. Communicators, then, must understand what motivates the media in their pursuit of a story if they hope to use the media as a conduit for their message.

NEWSPAPER READERSHIP IN CANADA

According to NADbank Inc. (the Newspaper Audience Databank) in the 2005 Study of 77 Canadian daily newspapers in 54 urban markets there were:
- 11.8 million adults readers weekly in the top 17 markets;
- 8 million adults readers weekly in the Vancouver, Calgary, Toronto, Ottawa-Gatineau and Montreal markets;
- 2.4 million adults readers weekly read the *Globe and Mail* and 1.5 million adults read the *National Post*.[1]

The Nature of Media: Their Preoccupations

With sponge-like efficiency, the media soak up information, filtering out what is not useful to the story they are building. They do so by lining up the reams of data they receive, measuring it against the goal they have set for themselves in creating the story and then using that information to craft an article, news feature, radio clip or television segment that will sell — that is, a story that will have elements of human interest: excitement, danger or tragedy.

The media have long recognized that a good story will draw readers, viewers and listeners; as the American humorist Fred Allen said: "To a newspaperman a human being is an item with the skin wrapped around it." Anything can become an "item" — and a journalist's job is to find that bit of excitement, that "hook" that will draw a reader, viewer or listener into the story. Writers use this hook in the story's lead or first paragraph or, sometimes, as a headline. For example, if it's a plane crash, the story may lead with the number of people killed, or, if a famous person was aboard, that news will be part of the lead. Stories are also localized: Canadian media reporting about a plane crash in Indonesia will invariably mention whether Canadians were on board.

CANADIAN MEDIA: A BREAKDOWN

There are 5,614 media outlets in Canada. Among them are —

- 143 daily newspapers;
- 1,225 community newspapers;
- 843 consumer magazines;
- 832 business publications;
- 714 radio stations;
- 380 campus, farm and shopping publications;
- 147 television stations.

Together, their audience runs into the tens of millions. By comparison, the United States, with about 10 times Canada's population, is home to 1,500 daily newspapers, 7,200 weeklies and 75,000 periodicals.[2]

— Canadian Advertising Rates and Data, December 2005

In general, media are committed to balance in a story. They may write about the foreclosure of an orphan's home by a bank, but, in addition to describing the situation and getting a photograph of a dewy-eyed moppet, they obtain a comment from bank officials.

What Makes the News?

Take a look at the news around you. What's making the headlines? What is the lead story on the local broadcast? What story appears above the fold of the newspaper and what stories are given full-play on the Internet news websites?

News focuses on several factors. Thomas H. Bivins wrote in *Public Relations Writing* that what makes the news is decided by a number of factors including consequence, interest, timeliness, proximity, and prominence. I see these factors in a slightly different way, but I would like to acknowledge Bivins's work in laying the groundwork for these important concepts. The following five factors have the most to do with the way stories make the news.

Significance to the public. What does a story mean to people's families, jobs, shopping, recreation, business activities or safety?

Entertainment value. Is the story unusual or entertaining?

Currency of the story. Is the story timely or is there a new angle that can be created for an old story?

Local angle. What's the local perspective? Media look for proximity in a story, working to find the local angle in just about every story they approach. They will ask questions of how this affects people in their media outlet's community. National and international stories are also brought home by media: whether it's a situation in Afghanistan or a national health scare, media will look for a hometown perspective on the story.

Profile. How big will the story be? Media look for a story that has a high profile, often involving famous people. They look for the prominence of the story's featured performers and use that profile to drive home the story's main points.[3]

WHY MEDIA LOVE A CRISIS

Despite a general profession of high moral values, people are drawn to tragedy and drama — they love to read the lurid details of crimes, while at the same time sympathizing with the victim and hating the perpetrator, even though they may not know much about any of the three. (For instance, the creation of overnight shrines at the scene where people have been shot is an example of how an extreme situation creates a desire in people, usually total strangers, to relate to the victim of the crime.) Crises are likely to directly or indirectly impact the well-being of many more stakeholders than a single, even dramatic, crime.

As it is with crimes, so it is with crises in which organizations or their executives may be guilty of wrongdoing, or in which stakeholders may be harmed, physically or financially. Crises have a similar dynamic to crimes in terms of how they are presented in stories — they involve the same simple polarity of roles: a victim and victimizer, a crook and a cop or other public crusader, a corrupt company and a whistleblower, a hero and a villain. The media know that crises sell, and they certainly play to the audience.

EXTREME SITUATIONS AND CONTRASTS ARE ATTRACTIVE

The downtrodden, the cheated, the wounded, the lost, the dead, the suffering: media love to draw out stories that play up human emotion, tragedy and suffering. Media love the contrasts that can be drawn between who's right and who's wrong. They are drawn to extreme, dangerous situations in which these polarities are most easily suggested. News is almost always played out in black and white, rarely focusing on the grey areas where there might be doubt about which party is at fault. Even feature stories, which tend to elaborate more on those grey areas, present issues in a way that clearly delineates roles (good guys and bad guys, crooks and victims, victims and victimizers), with an emphasis on action and reaction, creating an emotional tone to draw an audience into the story.

A direct result of this preoccupation with dramatic contrasts is the media's love of speculation. The questions "why did this happen?" "how did this happen?"

and "who is at fault?" serve as great starting points for suggesting drama and all the attendant polarizations of issues and roles. Speculation serves the journalist by suggesting a black-and-white view or a sharp contrast of viewpoints where the situation is still too murky to be presented in a definitive way. A journalist cannot write a news story without an angle, without a narrative structure. When too little has become clear to form a coherent story, a journalist can really prepare a story of speculation only — all the things that might be the case. When journalists do this, they will most often frame their speculations in these sharp role definitions of hero and villain, and the dramatic contrasts these roles represent.

In a factory explosion, for example, journalists will immediately speculate about the number of injured or dead, and how much danger the resulting fire poses to the surrounding community. They will also search out information from other sources, such as emergency response personnel, for an opinion and use that information to embellish their story.

© Brooke McEldowney/Dist. by United Feature Syndicate, Inc.

The Hazards of Cool Media

In his analysis of media, Marshall McLuhan, in *Understanding Media,* spoke of hot and cool media. A hot medium is a means of transmitting information that delivers highly defined, densely packed information — there's lots of "stuff" in it. Radio, by McLuhan's definition, is a hot medium; it delivers information and it also really engages the listeners, demanding that they participate and think. The newspaper, too, is a hot medium. The information it contains is precise and concrete, and the writing requires a high degree of criticality of the reader.[4] New York University professor and culture analyst Neil Postman, in *Amusing Ourselves to Death,* speaks of the power of the written word in ensuring complete meaning: "[T]here is no escape from meaning when language is the instrument guiding one's thought. Though one may accomplish it from time to time, it is very hard to say nothing when employing a written English sentence … words have very little to recommend them except as carriers of meaning."[5]

A cool medium, on the other hand, like television, gives pictures but it doesn't engage people in the same way a hot medium does. It provides scant information, its data washing over you as you become a mostly passive receiver (should we even enter into a discussion of actively engaging viewers, making them "hot" participants, as many reality shows are now doing by asking their national audiences to text-message their favourite entertainer?).

Speech and telephones and writing are all cool media according to McLuhan; most likely, so is the Internet, though it might be tagged as "lukewarm" for its presentation of fast, cool images sandwiched between passages of in-depth writing. The risks of cool media are the interpretive gaps the receiver is left to fill in. An image of a burning building or angry strikers on a picket line certainly provokes emotions, but there is no chance for explanation, conciliation or key messages. Images on the Internet, in print or on television provoke emotions in publics immediately, often in obviating any criticality on their part.[6]

During the events of 9/11, the graphic moving picture — often shown in slow motion — of two jets crashing into the twin towers of the World Trade Center, was an image that was replayed, over and over and over, for days, weeks and months. The public filled those images with meaning, even while the hot media professionals were filling the pages of newspapers with commentary that sought to provide context and guide the thinking of readers to logical conclusions.

It is precisely because cool media have such a capacity to incite emotion that media firms are moving with ever increasing speed to cool media. Media watchers have applauded the advent of television for its directness while also criticizing it for its loss of "meaning delivery." Postman also discusses television's influence on other news: "In presenting news to us packaged as vaudeville, television induces other media to do the same, so that the total information environment begins to mirror television ... *USA Today* is modeled precisely on the format of television."[7] And look at the advent, particularly in larger Canadian cities, of the quick, short, snappy commuter papers that provide an entire story in only three paragraphs, wrapped around sharp colour photographs. This is media aimed at a consuming public characterized by a short attention span coupled with a need to receive information instantly in the most easily digestible form.

IMPLICATIONS FOR COMMUNICATORS

What do the nature and function of the media and the advent of cool media mean to communicators' relationship with them? It means that communicators need to understand how the media work and learn to work effectively with them in order to get their message to their publics. It means communicators need to ensure that their words have meaning, making certain that their sentences are short and have visual impact but are meaningful enough to convey plenty of information about the context of the events. The words must be powerful enough to *fill in the information gaps* between the communicator's organization and its publics that crisis events inevitably create. The writing accomplishes this best by using action-oriented and highly visual language, just as reporters use. By creating dynamic pictures with writing, communicators are using the powerful tools of images, albeit housed in words — the same tools of cool media. A combination of the dense information we can pack into a hot medium with the fascination and power of cool images is the strongest combination communicators can use to close any understanding gaps created by cool media.

Case Study:
Small-Town Crisis at Horizon Plastics, Cobourg, Ontario

Media are in the business of localizing stories and pulling out the elements that will have the greatest draw for their audience. In this case study about a fire at a small-town plastics company, we'll examine what was said and how the crisis was covered by the media. The purpose is not necessarily to look at how the company would have/should have responded (the officials were never asked for commentary and there was no ensuing negative fallout) but to see how the media approach a story. The focus is on getting a sense of how media see a story and what they focus on when reporting it. *This is essential to communicators because it allows them to get a better read of their media audience.* Understanding what the media look for in a story helps communicators determine how best to project their company's image, and how best to handle media inquiries during a crisis.

In late April 2005, in the town of Cobourg, Ontario (population 17,000), a fire at a plastics plant, Horizon Plastics, resulted in the mayor calling for a state of emergency. Three hundred people living near the plant were evacuated. Media played up the human element in the story. Several days later, two youths were arrested and charged with arson. Interestingly, media did not interview the company owners or executives, confining their quotes to local residents and emergency officials. This was the human element that they may have recognized would result in maximum interest for their audiences. It also might reflect a decision to steer away from what may have been considered too risky — there was the potential of getting dry or unexciting quotes from company officials and being obliged to put them into the story.

Pulse24.com, April 25:

The headline: "Raging inferno."

The lead: "A billowing mushroom cloud of black choking smoke rose as a fierce fire raged at a plastics plant in Cobourg on Monday. A state of emergency was declared by the mayor in the eastern Ontario city as scores of fire crews rushed to the scene."

In the story: "I got off work about four and about seven minutes after four there was somebody at my door," Jennifer Magee said from the evacuation centre at the Salvation Army, where she was whisked away with her two children.

Commentary: Note the language used — this is a website news centre, and the words (billowing, choking, fierce) create an effective word picture for readers. The quote from the local woman — and the mention of the children — brings a dramatic, family-oriented human element to the story, emphasizing the danger to the community.

What could communicators do? They could emphasize in their key messages that company officials worked closely with emergency personnel to ensure a safe evacuation from the plant; they could also express the company's overriding concerns for safety in the community.

Canadian Press, April 26:

The headline: "Air quality around scene of Cobourg factory fire improves: Dombrowsky."

The lead: "Provincial government scientists tested the quality of Cobourg's air and water Tuesday, a day after a massive seven-hour blaze at a plastics plant blanketed the eastern Ontario town in thick, black smoke."

In the story: "Cobourg residents have nothing to fear from the quality of the air, [provincial] Environment Minister Leona Dombrowsky said before the Liberal government's weekly cabinet meeting."

Commentary: The Canadian Press took an interesting tack in approaching the story from the environmental angle, quoting the Ontario government's environment ministry. Again, the story comes back to the effect on human life with the talk of air quality — a valid and effective way of approaching a pretty standard story from a slightly different direction.

What could communicators do? This is a story that talks about environmental issues, and communicators could easily assert the company's environmental values and its contribution to local environmental groups. With approval from senior management, they also could confirm a commitment to work with the Ministry of the Environment to reduce the negative effects of the plant fire.

Relationships with Media

Media relations is the relationship that communicators build, nurture and maintain with the media, with both sides gaining a net benefit from the relationship. Media go in with the expectation that they will gather information from reliable news sources and be able to put together a story that fulfills their goals of a balanced story in time to meet their deadline. Communicators rely on media for earned media coverage (the coverage the company gets in news stories in print or other news vehicle, as opposed to media presence in paid advertisements in those same vehicles), for an honest and balanced approach to the way the company is portrayed to its publics and stakeholders, and for a working relationship that allows them to provide sound and effective information to media contacts. It should be clear, however, that communicators' expectations shouldn't be based on the anticipation that they will *always* get positive media coverage — that just isn't going to happen. They can only expect to be treated without undo bias and in a balanced way.

Media Relationships during a Crisis

In a crisis, communicators have to expect that questions will come faster, deadlines will be tighter and media will be more demanding than usual. A media outlet that might have one reporter assigned to a communicator's company on an average day might now have two or three assigned to talk about different aspects of the crisis.

Communicators who normally deal with only a half dozen media outlets on a regular basis, based perhaps on the industry niche the company occupies or its location, might find themselves dealing with three times that number. And their day will be filled with more exacting demands and a great deal of pressure to meet those demands. Their relationship with the media is a business relationship that will sometimes be conducted under stressful or emotionally charged circumstances.

Reporters have a responsibility to clearly outline what they are expecting from communicators — the questions they ask both create and reflect the parameters under which communicators conduct their job as media contacts. Communicators can always ask reporters for clarification of what they want — is it information about the company, an interview with the company president, an update on what the company has done or a copy of the latest news release? Communicators should never shy away from asking reporters to explain why they are calling or the purpose behind their news story. Reporters do not call communicators to fish for generalities: they have a specific purpose, and communicators have a right to know that purpose if they are contacted. Clarity is important on both sides, and clarity of the media's purpose will establish the foundation for a positive long-term relationship. It will also mean greater credibility for communicators, as they are able to specifically respond to the points reporters are raising.

The best ways to maintain media contact in a crisis depend on the conditions of the crisis and the communicator involved. Communicators tend to adopt an approach fitted to each reporter they deal with. Some reporters are approachable; others tend to maintain as much distance as possible. Yet others ask generalized questions, allowing the communicator to take the lead in the way the topic is approached. This can work especially well for communicators, because it allows them to easily deliver the information they want to get into the public domain.

> "You have to give media a road map; you have to give them a sense of where you are going to go; if you're going to say 'I can't speak to you right now,' you have to let them know *when* you're going to speak with them and you better damn well be able to do that. Media are just doing their job, and they can be relatively understanding and quite fair, but if you give them a stock response that doesn't show any sign of humanity, they're going to eat you alive."[8]
> — John Larsen, communications consultant and principal of Corpen Group.

GUIDELINES FOR DEALING WITH THE MEDIA DURING A CRISIS

Following are guidelines communicators should keep in mind when seeking publicity or responding to media queries.

Be mindful of the past relationship with the reporter. What did the reporter say about the company in the past? What kind of relationship does the communicator have with this media contact? Although some communicators may question the idea of friendship with media, a positive business relationship can nevertheless be created, nurtured and maintained — and their communications can certainly reflect the general tone of that relationship. If they know the reporters by name, if they've met them personally and if they have had an opportunity to talk about things in general — the newspaper or radio or television station the reporters work for, their thoughts on the business community and so on — they are building familiarity with them. This gives communicators a sense of how the reporters may handle the issues at play if a crisis or issue breaks. It doesn't mean that the media are going to go easy on the company, and communicators can't expect that a friendly business relationship will guarantee a soft landing for the company during a crisis; it simply means that they are likely to face a less hostile media environment, since a comfort level has been established — the reporter knows the communicator as a person, not just a faceless media flack, and the communicator sees the reporter as someone working hard to get the facts right and meet a deadline.

For several years, when I worked for the Ontario government's Ministry of Economic Development and Trade, I made a point of contacting business reporters, occasionally going for lunch or coffee with them — it was what I would call a "getting to know you" meeting or a "maintaining contact" meeting. Invariably it worked well — reporters often appreciated that they were being recognized for the stories they wrote. From their perspective of dealing with a large and often bureaucratic government, the reporters had a face with a name, they knew whom to call for information and, in the case of a crisis, they would have a direct contact within the organization, something that is usually greatly appreciated. It meant less fishing for information and a quicker route to getting their stories filed.

Maintain a centralized location. One place should serve as a one-window, single-source location for delivering messages to the media. This involves:

- Ensuring all members of the crisis communications team can get to this location easily;
- Holding all news conferences in that place only;
- Posting at least one communications staff member at that location during business hours, even when a news conference isn't being held. This team member provides previously released news releases and backgrounders and notifies media of upcoming news conferences or changes in schedule.

Get the facts straight and don't speculate. Communicators need to work quickly to pull in facts and have them approved. Those facts have to be worked into key messages that reflect the overall direction of the company and they need to be approved by senior staff. It's often difficult to get all the facts in time to meet the media's timetables. This is where companies often run into trouble — as media outlets wait, and speculate, about possible answers.

Most organizations will say after the fact, when they are in the post-crisis analysis phase, that they would rather have the facts straight than go early with a response to media that contains incorrect information. And that is true, to a point. However, it's also essential to be responsive, and media are likely to spend the waiting time speculating: "Does the company have something to hide?" "Where is the president of the company?" "So many people are affected … why isn't the company responding?" Rather than dragging out the response time, it is often better to open with an interim or holding statement that emphasizes sensitivity to the situation and acknowledges both the urgency of the situation and of reporters' deadlines.

"We are concerned about this situation and we are taking steps to investigate it. We will have more information for you later today" — this is the essence of what a holding statement is meant to convey.

A holding statement is a way of saying: "We're here, we're listening and we're taking action" without committing to a set course of action at that time. It allows communicators to take a measure of control of the crisis — and it establishes a relationship with media from the outset, letting them know communicators fully intend to cooperate with them. Communicators must then follow through on their commitment, even if that means, later in the day, simply providing another update on how the investigation is going.

> "Don't let your mind go to the 'whys' — keep your mind on the 'what.' The media will usually be one step ahead of the crisis response. As crisis communicators it's incumbent upon us to provide correct, accurate information. Media will always want speculation — and the way I dealt with that (in the event of a Snowbird crash) was by saying that 'speculating would be unfair to you and to me. I can't offer conjecture on that. Our priority is the recovery and the families of the pilots involved in the crash.'"[9]
>
> — John Larsen, principal of Corpen Group

Be upfront and direct. Ensure that the top spokesperson or spokespeople are there, in front of the media, representing the organization; that they speak openly but do not speculate. If the company doesn't have an answer, communicators need to tell the media that it doesn't have one at this time but that they will get back to them. The media are looking to communicators for answers, and communicators have a responsibility to provide them.

PRESENTING KEY MESSAGES TO THE MEDIA

1. Create three or four key messages: these should be concise and must deliver the main message that communicators want to get across to the media. Keeping them to a minimum of three or four ensures that they deliver the undiluted ideas the company wants to get across to the media, without any loss of impact; more than four and communicators risk watering down the significance of what they are trying to say.
2. Keep each key message to one sentence, about 17 to 20 words in total. Each message must be action-oriented.
3. Come back to the key messages throughout the conversations with the media.
4. Work through the "bad news" message up front in a way that acknowledges the situation, and then build toward a positive outcome that clearly demonstrates that the company is in control and taking action.
5. Deliver bad news first, but do not mix messages in the same sentence — don't give a negative message followed by a positive one.
6. In delivering the news, use the guideline of three positive messages to one negative message.

Avoid spin by focusing on positive key messages. There are few things worse than lying, especially when the company's credibility, profile and reputation are on the line. Using slanted language designed to mislead through ambiguity or bias can be just as damaging to a company as lying.

For instance, a company that is saving money by laying off employees might say, "Our company has made some bad decisions operationally in the past fiscal year. We are in a position to lay off 500 employees, but this is really part of our company's need to look at enhancing efficiencies in our operations. It's just a part of doing business."

Enhancing efficiencies is the offensive term. Clearly, the organization is trying to weasel out of a tight situation — and the use of such a term won't lead the media to do anything but run out and find disgruntled employees whose job losses will help in that "enhancement." As well, the coldness of the phrase "just a part of doing business" shows insensitivity to the organization's workers. The company would be better off just saying that it is in financial difficulty and needs to save money.

Here's a different approach:

"Our company is facing a series of financial losses. As a result, we are being forced to lay off 500 workers. This immediate step will allow us to right the balance in our operations. It means that, as a vital member of this community's business sector, we can continue operating, preserving more than 1,200 jobs that are in place now — and it gives us a chance to invest in improvements that will make our company a better performer. On a positive note, some of the laid-off workers may be called back — and those who aren't will have the benefit of either an early retirement package or other benefits."

In this version, the company shows compassion for the laid-off employees and delivers messages about what the company *can* do for its employees: pension packages, reassignments and other initiatives. All these things can help boost the organization's profile. Notice how the message's wording includes the phrase "being forced to," giving the sense that the company had little choice in the matter and that it values its employees.

Be consistent. Any announcement that deals with a highly charged emotional situation is not the place to float a "trial balloon" — an idea that an organization puts in front of its audience, through the media or stakeholder meetings, to gauge the response of its publics, waiting to see how the public and stakeholders might react before either implementing the idea or vetoing it. The trial balloon should be reserved for a more stable period in the company's life, not when a crisis is either looming or underway.

For instance, a company might float a trial balloon about expanding its operations; a comment from the company president might involve a statement such as: "Our intent is to investigate the possibility of entering new and exciting overseas markets." The company can then talk to stakeholders, business associations and the media and find out what they think of the idea before deciding whether or not to go forward with the expansion plans. But this is business that should take place on a quiet day — not in the middle of a crisis, when the media, the community, stakeholders — especially in a smaller community — might speculate that this means the company will move its entire operation to another location, adding to a perception of instability in a company striving to bring itself back into balance.

© Scott Adams/Dist. by United Feature Syndicate, Inc.

Avoid "no comment" and "off the record" statements.

A "no comment" statement implies that the company is trying to hide information. Communicators should be able to provide an update and must always be ready to say to a reporter, "I don't have that information for you right now, but I will get back to you."

Communicators should never bite at a reporter's request that they speak off the record. *There is no such thing,* and communicators don't want to find themselves trapped in that kind of situation. Often reporters will be folksy, friendly or desperate-sounding, making a statement such as, "Listen, I'm really trying to get a handle on this situation and my deadline is looming. Off the record, what's really happening here?" Making an off-the-record statement or speculating off the record not only hurts the organization, it could lose a communicator his or her job.[10]

It sometimes astounds communicators to see their off-the-record comments appear in print. Each and every time they are with a reporter, they must assume the discussion is on the record, even if they have a positive and proactive business relationship with that journalist.

Respect the deadline. When communicators agree to provide information to a reporter, it is tacitly understood that they are providing a service to that member of the media. While there are legal issues as well as sensitivities that may preclude communicators from sharing some information, they will want to be as sensitive as possible to the reporter's need to pull a story together by deadline. Responsiveness is the basis for building strong and consistent long-term business relationships; communicators' ability to help journalists get the information they need will create a more positive, mutually supportive working relationship for the future. It has tangible long-term impacts — if communicators are able to get information to reporters in a fast-paced, time-crunching period, those reporters will be more receptive to them in the long run.

Follow Up. From an organization's perspective, it's vital to understand that, as the old saying goes, "We can't know where we're going unless we know where we've been." Communicators must review what was said about their organization and then use that information to help them plan for the next potential crisis. They must also be willing to scan the media to see how the story was handled and be willing to make contact with reporters to let them know what they are doing post-crisis, and to see if there is any other information they can provide.

Case Study: The Mississauga Train Derailment

Do all of these guidelines actually work in practice? To test their effectiveness, let's take a look at the granddaddy of crisis management in Canada: the Mississauga train derailment of 1979. From the moment the accident occurred to the follow-up that took place after it was all over, the stellar work of the media relations team from both the police force and the Ontario government garnered a great deal of attention — and praise.

It happened on Saturday, November 10, 1979. Twenty-two of 104 cars of a Canadian Pacific train, carrying 80 tonnes of chlorine as well as loads of other dangerous chemicals — caustic soda, propane, styrene and toluene — skipped off the tracks in suburban Mississauga, just west of Toronto.

It came to be called the "Mississauga Miracle" because there was no loss of life and no serious injuries. In the immediate aftermath, firefighters were kept busy fighting flames from propane tankers that shot 1,500 metres into the sky and could be seen 100 kilometres away. From the sky, the rail cars looked like a pile of matchsticks, according to Ontario Provincial Police and media reports. Styrene and toluene spilled onto the tracks from punctured rail cars and added fuel to the flames. Residents who heard the explosion called the fire department immediately; emergency crews were dispatched and roadblocks established. Peel police chief Douglas K. Burrows, Mississauga fire chief Gordon Bentley and Mississauga mayor Hazel McCallion were on hand quickly to take control of the situation. For 11 days, crews worked to clean up the site. In the long term, the Mississauga Miracle would lead to legislation to control the transportation of dangerous goods by rail, air and road.

More than 218,000 Mississauga residents (of a total population of 284,000) were evacuated during the crisis, making it North America's biggest peacetime evacuation. Emergency planning went into effect; the Peel Regional Police had an emergency plan developed because they are responsible for Pearson International Airport. "They were able to use that model when they set up for the rail disaster," says Allan Dickie, the director of communications at the Ministry of the Solicitor General under Solicitor-General (now Chief Justice) Roy McMurtry at the time of the derailment.

Not only were there no deaths or injuries but there were no crimes: no theft or looting. The emergency crews were able to do their job and members of the public who had been evacuated cooperated by staying away from their homes — for more than a week — while crews cleaned up.

Communicators ensured that the public and the media were kept informed of new developments during the crucial cleanup week, often helping to placate public fears over the possibility of exploding tanker cars or toxic fumes.

BUILDING THE COMMUNICATIONS TEAM

The communications team was assembled in the early hours of the crisis and
included Peel Police superintendent Karl Barnhart and Sergeant Barry King,
Dickie, and David Allen, director of communications for the Ministry of the
Attorney General, along with other police officers and government communicators. In an era long before BlackBerrys and email, Dickie and the communications team relied on telephones, fax machines and typewriters as their
main tools of communication.

"What the operation also had going for it was a superb emergency plan
assembled by the Peel Regional Police, primarily to deal with airport emergencies," says Dickie. It was adapted to fit the circumstances of the derailment."[11]

During the crisis, Dickie was the "outside guy" for the Ontario government who was in contact with reporters, connecting with them to determine
the questions they needed to have answered, updating media on developments and fulfilling their requests for interviews. The "inside guy" was David
Allen. Allen's job was to attend the command post meetings and write news
releases, while Dickie acted as liaison with the media. Both communicators
attended all the meetings, because it was essential that both were fully briefed
on all aspects of the derailment and the actions officials and crews were taking. With the influx of media and the demands for information, the job of
gathering information, assessing it, coordinating it and incorporating into
strong and compelling news releases was shared by the ministries of the

Solicitor General and the Attorney General, as it would have been too much work for one person to handle. For the practical purposes of coordinating responses to the media, Dickie and the police officers directed media queries to appropriate sources and fed information gathered by Allen to the media. Dickie coordinated the media sessions and, using the information gathered and written by Allen, presented it to the media.

According to Dickie, a cornerstone of the strategy was to let the elected officials and chiefs of police and chiefs of fire departments deal directly with the media once or twice a day through press conferences and make them available for interviews with major media at strategic times. Roy McMurty and Hazel McCallion were front and centre at every news conference and their presence was essential to the success of the communications plan.

THEY GOT THE FACTS OUT

The need to gather accurate information and get it out to the media quickly was paramount. Local media responded quickly and were, after the firefighters, the first on the scene. Other media representatives, first regional, then national and international, began pouring into the site on Sunday, November 11, the morning after the derailment. The media expected officials to provide them with accurate information that would help allay the fears of local citizens. Communicators from the Ontario government, as well as the police and fire departments and the City of Mississauga, knew that what their officials said would be quickly relayed to an anxious public, both within the hot zone of the derailment and provincially and nation-wide. Accuracy and timeliness were essential.

"The question was one of letting people know what was happening and what they needed to do to be safe," says Dickie. "It was clear that crews could contain the chlorine spill but the cars were still burning immediately after the crash. If the chlorine car exploded, it would have been a disaster. It was obvious early on that this was a major crisis — you could see the flames from several miles away — and it didn't take a lot of convincing to get people to evacuate."[12] The information that communicators dealt with ranged from how firefighters were handling the fires (in many cases containing the fires and allowing them to burn themselves out) and removing the remaining hazardous chemical tanks to prevent further explosions, to letting evacuees know when it was safe to return to their homes and providing information about the rerouting of highway traffic around the site.

THE MISSISSAUGA TRAIN DERAILMENT: WHAT THE COMMUNICATORS DID

- Within the first hour, a senior police officer was assigned to handle on-the-scene news requests.
- Two media centres were established: one at Peel Police headquarters in Brampton and one near the emergency site.
- Meetings of communications staff from the Ontario government, Peel Police and the City of Mississauga were held each morning. Pertinent information and updates was gathered and reviewed.
- Information from scientists was rewritten in plain language and approved by technical experts, communications staff and senior officials.
- All senior officials were involved in reviewing information and approving it before news conferences were held.
- News conferences featured elected officials, who would speak on that day's events.
- The news conference was followed by a Q&A from reporters.
- After the Q&A, a follow-up technical briefing from scientists and technical staff was held, giving reporters a chance to ask for clarification on scientific and technical questions.
- Media representatives were hosted in a media centre located in a truck stop across from the regional centre (discussed below).
- Communicators monitored media reports daily and ensured that what they were saying to media was accurate. In the case of inaccurate reporting, the appropriate media outlet was called, informed that their story contained inaccuracies and asked to ensure that correct information was provided in a subsequent story.

Communicators also produced remarks for the spokespeople on site, often working 14-hour days and in shifts to ensure 24-hour representation during the week that residents were evacuated. In addition to that from the media, this information, vetted by senior spokespeople, was made available to citizens on a request basis in the form of phone call responses and bulletins. News reporters were provided with media advisories, letting them know when the news conference was taking place. As well, daily news releases were sent out to all media contacts establishing the direction the emergency response officials were taking on that day.

THEY HAD A PLAN

As one of the key provincial government communicators, Dickie met with his counterparts from Mississauga, other provincial government officials (including those from the Ministry of the Environment and the Ministry of the Attorney General), and the police and fire departments to put a plan together that included delegates from each organization. The plan was to ensure that all information flowing to the media from the site was carefully coordinated so that the message was consistent: information from the Ontario government would be shared with the media relations representatives of Mississauga and the Peel Regional Police and the messages delivered to the media would be consistent and understood by all the spokespeople.

Each component of the media relations team — government, police, public health, fire and city — knew what information the other team members had, what they planned to say and when they planned to say it. This allowed them to speak with one voice.

THEY ESTABLISHED OFFSITE AND
ONSITE COMMUNICATIONS CENTRES

An offsite media centre was established at the Brampton police headquarters to link all parties involved in handling the emergency, including the City of Mississauga, the provincial and federal governments, and government agencies such as the public health department. A senior police officer trained in public relations was assigned to lead the handling of on-the-scene media inquiries. Up to 12 officers, all well versed in media relations as well as emergency response, coordinated media relations. Dickie coordinated media relations duties ranging from answering basic questions to tracking down answers to specific questions about the disaster and setting up media interviews for senior staff.

Following first-day meetings, the communications team also established what came to be called an onsite regional communications centre: a Bell telephone building in the area. This regional centre complemented the Peel Police communications office in Brampton, and became the main centre for handling media inquiries. The Peel Police centre, initiated at the front end of the crisis because police were first on the scene, began to funnel media requests to the regional centre. Peel Police media contacts continued to handle basic questions from the public at their office, but media questions were managed by Dickie and staff at the regional centre. This was significant, because of the number of media that were beginning to arrive to cover the story.

"We had 200 to 300 media representatives from around the world suddenly showing up, and that building was just right for us to hold our regular press conferences," says Dickie. "It's important to have a place where you can set up and deal with that number of media and also have a place where you know where the media are; this is essential, because you have restricted areas and you don't want media wandering around the emergency site — it is already a dangerous situation and you run the risk of creating more problems if a reporter got hurt."[13]

Keeping reporters confined to one building but close to the site, where they could gain access to spokespeople, was a direct way of providing information while ensuring safety, because all the resident experts were on hand to offer commentary and perspective. "Everything was done on site," adds Dickie. "We had enormous resources in the form of telephone lines set up for the duration of the crisis, communications staff who could turn out briefing materials for senior staff based on information coming from the emergency site. The Peel Regional Police had a great team of communications people and so, all together, we had all those remote resources on site and were able to both keep track of news reports — what the media were saying on a daily basis — and prepare for the next news conference." This approach ensured a consistency of message throughout the crisis.[14]

THEY WERE OPEN AND DIRECT

Communicators at the crisis site settled on a straightforward process that meant information was rapidly gathered and shared. During early morning briefings, scientists met with elected officials, senior police representatives and the Ontario government communications team; the team then distilled the information provided. Scientific language was simplified and written up into news releases, which often included diagrams of the site and an explanation of hazards. Technical experts were on hand to explain particular components of the cleanup to reporters, if called upon.

This rapid assembly and sharing of information could be achieved only through ongoing media contact. "Communication had to be as open as we could make it," says Dickie. Because the information dealt with a direct threat to people's lives, the approach to communicating with publics demanded a clear and open conduit for relaying information to the media and stakeholders. "We wanted to develop a sense of trust on the part of the public," says Dickie.[15]

Dickie's priority was to make sure his staff could enable the media to understand what was being done to keep the situation under control. This was essential because the high-profile, highly visible emergency could easily inspire wild speculation on the part of the media and the public. There was a need to be transparent and direct and to engender a sense of trust in the public that the agencies involved were able to handle the crisis effectively and would allow people to return home safely and as soon as possible. In a scary situation, media and other publics will begin to speculate the moment an information or understanding gap opens — and often even during a communications lull, even if only a brief one.

Dickie elaborates:

We had "inside notes" that were distributed at the crisis communications team meetings and then decisions were made on what we would include in news releases. I worked on the outside, dealing directly with the media, setting up interviews, checking out rumours, finding out which reporters needed information and who needed to get into the news conferences. We kept the major players of the control team — the police chief, the Solicitor General and the mayor — close at hand. The most important thing was making sure that the media messages were accurate. The worst thing is for the media to think you're not levelling with them. The lesson: keep your control team in a positive environment and keep the messaging consistent.[16]

THEY GOT THE FACTS STRAIGHT AND PREVENTED SPECULATION

The communications team worked to track down and dispel rumours. "In a major crisis, the thing that often happens is that someone starts a rumour," says Dickie.

For instance, there was one rumour from a federal official about a cloud of chlorine gas. There was in fact no cloud of gas. We had to track that rumour down and then correct it in the media. It was a question of getting accurate information. We went to the reporter who had received the rumour and took him to the environment officials and got him the right information. We made a point of tracking that stuff and dealing with it right then and there rather than letting it slide.[17]

THEY MAINTAINED CONTACT

News conferences were held at the same time each day. "We were cognizant of reporters' deadlines, so we would have a late afternoon press conference, and these would be built around the regular meetings that were taking place at the site, which included the principal people from Peel Region, Mississauga, firefighters and the environment ministry," says Dickie.[18]

By the early days of the week, news conferences developed a regular pattern. "These were chaired by the leaders of the crisis team; in attendance were spokespeople for the direct agencies involved: [Solicitor General] Roy McMurtry as well as the fire chief, the police chief, Mississauga mayor Hazel McCallion, the chief environmental officer and the medical officer of health," says Dickie. "The media were able to question all these people to ask them about various aspects of how they were dealing with the crisis at the time. The main thing was to keep that team together, make sure they were together for the news conferences and to hold those news conferences on a regular basis."[19]

THEY FOLLOWED UP AFTER THE CRISIS WAS OVER

Communicators conducted a survey of the affected citizens. "That survey showed that 86 per cent were happy with the information that was given to them," says Dickie:

> They trusted us. There was also a study conducted by the emergency measures people in the United States. They must have taken some lessons from it, because you saw it in 9/11, in the controlled news conferences that they had, with the police chief and the fire chief and all the other necessary spokespeople on hand. It helped set the standard in crisis response.[20]

In addition, in the wake of the crisis, every municipality in Ontario was urged by the province of Ontario to develop an emergency plan for evacuating citizens and handling a crisis.[21]

THE MISSISSAUGA MIRACLE: THE HEADLINES

"Welcome home" — MISSISSAUGA TIMES, November 14, 1979
"The week they closed Mississauga" — TORONTO STAR, November 18, 1979
"Mississauga's lost week" — TORONTO SUN, November 18, 1979
"City in crisis: day by day" — MISSISSAUGA NEWS, November 21, 1979

THINK TANK

In a group of two or three, discuss Allan Dickie's description of how authorities handled the Mississauga train derailment crisis. Is there anything that might have been improved on? Did they miss anything?

1. How does the derailment compare with crises today in terms of the scope of the crisis and how it was handled?
2. What are some challenges today that weren't present in 1979?
3. How would the crisis plans and tactics be different had the crisis happened today?
4. What are some of the lessons learned from the handling of this kind of disaster?

A Journalist's Perspective

Marlane Oliver is a broadcast journalist, reporter, media consultant and radio host for 680 News. In the Q&A that follows, Oliver mentions many of the strategies that we have discussed regarding media relations, as well as what communicators need to do during a crisis and the importance of putting a leader up front to deal with external stakeholders.

MARLANE OLIVER, JOURNALIST: CURRICULUM VITAE

Mainstay of Toronto's all-news radio station 680 News since 1993. She has covered thousands of stories for 680 News, many focusing on crisis events.

She has a background in public affairs and politics, with a special interest in health stories.

From a media perspective, are websites useful during a crisis?

An updated website can certainly reduce the number of phone calls that we have to make to PR people. We in the media find them particularly useful when the public needs to be informed immediately, [when] there is no time for a news conference and the media have to scramble to get information as quickly as possible. An excellent example of this is the Peel District Board of Education, which used its website when a teacher was shot at a high school in Brampton and the school was in lockdown. For media, we were able to get information quickly about the situation. I think as well that the website probably reassured parents their children were safe, that police were on the scene, that the shooting took place outside the school — and it also gave parents the information they needed on when to expect their children to be released. In that way, the board communicated directly with the people who needed to know most; that is, the parents of the children involved.

For us in the broadcast media, we were able to draw information from the website and use it to provide listeners with updates on the situation.

Updates are essential, and the speed of information today dictates that updates be provided as soon as they are available. This helps reassure stakeholders and the public that the organization undergoing the crisis is taking action; as well, it underscores a sense of trust on the part of the media, a feeling that the organization is moving in the right direction in handling a crisis. Websites are effective in doing this because reporters have 24-7 access to them — they may not always be able to track down communicators for comment; and communicators can update website information at any time.

Are news releases useful in providing updates?

Yes, but they tend to be used for less urgent, ongoing situations. For example, we got them regularly from the health departments for West Nile virus during the summer of 2004, which was important. There is an essential fact-based element to news releases and they are great for conveying numbers — we can access news releases easily, from websites or Canada Newswire, and get the numbers we need to ensure that our stories have the most correct, up-to-date information. They also help to spell out clearly — no guessing, no conjecture — what steps an organization is taking to handle an issue. Finally, they are a great heads-up for us, as to when an organization will hold its next news conference and what it plans to say.

Nothing upsets an organization's senior people faster than seeing one media story with one set of numbers and another with completely different information. A news release with accurate, approved information delivered to media contacts will ensure consistency of message. In urgent situations, communicators can keep tumbling out the news releases, but they have to ensure that the numbers are correct, and it can be a challenge for media to keep track of which news release they are looking at — is it the most current one?

What are the biggest mistakes you have found organizations making during a crisis?

First and foremost, not responding quickly enough. That's key. It speaks volumes as to lack of leadership and direction, [and it suggests] that there is confusion and potentially cover-up. Second is having too many spokespeople. The public and media have to know who is in charge. He or she has to become the face and voice of the crisis, for example Rudolph Giuliani during 9/11.

Hiding the spokesperson only leads to the media doing more digging (such as the situation at Enron and WorldCom, where information that was buried eventually came to the surface, leading to bigger crises for the leaders of those organizations). The spokesperson should ideally be the one calling the media in the morning — the key radio stations first, then television, then the papers — if the information needs to get out urgently.

Oliver makes a valid point in talking about the hidden spokesperson. Media will persist until they find someone who will speak to them and answer their questions — even if that spokesperson is far from the centre of activity within the organization. This can fuel rumour and speculation: the farther one gets from a designated spokesperson, the more diffuse or diluted the organization's actual message (the one the organization wants to get out) becomes. Such a situation is the result of having no one within the organization stepping forward and taking charge during a crisis.

Has a leader ever failed to show up for a crisis that you have covered?
I think that during SARS, the federal Health minister, Anne McClelland, was not visible enough. There seemed to be a decision to make this a Toronto problem and not a national problem, which it was, so she didn't step up and take charge. The fact, is, during a crisis you really have the chance to not only make your organization look responsible and in charge but also minimize the risk of lawsuits.

Criticism of the handling of the SARS crisis included hospitals casting blame on the provincial health ministry for not taking charge quickly and decisively enough, and comments that the federal government was simply out of the loop. This failure to respond reflects a panic mode wherein the distress of the situation causes those who need to step up to instead run away from the problem. In McClelland's case, the information gathering should have been done faster and more effectively than it was. Because they appeared ill-prepared, both the federal and provincial governments lost the chance for a more positive media profile.

Even if they didn't have the most current information, the governments should have recognized their roles as leaders (even minor ones) and established for the media that they had linked in to the communications channels with other agencies, organizations and departments, and that they were prepared to come back to the media with information later. Common sense dictates that if you have a responsibility for the issue, even if you're not the main leader in handling the crisis, the least you can do is demonstrate that you are a team player.

Conclusion

As we can see from the Mississauga train derailment case study, communicators must create effective channels of communication between themselves and their stakeholders and the media — and that means building and maintaining strong, long-term relationships. It's a case of *build, build, build* followed by *maintain, maintain, maintain.* It's not enough for communicators to see their relationship with the media as a series of one-offs, whereby they slingshot information to them, then sit back and expect reporters to take care of first getting the message right and then getting it out the door. Communicators must view themselves as providers of one-window service in gathering information and getting it out to media contacts. Communicators must have a hand in all aspects of the communications cycle, from brainstorming ideas to crafting the message, and then delivering it and following up — and all these functions reinforced by the creation and maintenance of positive, strong, day-to-day business relationships.

To deliver a powerful message to the media, communicators must —

- Understand what the media look for in a story: drama, conflict and contrasts. Communicators must address these elements if they hope to have the media act as a conduit for their message and ask questions to determine the company's strategy in handling whatever crisis it is faced with. Understanding what motivates the media in the pursuit of a story will help communicators determine how best to project the company's image and how best to deal with a company crisis that will be covered by that same media.
- Ensure that their words are strong enough to create compelling pictures, just as cool media do. These words must be informative and potent

enough to close the gaps in understanding that cool media can create.

- Have guidelines in place for dealing with the media.
- Have a plan:
    - Maintain a centralized location;
    - Get the facts straight;
    - Be upfront and direct;
    - Be consistent;
    - Avoid "no comment" and "off the record" statements;
    - Maintain contact;
    - Respect the deadline;
    - Follow up.

Part III: Interview and Exercises

Bart Mindszenthy,
APR, Fellow CPRS

Bart Mindszenthy, an Accredited Public Relations Professional through the Canadian Public Relations Society and a partner in the niche communications firm Mindszenthy & Roberts Communications Counsel, has more than 38 years of experience in public relations. He has specialized in crisis communications, change and issues management, and conflict and crisis management since 1988. A graduate of Detroit's Wayne State University, he worked for the Detroit Convention Bureau (arriving at the time of a major crisis, the Detroit Riots of 1967, which left 43 people dead and 1,189 injured, with more than 7,000 people arrested after five days of rioting) and for the Detroit-Macomb Hospital Association.

In Toronto, Mindszenthy worked at PIR Communications and at chemical manufacturer CIL, a maker of paints, fertilizers and other products. At CIL he dealt with the issues threatening the chemical industry following the Union Carbide disaster in Bhopal, India, as well as with situations such as chemical leaks, fires and derailments. In the mid-1980s, Mindszenthy co-authored a book on crisis communications called *No Surprises,* and in 1990, with partner Gail Roberts, formed Mindszenthy & Roberts, a company focused on crisis and issues management and strategic communications planning. A proponent of common sense in handling crises, he met partner Gail while both were consulting on crisis communications around disgraced Canadian sprinter Ben Johnson in 1988, following Johnson's positive test for steroids at the Seoul Olympics. In 2003, Mindszenthy's company effectively managed communications for a crisis-free Rolling Stones concert in Toronto.

ON HANDLING STAKEHOLDERS IN A CRISIS

"Communicators must ensure that stakeholders hear from them directly whenever possible rather than from other parties — particularly the media. They need to have the process of stakeholder relations in place ahead of time, before a crisis, along with the ability to gather information quickly. They must also make sure that they are linked to other people in the organization through open channels of communication.

"During a crisis, communicators often don't do nearly as good a job of communicating internally as they should, especially given the technology that's there to support them. They often don't make the effort or they take internal communications for granted — they assume that employees know what's going on. When employees are surprised to find out that 'this is what my company or organization is saying,' they feel a sense of betrayal, frustration and anger. As a result, the company can have some pretty unhappy employees — and how can such employees be supportive ambassadors?"

ON EXTERNAL STAKEHOLDERS

"External stakeholders will always want to know what happened and what the implications for them are. They'll want to know the consequences of the crisis on three levels: emotional, physical and financial. Communicators need to be aware of what combination of these three elements there will be, and how significant each is. Let's remember that in a crisis, external stakeholders are almost always involuntary participants — they don't want to be part of the crisis and will depend on communicators to get the right information to them."

ON THE INTERNET AND CRISIS COMMUNICATIONS

"Practice crisis scenarios are important because they teach communicators to think on the fly. The other element that is now all-pervasive is the movement of information globally … almost everyone has a digital camera or a cell phone in his or her pocket. Let's face it: information moves fast!"

ON COMMON SENSE DURING A CRISIS

"Communicators have to use common sense. During the Molson Rocks Rolling Stones concert at Toronto's Downsview Park in July 2003, my partner and I used our collective experience to think ahead on every issue that could come up. It was a hot day in the sun for music fans, and common sense came into play when we saw that the nearly half-million concertgoers were thirsty but did not want to move from their choice spots. The solution? Before a crisis hit — before concertgoers began dropping from heat stroke in the heat wave — we told organizers to pass out bottled water. Crisis averted."

ON PLANNING

"The best crisis plans in the world are never going to do exactly what communicators would like. They have to be flexible and intuitive.

"There are two questions communicators must ask themselves: 'What can we say?' and 'What are we willing to say?' Contrast that with 'What can't we say?' and 'What are we unwilling to say?' Communicators can play with the combination of what can be said and what they are willing (as an organization) to say, but they are often limited in a legal way, a governmental way or by what the media may or may not do with the information they provide. That's why it's important to plan and practise."

Exercise: The Stakeholder as Customer

Choose an organization, preferably a company you've done business with. Using the company website's customer service link, submit a question related to the business — about product quality, service or timeliness, for example.

YOUR TASK

After waiting a maximum of one week for a response from the company, answer these questions:
1. How quickly did the company respond?
2. Were you satisfied with the response? Where did it fall short?
3. How do you feel about the company now? Has your opinion of it changed?
4. How can you use this experience to guide your interactions with stakeholders?

Exercise: A Hiring Crisis

You are the communications manager of a medium-sized company, Angstrom Personnel, which provides staffing solutions to business. Your company works for a range of clients in the technology and manufacturing sectors to match them with qualified workers, especially engineers, accountants and computer technicians. Workers are expected to have clean work records (i.e., no criminal record), appropriate credentials and experience in the field.

THE CRISIS

Six months ago, an Angstrom employee engaged the services of an accountant for a client in the manufacturing industry. The client has just discovered that the accountant was embezzling, setting up false accounts and funnelling the client's money into them. To compound the problem, the accountant, it turns out, has a criminal record: she was convicted of defrauding a company in the manufacturing sector about 10 years ago, and the story had been reported in the media. Several clients who have heard the news, as well as the Canadian Association of Personnel Agencies (the business association to which your company belongs), are now asking you why a criminal check wasn't conducted. You know that the answer to that is "human error": the criminal check was overlooked. The negligent Angstrom Personnel employee has been fired as a result. However, you need to spell out to the company's stakeholders how the company is handling the situation and what it is doing to ensure that such an incident doesn't happen again.

YOUR TASK

1. Identify the external stakeholder groups and list them according to their significance to the company.
2. Develop a set of key messages to deliver to stakeholders.
3. Develop a game plan for dealing with each stakeholder group. How are you going to get your messages across?

IV

Crisis Communications Tools

8 | Tools I
Leadership and the Message

A dog is not reckoned good because he barks well, and a man is
not reckoned wise because he speaks skillfully.

— CHUANG TZU

Since the Johnson & Johnson poisoned-Tylenol crisis in 1982, the
methods for handling a crisis have changed. The communications environment has shifted from one in which communicators were learning on the go
and establishing new practices as they moved from one crisis to the next, to
one where those practices have been used to create more or less reliable principles and approaches to use, but customized for each situation.

The Internet has dramatically changed the way we share and transmit
information, and in turn has affected the acceleration and proliferation of crisis situations. Crises can sometimes spark and spread much too rapidly for a
communications team to contain them. As a result, today's communicators
emphasize preparation and planning ahead. Those who don't plan for a
potential crisis are going to be in the same position that companies such as
Johnson & Johnson were in back in 1982, either trying to create the steps to
handle the crisis in the midst of the crisis, or scrambling for examples of how
to control it. Communicators have numerous successful examples to learn

from, but their approach must always be proactive, creative and fresh.

At the centre of this forward-thinking approach is the leadership role, a role that communicators may occasionally perform but more often a role taken on by executives, with communicators working as their coaches. The leadership role is best thought of by communicators as a performance task and, in this sense, a formal tool for delivering messages to publics and a means of healing relationships with them during a crisis period. The role is generally best performed by a single person in a position of high-level authority. To say that leadership during crisis is a *performance* is not at all to say that the role is false or disingenuous. Rather, the role of leader in crisis is defined by the many expectations and needs that publics have for information, help and reassurance during a crisis. In practice, few of the people called on to perform this role appreciate all the expectations of this performance, and it is communicators who must ensure they are ready to fulfill them.

Leadership, as we use the term here, also includes the ability to organize and focus the efforts of a crisis team. Leaders must have a great understanding of the needs of stakeholders and an ability to organize effective crisis response from company employees, but they must also recognize the need to occasionally enlist the aid of outside experts and organizations. This chapter addresses both the organizing and performance dimensions of the leadership role. Communicators will require at various periods of their careers a competency in both dimensions of leadership, though most often they will focus on preparing leaders to fulfill the demands of the leadership role.

The leadership role, effectively handled, allows a company to directly inspire trust and understanding in all of a company's publics from the start of a crisis through to its resolution.

This chapter explores:

- The expectations of the role of leadership;
- The role as it is divided into its major tasks and tactics;
- The role versus the person performing the role, and opportunities to succeed in bridging the gaps between the two.

As we will see, leadership is instrumental in presenting communicators' message to the media and to their stakeholders. We will study the use of the leadership role in two key cases in which leaders used the role effectively.

Expectations of Leadership

It was common for leaders in the past (for instance, Pierre Trudeau, Lester B. Pearson, Mahatma Gandhi, Sir Winston Churchill, Martin Luther King Jr.) to be judged on their overall qualities — there was an assumption that they could and would handle themselves with forthrightness and distinction every time, all the time. It was the archetypal idea of the "single combat warrior" that writer Tom Wolfe characterizes in *The Right Stuff,* a book about the early U.S. space program — the notion that a single savvy, brave and intelligent individual can save the world. In *The Right Stuff,* astronauts are chosen for their singular qualities: they are chosen not only for their intelligence and great physical conditioning but also for their courage, their ability to focus on a multiplicity of tasks and their adeptness at being able to talk easily to the public, being able to relate to the common person despite the role they had taken on, of doing something no one else had done before.[1] Such was the nature of leadership yesterday — being able to face multiple uncertainties and unknown dangers and to lead people through those challenges until the goal was achieved, whether it was blasting into space, walking on the moon, staring down Communists, beating the Germans in World War II, gaining civil rights or taking on terrorists.

"The first thing we need to do is to hear from the CEO or president responsible for the business, organization or the government department. It's not good enough to hear from a public relations spokesperson. When there is a crisis, the public has the right to hear from the person in charge and to hear from that person quickly, within the first 12 hours if not sooner. The information should be presented in person, not by issuing a statement. If the situation warrants it, there should also be mention of when the next update will be provided, [such as] the next day, in six hours, etc.

"The president can also be accompanied by experts who can answer detailed questions but first and foremost the president should come clean and explain exactly what happened, how [the company is] taking responsibility for it and what is being done to fix it."[2]

— Marlane Oliver, Toronto radio host, 680 News

With the speed of media today, however, leadership is often reduced to simply having the ability to tackle a single crisis or issue head-on. The public is not looking for a hero, just a competent professional who can answer their questions (but, like the hero of yesterday, someone who *is* able to offer assurances that their corner of the world will be safe). Paparazzi, blogs, business books that drill down into not just the organization but the *personalities* behind the organization and reality television shows such as *The Apprentice* and *The Rebel Billionaire* have all steadily eroded the image of perfect corporate and political leaders. The speed of communications today means that the leader is not the single combat warrior of the past — the leader may be a generalist, but his or her role is reduced to leading one specific entity — the company. At the same time, the leader is expected to be able to talk on a variety of subjects, and on a variety of levels, encompassing the company's work, as well as its relationship to the community at large, its immediate actions and its plans for the future. In a way, the corporate leader has to be a smaller-scale Winston Churchill, able to understand the emotions of the publics and understand his or her role in taking the company and its publics forward through troubles. Today, a leader has to be able to talk to publics as well as act for their benefit, and his or her words must have meaning. That meaning must in turn be demonstrated in the actions taken by the leader and by the organization he or she represents.

Rudolph Giuliani's profile was raised immeasurably by his actions during the crisis of September 11, 2001. It was crisis that became the subject of books, speeches, and movies, and one that redefined the way the United States saw itself and the world. Giuliani demonstrated leadership during a time of crisis and proved to be a good administrator who could competently answer the public's questions. His focus was on explaining not just what he was doing, but *why*, and in a way that linked each message to a demonstrable action being taken by the city. For instance, in the immediate aftermath of 9/11, when the tunnels into Manhattan were closed, Giuliani explained that it was a precautionary measure; it would ensure that no other terrorist activity could take place in the tunnels. This was a response to overwhelming public concerns over the possibility of transportation corridors such as the tunnels becoming a conduit for terrorist activity into New York City. Giuliani demonstrated leadership in taking a stand and explaining decisions in a way that was clear; and yet, he also welcomed the opportunity to be questioned, criticized or even condemned. As he writes in his autobiography *Leadership*: "Whenever I communicated, I explained the overriding philosophy behind what I was saying. This way people could understand and agree or disagree with my thinking. My goal was to integrate even the simplest policy decisions into my basic ideas."[3]

It's clear that a lot of crisis management is about leadership, and that what leadership amounts to is that someone has to be *seen to be taking charge* and be consistent in making the organization's actions during a crisis clear to stakeholders. This role in the crisis management equation is as much about image and actions as it is about words.

The Leadership Role in Crisis Communications: Tactics and Tasks

INSPIRES TRUST FROM PUBLICS

Comes forward and deals with the bad news first. The leader in a crisis will take charge, not unseen in a backroom but by coming forward and being seen to be handling the crisis in an open forum. As the saying goes, "It's not enough to do the right thing; you have to be *seen* to be doing the right thing." The effective leader tackles the tough issues first, never avoiding them. The challenge for communicators is in ensuring that their leader is well briefed and ready to take on this role when he or she comes forward. The leader must be comfortable with the communications messages and comfortable in assuming a role in which he or she will tackle issues that might cast the organization in a negative light. Communicators are involved in preparing the leader, making sure he or she knows the facts, the messages, where the organization stands and where it's going. Communicators must also ensure that the leader knows when to delegate supporting roles to others, especially when technical expertise is required.

Connects emotionally with publics. The effective leader recognizes and responds to the impact the crisis has on the organization's publics. The effective leader acknowledges and understands the pain the publics suffer and will demonstrate that the organization is in tune with their publics' feelings about that pain. A leader connects on these important points through key messages acknowledging those emotions. Communicators face challenges with a leader who is out of touch with internal and external stakeholders or does not come across as sincere. Communicators are then obliged to demonstrate to the leader the real human impact of the crisis and offer him or her information — the images, facts and figures of the crisis — to help them relate to the organization's publics.

Is accessible. The leader will make him- or herself accessible as often as necessary — to internal stakeholders, to media and to external stakeholders. The leader will adopt the mindset of "I'm available any time, give me a call," rather than, "I'll be ready to talk when I'm ready." For communicators, it means ensuring that the leader has the most up-to-date information and that their schedule is in synch with that of the leader for the duration of the crisis.

Appeals to higher authority, expert advice or testimony. A strong leader is one who will be able to delegate with confidence and who has the ability to say, "I'm not an expert on the science of what happened during the crisis. However, I can tell you that our research director has done extensive work on this issue. Here are the results …"

TAKES COMMAND

Immediately takes charge; immediately takes responsibility. The leader assumes command and issues a statement that he or she is working to maintain control and a positive direction during a difficult time. The leader works with experts both within and outside the organization to gain a measure of understanding of what happened, and then makes the appropriate decisions to take the organization forward in a direction that will resolve the crisis and prevent a similar crisis from happening in future. In this case, the leader is telling the organization's publics where the organization is planning to go; he or she might also be letting them know that although it might be rough getting there, the destination will be reached.

Understands the media's and stakeholders' interests. A leader who has a keen understanding of the organization and its relationships to its publics will be able to see all the impacts of the crisis on most or all of the organization's stakeholders. In doing so, the leader has a good sense of the kinds of questions the media and stakeholders will ask, because he or she knows how it will affect them. The leader knows that the media look for human-interest angles and understand that customers and other stakeholders will be most concerned about the crisis's impact on their safety, health or business. Knowing this, the leader is able to respond with appropriate messages that demonstrate knowledge, understanding, empathy and direction.

Is ready for a crisis. The capable leader is ready for a crisis because a crisis scenario has already been played out within the confines of the corporate boardroom, the communications office and the branch plant. The leader knows what to expect and is unruffled by uncertainties that may come his or her way. Being crisis-ready means being practised and confident in handling a high-pressure situation.

Is able to answer questions. Working through mock scenarios with an effective Q&A as well as developing and nurturing a sound knowledge of how the organization works will mean that the leader is ready to answer any question that comes his or her way. The leader will be able to think on his or her feet and handle questions about what is happening as well as capably handling inquiries as to where the organization is headed.

PROVIDES DIRECTION FOR PUBLICS AND GUIDES EXPECTATIONS

Follows through. The effective leader will not deliver a promise, then sit back and wait to see if that promise can be fulfilled by staffers; he or she takes responsibility and ownership and follows through on everything he or she says. Communicators can assist by keeping track of what is happening during the crisis; a listing of these promises often forms a very effective checklist at the end of the crisis, something the leader can make reference to in end-of-crisis media sessions: "I am pleased to tell you that we took the following actions during the crisis …"

Communicates message directly. A strong leader goes out to the organization's publics to directly deliver a message, rather than leaving the message to words on a news release, issued at midnight and hopefully picked up by media and run the next day. The effective leader recognizes that we live in a visual world and that the media and stakeholders need to see an image of a positive, take-charge leader delivering a promise of positive change.

Creates a sense of teamwork and shared responsibility. A capable leader knows that he or she alone doesn't have all the answers. He or she looks to a team of professionals who can research, create and refine the key messages the leader needs to deliver to the organization's publics. During that process, the leader delegates effectively, creating a sense of teamwork and a workplace where everyone has a role to fulfill and where everyone's contribution is valued.

Promises future action and ensures accountability. The experienced leader will not say that ending the crisis was enough — there will be a promise of future action to ensure that safeguards are in place to prevent a similar crisis from happening in future. The leader will also hold him- or herself accountable for gaps in communications, problems that led to the crisis and other mishaps, with the proviso that those issues will be identified and rectified.

Four Stages of Leadership during a Crisis: Building Momentum

The leadership tasks and the tactics that accomplish them, when carried out well, tend to group neatly into stages of leadership as a crisis progresses. These stages are often pronounced enough to form something like a story arc in the media, with headlines that may sound similar to the titles of each stage. These stages can be of help to communicators in conceptualizing the progression of a leader through different stages of perception by the general public and the media. It is often a strong indicator of how the organization itself is moving through the crisis.

Recognition. The leader recognizes the crisis and the interests of various publics involved. The leader recognizes formally that he or she is responsible for the negative events and for finding solutions and, if necessary, making reparations.

Taking action. The leader spells out specific measures and plans to deal with the crisis and bring it under control. This phase is characterized by numerous press releases and updates, as well as by active participation in news conferences and interviews as new actions are taken.

Building trust. This phase may overlap with the taking action phase, but more often it follows it. The leader presents numerous messages created to emphasize a connection with the publics that have been harmed or affected and offers opportunities for publics to participate in the crisis, even if only to monitor or audit the actions of the leader or the organization.

Moving Forward. The crisis has largely been controlled, with the leader having already made strong connections with stakeholders and earned a measure of patience with hard work and promises kept. The leader now spends time demonstrating a desire to fully heal the organization's relationship with its publics and make improvements in a way that demonstrates that the organization has learned from the crisis.

In fact, it is often desirable for the leader to present explicitly, in the opening communications, these four stages as checkpoints in the plan for dealing with the crisis. This gives media and other stakeholders a road map for the company's route through the crisis and ultimate destination. It can be paraphrased along these lines:

I recognize that we are accountable for these events. We will be taking steps immediately to bring the matter under control and to determine how it happened in the first place. I invite you to keep in touch with us as we work toward a resolution and to consult with our team. Once we succeed in dealing with the problems, we will work toward compensation and improving our relationships with our stakeholders in the following ways …

Each of these tasks constitutes the major elements of the leadership role as a tool in crisis communications. The tactics that best accomplish these tasks are evinced in the case studies that follow. The first case examines the performance of Rudolph Giuliani during the 9/11 crisis and demonstrates how a leader may put these tactics to work in a way that reflects his or her style, allowing the gap between a role and the reality to be filled by the authentic personality of the performer.

Case Study:
New York City Mayor Rudolph Giuliani's Triumph

On September 11, 2001, terrorists hijacked four commercial airliners; two were crashed into the twin towers of New York City's World Trade Center, which collapsed within two hours of the attack. A third aircraft was crashed into the Pentagon in Virginia (the headquarters of the U.S. Department of Defense) and a fourth plane crashed in a Somerset County, Pennsylvania, field. Almost 3,000 people died as a result of the hijackings, among them 265 airline passengers, 343 New York firefighters and 23 New York City police officers.

9/11: WHAT THE MEDIA SAID

TORONTO STAR, September 15, 2001:
THE HEADLINE: "Giuliani becoming city's 'symbol of hope.'"
THE LEAD: "[Giuliani] is the city's grief counselor, the disseminator of information, and a tireless cheerleader. Once contentious as a politician, he is emerging as the city's symbol of hope."

TIMES (UNITED KINGDOM), September 19, 2001:
THE HEADLINE: "Finest hour of a mayor who may go far."
THE LEAD: "Within minutes of the first aircraft hurtling into the World Trade Center, Rudolph Giuliani joined his beloved firemen and police running towards the inferno as the public fled past his office in City Hall in the opposite direction ... [Giuliani] has become a national hero with a stoic, yet soothing, response to the calamity that could carry him to high office — even the presidency itself."

CHRISTIAN SCIENCE MONITOR, September 28, 2001:
THE HEADLINE: "Giuliani as Gotham's phoenix."
THE LEAD: "He transformed the city during his time in office (helped by a booming economy). He's created a better sense of community, made even stronger by the tragedy."

The 9/11 crisis thrust a widely disliked and mistrusted mayor, Rudolph Giuliani, into the spotlight. And it is an example of how tuning in to your publics makes a difference in how you're perceived. Before the crisis, Giuliani's reception from stakeholders ran from lukewarm to dislike to outright revulsion. New York newspapers criticized him as a clown, a bigot and an arrogant, abrasive politician with no ability to reach out to his sometimes marginalized electorate. His relations with the media were not exemplary; although he initiated a weekly phone-in show on local radio after his election in 1993, he was averse to one-on-one interviews with the media, preferring to deal with media questions in press conferences.

That changed after 9/11, when he became to many nothing less than a hero; he will be viewed as a hero in most circles for the rest of his days, his life backlit by the dynamic, fearless and human approach he took in handling events following the terrorist acts of that day. Giuliani employed many of the tactics in our leadership model.

CORPORATE GLANCE: NEW YORK CITY

THE CITY: With an area of 1,214 square kilometres and a population of 8.1 million (a metropolitan area population of 18.7 million,) it is the largest city in the United States and the most densely populated city in North America.

ECONOMIC CLOUT: In 2004, New York's metropolitan area had an estimated gross metropolitan product of US$901.3 billion, larger than the gross domestic product of India and slightly less than that of Canada.

MEDIA CLOUT: Home to 200 newspapers and 350 consumer magazines, New York is also the headquarters for the *New York Times* (circulation 1.1 million); the *Wall Street Journal* (circulation 2.1 million); *New York Daily News* (circulation 730,000) and *New York Post* (circulation 650,000). It is the largest metropolitan media market in the United States, comprising 7 per cent of American television-viewing households.

THE MAYOR'S OFFICE: Elected by direct popular vote, the mayor of New York appoints deputy mayors to lead major offices reporting to the mayor: First Deputy Mayor's Office, Economic Development and Rebuilding, Health and Human Services, Legal Affairs, Governmental Affairs, Administration, and Education and Development.

A communications director oversees a staff of senior communications and press officers to handle public and media inquiries. The mayor oversees several agencies and advisory committees handling a range of matters, from arts and libraries to issues on aging, building codes, taxes, education and sanitation. The mayor is limited to two four-year terms, as are the councillors. Rudolph Giuliani served two terms and was replaced by Michael Bloomberg in September 2001; Bloomberg was re-elected in November 2005.[4]

Timeline of Events on September 11, 2001

At 8:45 a.m. on Tuesday, September 11, 2001, New York had a so-so mayor; a minute later and Giuliani was front and centre. To use the old baseball cliché, he stepped up to the plate. The timeline of events of that day tell it all:

8:46 a.m. American Airlines Flight 11 crashes into the north tower of the World Trade Center.

9:03 a.m. United Airlines Flight 175 flies into the south tower of the World Trade Center.

9:43 a.m. American Airlines Flight 77 crashes into the Pentagon. The White House is evacuated two minutes later.

11:02 a.m. Just two hours after the crashes in New York City, Mayor Rudolph Giuliani makes his first statement, urging the citizens of New York to stay at home; he also orders an evacuation of the immediate area of the World Trade Center.

1:04 p.m. President George W. Bush makes his first statement, two hours after Giuliani and four hours after the tragedy began unfolding. His quote: "Make no mistake, the United States will hunt down and punish those responsible for these cowardly acts."

2:49 p.m. Giuliani holds a news conference, announcing the partial restoration of transit services in New York. When questioned about the number of deaths, he refused to speculate: "I don't think we want to speculate about that — more than any of us can bear." It was the first of many heartfelt, emotional statements he would make.

3:55 p.m. Giuliani announces that the number of critically injured stood at 200 and there were 2,100 injuries.

6:10 p.m. The mayor speaks to the press again, urging New Yorkers to not go into work the following day.

8:30 p.m. President Bush makes a public address; part of his statement reads: "Thousands of lives were suddenly ended by evil … these acts shattered steel, but they cannot dent the steel of American resolve."

9:57 p.m. Giuliani takes to the podium once more, providing an update on school closures for the following day and expressing hope that some people at the World Trade Center site may still be alive.[5]

INSPIRES TRUST IN MEDIA AND STAKEHOLDERS

Comes forward and deals with the bad news first. Giuliani did not hesitate in coming forward and speaking to the public. From a public relations perspective, he had the advantage of being close to ground zero, of having staff on the ground who could find the information he needed and of being able to organize and deliver a news conference shortly after the attacks took place. The big question in many leaders' minds would have been: "Do I need more time?" Giuliani came out with a statement telling people to stay at home and ordering an evacuation of the World Trade Center site — these were safe messages in that he was echoing what the police department was also saying, and yet they also positioned the mayor early on as a key figure in managing the crisis. Stepping up early would make the next news conference easier. The first statement is essential in getting established and setting a rhythm for subsequent sessions.

Remains accessible. Giuliani stayed in front of the media and stakeholders, making five major statements in the same day. Had he stuck to a standard communications plan, he might have made two: one in the morning and one in the afternoon. But his communications team recognized that these were unusual circumstances and the mayor kept coming forward, demonstrating that he was taking control of a situation that was dangerously out of control in its first few hours.

Appeals to higher authority, expert advice or testimony. Giuliani recognized that his role was that of leader of the people of New York and he recognized the importance of that role in directing activities. He was fully confident in turning the podium over to experts from the New York City police and fire departments when necessary and worked seamlessly with federal and state government officials as well as disaster experts, who could fill people in on the particulars of the crisis. He was a leader who was comfortable sharing the spotlight with a range of highly qualified people and saw that the crisis demanded just such an approach.

Connects emotionally with stakeholders. As the first major leader to speak out after the crash, he immediately connected to the people of New York. He got out into the public eye and into the street, wading into the sea of confused, frightened humanity that drifted through the streets of New York, mingling with those suffering from the shock of the attack on the World Trade Center. It wasn't surprising that accolades came his way.

Many leaders either overplay or underplay their emotive role. Giuliani was effective in that he did not shy away from striking an emotional chord each and every time he talked about the tragedy, either during press conferences or when he met with citizens' groups. There is continuing debate over whether it was just "good acting"; still, Giuliani did not come across as phoney or out of touch with the public, nor did he get into overblown histrionics when faced with the sadness and uncertainty that played out after 9/11.

The media loved the effect and played it to the hilt, as *Newsweek* reported in its September 24, issue: "[in the moments after the attack,] Giuliani and a small group set off on foot for a mile hike up Church Street, urging the ghostly, ash-caked survivors to 'Go north! Go north!' A distraught African-American woman approached, and the mayor touched her face, telling her, "It's going to be OK."

As quoted in the same article of *Newsweek,* President George W. Bush spoke to larger issues: "This conflict was begun on the timing and terms of others. It will end in a way and at an hour of our choosing." Giuliani brought the message home in a simple way to New Yorkers: "We're going to rebuild and rebuild stronger."[6]

That formed the core of one of his first statements, capturing the sense of shared tragedy and melding with a resolve to stay strong and move on: "Tomorrow New York is going to be here. And we're going to rebuild, and we're going to be stronger than we were before ... I want the people of New York to be an example to the rest of the country, and the rest of the world, that terrorism can't stop us."[7]

TAKES COMMAND

Immediately takes control; immediately takes responsibility.
Giuliani played a leading role, but it was a role that could easily have been delegated to a team of subordinates. He took on the responsibility for coordinating the work of the various city departments that were responsible for maintaining control after the attack. And he spoke directly to the authorities at both the state and federal levels, keeping them apprised of what help the city would need to rebuild the site around the World Trade Center as well as prevent further terrorist attacks. To the public he became the one window of information, delivering news on road and tunnel closures, making decisions on handling immediate issues and taking the time to visit injured New Yorkers and offering comfort to families who had lost loved ones.

Is ready for a crisis. Before September 11, Giuliani and his staff played out crisis management drills for 10 scenarios, from anthrax terrorism to poison gas attacks and truck bombs. It meant that the entire crisis management team at City Hall was ready when a crisis occurred. It could have been any disaster and Giuliani would have been ready. Here, we see the importance of having a crisis plan in place, ready to be implemented at any moment of any day. *Giuliani had already walked through crisis scenarios, which gave him a sense of the process of managing a crisis.* There is a rhythm that builds in a crisis, the steps of recognition, taking action, building trust and moving forward, that can serve almost as a template. Knowing the process without knowing the details means filling in the template of action with the details as they take place.

Understands the media and stakeholders' interests. By the time 9/11 hit, Giuliani was already a media-savvy mayor. He was also very aware of the media's and public's need to know. As mentioned earlier in this chapter, he was simple and direct in his approach, and explained the details of what he was saying to both media and stakeholders. He brought his messages down to effective sound bites that encapsulated his policy decisions. In this way, he was not just *saying* that action would be taken — he was demonstrating that it was being taken and also telling people why. He showed people that the public's need for safety and business stakeholders' need for business continuity were being looked after. Among his initiatives was the quick creation of a task force of New York business leaders.

Giuliani established and chaired the Twin Towers Fund to funnel donations to families of police officers, firefighters and government workers, and *BusinessWeek* on October 19, 2001, reported that the money would likely also go to education, legal services, housing and counselling.

PROVIDES DIRECTION FOR STAKEHOLDERS AND GUIDES EXPECTATIONS

Creates sense of teamwork and shared responsibility. New York is the financial capital of the United States, an icon both nationally and internationally. Giuliani was able to generate a feeling among many levels of government and the citizenry, from the person on the street through to police and fire departments and state and federal officials that they were all in it together. Jingoism? Perhaps. But Giuliani recognized what people needed to hear, what they wanted to know, and pulled those messages into compelling gestures that drew an emotional thread to anyone connected with 9/11.

Promises future action and ensures accountability. In his words and in his actions, Giuliani was able to make commitments without promising actions that couldn't be delivered on. He promised to work with all other governments to rebuild New York's infrastructure and especially its confidence. He was able to be boldly confident and responsible without drawing blame.

Communicates message directly. The mayor had prepared his responses to the tragedy and was in a position to meet with people on a direct, one-on-one basis. He was also unafraid to be himself in the aftermath. Giuliani was the first to say that the impact of the crisis made everything else seem small; he was able to admit his weaknesses and his vulnerability in feeling the pain that all New Yorkers must have felt. It is understood that leadership is often a performance, and skilled politicians are great actors, tugging at the emotional threads of the audience and delivering their lines with aplomb. Giuliani certainly performed well, but clearly his expression of his own feelings and experience of the crisis were genuine. That they enhanced his performance is simply another way of saying that he added himself in a genuine way to the script. As a result, people were not about to blame him for any shortcomings; they were in fact able and willing to identify *with him* as the person with the huge burden of leadership in a terrible crisis. We often talk about the concept of the roll-up-the-shirtsleeves leader who can relate to his or her audience on the level of the common person. Very few are able to really effect that role with any level of skill and, if they do initially, it's often hard for them to maintain that veneer of "I'm just a regular person" honesty. Giuliani, by having practised his role and knowing his audience, was able to make the leap from skilled actor to fellow New Yorker.

As Giuliani notes in his autobiography *Leadership*: "One of the great advantages of being New York City mayor was that I could communicate directly. Because it was such a visible job, I didn't have to be a slave to press coverage. A leader who cannot access the airwaves or draw people to a meeting risks having the media shape the public's impression of him."[8] The information that Giuliani was provided by experts (on the number of deaths, on efforts to clean up the 9/11 site) as the days progressed, he in turn quickly provided to the public, in a direct and proactive way.

THINK TANK

Think about the events of 9/11 and what you have read, heard or seen about it. Then consider these questions:

1. How did Giuliani's stakeholders handle themselves on that day? Who seemed least under control that day? The media? The communicators? The public services? What does this tell you?
2. How did the media treat the crisis that day?
3. What do you remember about the way leaders handled themselves? What key messages did they deliver? Were those messages effective? What can communicators take from this? Was anyone in the media, public service or communications out of his or her depth? What tells you so?
4. What evidence of preparation for a crisis on this scale can you see in Giuliani's leadership?

5. If you were a leader of a city in such a situation, what would the greatest challenge be in this role? When would the gaps likely turn up in the performance of this role, in terms of the gap between seeming confident and in control and seeming to be just another stakeholder in a difficult situation? How would you prepare yourself to close such gaps?

6. What would the greatest challenges be as a vice-president of communications in serving such a leader? How would you best support him or her?

© Scott Adams/Dist. by United Feature Syndicate, Inc.

Rehearsing Crisis

The best way to prepare executives to perform the leadership role is to have them practise the role under as much pressure as possible. Many organizations employ an outside company specializing in providing these practice services, or hire journalists or former journalists to help them do this. An outside company can help the organization's leaders understand how to handle the crisis and provide tips on how to do so; it can work with experienced communicators to develop the format for delivering the messages and communications initiatives to handle the crisis; or it can work from a previously developed crisis plan that was created by internal communicators. Regardless of which approach is chosen, an outside company brings a set of fresh eyes to the scene and can often provide commentary and advice that will help the organization refine and improve its approach to the crisis.

If the organization is unable to hire an outside firm, scenarios can still be developed. Undertake these projects during a time of stability, but recognize that a crisis can come at any time. Many freelance journalists or former journalists offer services in crisis media relations. These range from advice and counsel — identifying the kinds of questions that will come from the media in a crisis — to peppering senior officials with questions in preparation for appearing in front of the media.

Here are the recommended steps for giving leaders the practice they need to succeed in this role during a crisis:

Step 1: Book time to practise and create the test. Set aside time (two to three days or a number of afternoons) and get a commitment from your organization to run a crisis scenario. If you are able, hire an outside firm to act as the media and stakeholders during a mock crisis scenario (to sit and pepper spokespeople with questions targeted to the "crisis"). Create a scenario from the most likely issue your organization has that could turn into a crisis, from an industrial accident to a costly computer glitch, using briefing notes or, if available, the completed crisis plan.

Step 2: Begin the exercise using the crisis plan. Pull up your crisis communications plan and review it thoroughly. How well does it match the current scenario? Turn the plan into a working document and update it twice daily. Make changes to the initial steps (appoint crisis team members, choose a war room, and so on). Have the next steps of the plan reviewed by senior communicators and returned quickly with amendments. Initiate the plan immediately, following the remaining steps, but ensure that communicators are empowered to revise and update the plans as often as necessary as the mock crisis plays out.

Step 3: Test communications products and internal communications. Take products written in advance as part of the plan (fact sheets, speeches, news releases) and have leaders and communicators review them. How much customization do they need? Do they work well? Are they too detailed and in need of further distillation before they are ready for their audiences, or for the leader to use for that matter? Have senior communicators and leaders test the internal communications links to other department heads to see how quickly information can be gathered from them in the event of an emergency. Do the internal communications lines function well to give you all the information you need as the crisis erupts? As it evolves? Is there too much information coming from departments or too little? Will new links to internal stakeholders be necessary to ensure a two-way flow of only the necessary information from management, communicators and staff?

Step 4: Prepare for media and answer questions. After reviewing the plan and before the full onslaught of the crisis, identify the key media the organization deals with and outline how they will likely approach your organization as the crisis begins to break. Gather brief profiles from staff on the history of all media with whom you expect to communicate soon.

Prepare media questions as well as questions that will come from stakeholder groups, then, posing as journalists or stakeholders, ask the organization's spokespeople these questions (or have the outside help you have hired for this purpose do this). Videotape the spokespeople, then review the videotape to see how they responded to the crisis. Much of the critiquing should come from the spokespersons themselves; ask them, "How do you think you did?"

Practice allows spokespeople, especially the company's leader, to become more comfortable with the kinds of questions that will come from the media.

Step 5: Follow up. At the end of the scenario, take your organization through the successes and failures of the crisis planning — then make the necessary corrections to ensure maximum success.

Case Study:
Taking Responsibility in a Crisis:
Paul Martin and the Gomery Inquiry

Another prominent example of a leader effectively taking charge in a crisis is closer to home. As a political crisis, the sponsorship crisis and the Gomery inquiry have a place in the current top ranks. As we examine the statement that then prime minister Paul Martin made on national television in response to the sponsorship accusations, we will try to relate what Martin and his communications team did to the tasks and tactics of leadership.

On April 21, 2005, thousands of Canadians tuned in to watch Paul Martin, enmeshed in the Gomery inquiry on the sponsorship issue, make a statement on national television to plead his case to the people. He had been battered in the media and in the House of Commons for days; the opposition forces were calling for an election in the wake of $250 million in misappropriated funds and alleged kickbacks to the Liberal Party.

Martin was aware that boosting his public image, as filtered through the media, would be essential to getting through this crisis — and he needed to deliver his message in clear and concise language.

His own communications team would have been charged with the responsibility of laying out a course of action, taking his publics from the "bad news" through to the position of getting information into the open, then building a sense of teamwork, before making a promise of future action.

In the speech one can see the broad stages of the four-stage model of leadership mentioned earlier in the chapter: recognition of the crisis and the laying out of a course of action; taking action by explaining in detail what had happened in the scandal; building trust by connecting with stakeholders, being clear and direct, and offering an opportunity for the public to respond; and moving forward by telling the Canadian public what the government was doing to rectify the situation. In Martin's case, the goal in the structure of the final product was to build momentum by telling a good story — creating a drama to draw in the audience and leading up to a climax, in this case, his promise of a better future.

Analyzing the speech from the viewpoint of communicators, we can see that Martin followed a key script for handling crises, using many of the key tactics of leadership:

- Dealing with the bad news first;
- Putting the issue into current context and outlining what happened in the past;
- Demonstrating a past proactive stance before promising future action;
- Taking responsibility, though not necessarily implicating himself;
- Creating an air of openness and integrity;
- Building momentum through the four stages of communication during a crisis;

- Creating a sense of teamwork and shared responsibility, i.e., "We all have a stake in this issue," even if the primary responsibility is his;
- Appealing to a sense of higher authority, expert advice or testimony — the objective third party that will be able to rise above the petty emotional issues that mark the crisis;
- Connecting emotionally with his stakeholders;
- Respecting the view of those stakeholders, valuing their perspective on the issue;
- Promising future action and ensuring accountability.

NOTES FOR COMMUNICATORS

As we know, at times communicators must be coaches of leaders; at other times, they may find themselves performing the role of leader, as, for example, a vice-president of communications. The analysis of the following speech (a slightly shortened version of the six-and-a-half-minute speech) by Paul Martin shows how the tactics of leadership that a communicator or the organization's leader will use across many hours of a crisis need to underpin even a short speech or written communication.

Let me speak plainly. What happened with the sponsorship file occurred on the watch of the Liberal government. Those who were in power are to be held responsible and that includes me.

Here, Martin gets the bad news out. He takes responsibility for the issue but doesn't implicate himself. From here on, Martin can move through his points in a way that offers clarity. Almost as though working from a checklist, he (and his communications handlers) can check off that he took responsibility for the issue in a public forum. For his audience, it is a moment when they can say, "Ah, finally some openness on the issue!" There is a tendency for people to reward honesty, and Martin is playing his cards from that perspective — be honest, open and direct, with no equivocating, and people will be more apt to listen and respond in a supportive way.

I was the minister of Finance and knowing what I learned in the past year, I am sorry that we weren't more vigilant, that I wasn't more vigilant. Public money was misdirected and misused and that's unacceptable. That's why I apologized to the Canadian people a year ago.

Martin offers a historical context to the crisis, establishing that public money went to the wrong hands and acknowledging that this action was wrong. This moral approach is an attempt to take the high moral ground on the issue and distance himself from the wrongdoing. The corporate apology he offers is seen as part of doing business: he makes it clear on public record that he is sorry for what happened. As a result, no detractor can come back and say he didn't offer an apology, nor that he refused to take responsibility. This approach is focused largely on issues of clarity and directness, but it also establishes an effective set-up for the rest of the speech. A standard dictionary definition of an apology is a statement or acknowledgement that brings with it an expression of regret or a request for forgiveness; the Latin *apologia* is a more formalized defence or explanation of one's actions. Martin's opening lines serve to set up his apology; later in the speech he introduces an apologia. The first statement says "I'm sorry," the next one says "Here's why it wasn't my fault" and offers details as to why, from Martin's perspective, it wasn't.

You will note, however, that in his speech, Martin doesn't offer his key messages all at once — his messages are delivered in short sound bites that offer up information in a clearly understood and succinct way. He is moving to speak to one issue at a time, simply and directly — using a standard of plain-language writing of one idea per sentence, and short sentences. He makes it clear that he will deal with all the issues in the course of the speech.

Taking responsibility is about more than words. I want to tell you what I have done as the prime minister to deal with the sponsorship scandal to make sure it does not happen again, to make sure that those who violated the public trust will be identified and will pay the consequences.

Note the words he uses: *taking responsibility ... deal[ing] with the scandal ... make sure it does not happen again ... make sure* [the wrongdoers] *pay the consequences.* These are words that demonstrate an intention to take action, offering a promise that Canadians assume will be fulfilled. If you make a promise, whether you are president of a corporation, head of a non-profit organization, or prime minister of Canada, you will be held accountable for it. Stakeholders don't need to be encouraged to audit your actions — they will do so, and so will the media. Clearly, though, Martin's government was on shaky ground and he had nothing to lose.

On December 12, 2003, I cancelled the sponsorship program. It was my very first act on my very first day in office. When the Auditor General's report was publicly tabled, I acted immediately by ordering a fully independent commission of inquiry under Mr. Justice John Gomery. Its mandate is to get to the bottom of what happened and to do it in full view of Canadians. He will report before the end of the year.

Again, Martin talks about taking action, and in so doing presents himself as a proponent, rather than an opponent, of the inquiry. In this way Martin links his own actions (his "first act" on the "first day in office") to the purpose of the Gomery inquiry and elaborates on the inquiry's purpose. The message: "I'm decisive, I'm fair, and I wasn't going to hide anything." Martin positions himself as moving forward, with a promise of accountability. The promise of a report before year's end sets up an expectation in the minds of Canadians — "We did something positive, we are doing something now and the results will prove to you that we did the right thing." The timeline of the inquiry might be seen as a play for time; indeed, that time could and would be filled with strong messages that supported the government's actions and reinforced the statements Martin had already delivered. But more likely and more importantly, the promise of a report gives his government a deadline to meet, and makes another concrete commitment.

And I think you will agree that Judge Gomery is leaving no stone unturned. In addition, I fired Alphonso Gagliano, the minister responsible for the sponsorship program, from his appointment to ambassador to Denmark.

Again, Martin adds to his record of taking action. And a note to those who want to avoid trite phrasing (such as "no stone unturned"): avoid it where possible but be aware that, very often, a hackneyed phrase works. People like to hear the tried and true expressions — they're comfortable with them. Communicators must judge the right balance and whether an old expression would enhance or obscure meaning.

I put in strict new controls on spending within every single government department. My government brought forward whistleblower legislation to insure that when public servants and others come forward with evidence of wrongdoing, they are protected, not punished.

More information is being provided, but not in a checklist format: Martin is clearly stating that each measure he took was aimed at a separate, important result; in this case, protecting public servants who reveal wrongdoing. This statement reinforces the taking action phase, as have the previous two chunks of his speech, and it helps build momentum as he works toward the next stage — building trust.

To recover taxpayers' money, money that went to those who did not earn it, I ordered my government to sue 19 people and companies for more than $40 million. I committed to acting on the recommendations of Judge Gomery when he brings forth his final report. And I myself testified before his commission, answering any and all questions.

Here, Martin is aiming for clarity, openness and honesty, and also a tough, take-no-prisoners stand. He talks about the actions that have been taken, steps that can be clarified with media if necessary; the bottom line is that these measures are concrete and real. Offering the numbers, the dollar figures and the number of people and organizations he is having sued, underscores that action.

Finally, I ordered that the Liberal party bring in auditors to conduct a forensic exam of its books and to call in the RCMP to investigate what took place during that period. Let me just emphasize that point. If so much as a dollar is found to have made its way into the Liberal party from ill-gotten gains, it will be repaid to the people of Canada. I want no part of that money.

Martin reiterates his promise to serve the people of Canada; again, he is using short, simple sentences to get his point across. He layers his sense of taking decisive action with a moral point, "I want no part of that money," to reassert his stance on the issue. The promise of repayment is a promise of rectification, of making things right for stakeholders.

As prime minister, I will never hesitate to describe what happened on the sponsorship file for what it was — an unjustifiable mess. It is up to me to clean it up. That's my job. I am cleaning it up. As people focus their attention on the commission's hearings, let us remember that the inquiry is being held in front of a judge for good reason. There is conflicting testimony. Only the judge is in a position to determine the truth. Only he can cut through the partisan politics. Only he can tell us what happened and who was responsible.

Here Martin reasserts that he is taking command; there is a promise of future action and, in appealing to a higher authority, he makes it clear that even if people continue to question his judgment as prime minister, they will certainly benefit from the authority of an impartial, third-party expert like Judge Gomery.

We all heard that the opposition might defeat the government and take the country to the polls for the second time in a year. I am prepared to face Canadians and have them judge my response to this serious test of leadership. I will be politically accountable.

Here Martin reiterates his message of personal responsibility and accountability and empowers the stakeholders — the people of Canada — to share in the responsibility. This is in line with the overall directive of teamwork and shared responsibility: as much as the Liberal Party may have messed up, the issue is not really about Martin or the Liberal Party, it's about Canada. As history shows, Canadians did judge the prime minister, and the Liberal Party, based on his job in handling the scandal. In the January 2006 election, the people put Martin's party out of office, although the Conservatives won by only a slim margin. Martin retired from his position as party leader on February 6, 2006. Yet, despite the fact that this leader lost the war, it could be considered that this tactic of creating a sense of shared responsibility was an effective one.

But I believe that, before there is an election, you are entitled to answers, to the answer that Judge Gomery is working toward. I believe that Canadians deserve a full and frank accounting of all the facts. Fairness and due process require nothing less.

Now, Martin appeals to the need for expertise. He acknowledges a huge information gap, and he emphasizes his publics' right to have it closed.

For that reason, I commit to you tonight that I will call a general election within 30 days of the publication of the commission's final report and recommendations. Let Judge Gomery do his work. Let the facts come out. And then the people of Canada will have their say.

Here he makes a firm promise of action; 20/20 hindsight may tell us that history did not play out the way Martin hoped it would, but he made a commitment and a promise of action.

In closing, let me say this: there are people who think that I was wrong to call this inquiry, wrong to expose my government to the political costs of the scrutiny that has ensued. They warn that we will pay a price in the next election and perhaps we will. But I trust your judgment. And I will not dishonour this office by trying to conceal or diminish such offensive wrongdoing. I have too much respect for this place. When I was young, I practically lived here in the Parliament Buildings. My father was a cabinet minister in four Liberal governments. He taught me that those who serve in public office have a duty to protect the integrity of government. I went into public life because I believe in the good that government can do and I will do my all as prime minister to make sure your government is worthy of your respect. The final judgment on whether I have done that will be yours. Thank you.

Here is the dramatic emotional link to the audience, in Martin's familial connection to government; it is intended to be a broad-ranging, sea-to-sea welling up of caring for Canada, placing him *well above* the partisan squabbling — and designed to clearly tell the Canadian people that he truly deserves to be looked on kindly by the electorate. Martin draws on the sense of teamwork and shared responsibility — Canada as an entity in which we all have a stake.

We've seen similar approaches with the private sector, particularly large, well-branded retail organizations. Eaton's had a 100-plus year run based on the emotional connection customers felt to the store; Wal-Mart executives wax poetic on founder Sam Walton's "small town" values, and Tim Hortons emphasizes and re-emphasizes its sense of appealing to a set of common, shared values as it serves up doughnuts and coffee at stores coast to coast. Martin's approach — "This is me, this is what I stand for" — is the kind of approach that works when you are in a position to lose it all, and yet it is common with politicians whose stock-in-trade is an appeal to the grassroots, to a shared perception of what it means to be citizens of the country. That same message will be delivered whether they are just starting out knocking door to door before an election or, in Martin's case, making a last-ditch appeal to the electorate. To draw on an image of a vulnerable little boy playing at politicking is an appeal, however simplistic, to the audience to relate to the speaker in an emotional way. Despite the scandal, the speechwriter for the Liberals knew that people make judgments, once the facts are in, with their emotions and not their intellect. The Liberals were betting that the facts of the case would not inculpate them too badly; that they would still be able to demonstrate that the party as a whole was an honest one. Even through a terrible scandal, a powerful appeal to emotions is essential for a public relations victory. It is necessary for the victory, but it is not in all cases sufficient, as was the case here. Martin's speech can be considered a battlefield victory, irrespective of the loss of the war.[9]

THINK TANK

1. How effective was Martin's speech? What can you take away from it?
2. Do you think the appeal hit the right note? Why or why not? What would you, as a communicator, have suggested to Martin?
3. Do a media search on the topic. How did the media treat Paul Martin in the aftermath of his speech? What does this tell you? Were his communications strategies effective?

Conclusion

As both Rudolph Giuliani and Paul Martin demonstrated, there are certain qualities and tactics that effective leaders have and use during a crisis, particularly in their handling of the media and stakeholders. Communicators need to ensure that they have a spokesperson front and centre during a crisis and that that person is well practised in wearing the leadership role, a special role unto itself during a crisis. That leader needs to be well briefed, to understand the nuances of what the organization does day to day, as well as its role in the context of business and the community. A lack of understanding of stakeholders and the media will mean that a leader is ill-prepared to go before the organization's publics and explain what is happening and where the organization is going in order to resolve the crisis and move forward.

Key Concepts

LEADERSHIP: The ability to direct an organization in its efforts to work through a crisis, and the ability to inspire trust and understanding in all the company's publics from the start of a crisis through to its resolution.

A LEADER INSPIRES TRUST BY:
- Taking charge and being seen to lead;
- Connecting emotionally with their publics;
- Being accessible;
- Appealing to a higher authority where appropriate.

A LEADER TAKES COMMAND BY:
- Immediately taking responsibility and directing staff to help him or her; understanding the situation and taking steps to make things better;
- Understanding the media's and stakeholders' interests;
- Being ready for a crisis and practised in the process of handling a crisis;
- Being able to think on his or her feet and answer questions effectively.

A LEADER PROVIDES DIRECTION FOR STAKEHOLDERS AND GUIDES EXPECTATIONS BY:
- Following through on promises made;
- Communicating messages directly;
- Creating a sense of teamwork and shared responsibility;
- Promising future action and ensuring accountability.

THE FOUR STAGES OF LEADERSHIP DURING A CRISIS:

RECOGNITION. Knowing the impact of the crisis on the interests of all parties involved.

TAKING ACTION. Spelling out the measures to bring the crisis under control.

BUILDING TRUST. Building the connection between the organization and its publics and inviting those publics to understand the process of handling the crisis.

MOVING FORWARD. A demonstration of moving forward to make things better, resolve the crisis and ensure that the factors involved in creating the crisis will not be an issue in future.

9

Tools II
News Releases,
Expert Testimony,
Environmental Scans

You cannot put a big load in a small bag,
Nor can you, with a short rope,
Draw water from a deep well.

— CHUANG TZU

The essence of the verse that opens this chapter is that the tool must be appropriate for and equal to the task. Communicators take this a step farther in thinking about a breaking crisis: to them, for each communications task, a unique tool must be fashioned. A news release must make a special appeal to publics during a crisis, and the company must find support from the right experts.

This chapter focuses on two essential tools in crisis communications: the news release and expert testimony.

The news release is both loved and hated by communicators, depending on who you talk to: some will say they are often overused, and so their significance in connecting with key publics is diminished. Others will say they are essential in delivering an organization's key messages and so need to be used as often as possible. Most communicators take an in-between approach — news releases are necessary for getting information for the public record out the door, but their impact (and as a result, the profile of the organization) is diminished if they are overused.

Expert testimony, too, can be thought of as a unique and carefully chosen tool that works in tandem with the communicator's standby tool, the news release, for dispensing information during a crisis and enhancing the power of key messages. Expert testimony strengthens an organization's position with its publics by aligning its message with positive or supporting commentary from high-profile stakeholders or opinion leaders. It gives the organization a third-party, arm's-length endorsement that tells its publics it is doing the right thing.

Our goal in this chapter is to:

- Discuss the news release — often seen as the ubiquitous go-to document for public information — and its significance in framing the messages an organization creates and delivers;
- Look at the way the news release can be used as a means of telling a story and answering the tough questions that may come the communicator's way;
- Examine a case where news releases were used to improve the subject's public profile;
- Discuss expert testimony and the role it plays in the communicator's approach to crisis communications management.

The News Release as a Crisis Tool

The news release has been around since 1907. Its significance as a vehicle for delivering information has grown in the past century. So just how many news releases do media outlets see? CNW Group, which provides news and information distribution services to organizations Canada-wide, estimates it sends out an average of 400 per day. CNW Group was established in 1960; it has locations across Canada and disseminates information from more than 10,000 information sources in Canada and internationally. Clients include public companies, all levels of government, not-for-profits and unions, and the company has active business relationships with many major trade associations, including the Canadian Association of Journalists, the Canadian

Federation of Independent Business, Canadian Investor Relations Institute, Canadian Public Relations Society and Public Affairs Association of Canada.

The news release can be an effective tool. If well written, properly researched and sent out promptly, it can help establish an organization's position with its publics quickly and effectively. A good news release is the foundation for subsequent communications activities. News releases are clearly a staple of doing business, but communicators need to be careful about using them. Receiving too many create a ho-hum response from an organization's publics; the media may decide the release contains nothing newsworthy.

But in a crisis the news release is indispensable because it allows communicators to get the information out quickly. Just as important, it allows them to track the information they deliver — what was said, when and by whom. It is a cogent public record of the organization's position during the crisis, allowing its spokespeople to see just what the organization said and did. Keeping a record of what was said to the organization's publics is important for gaining some perspective on the organization's actions: it helps communicators in the future learn from what happened here and now.

News releases also, as Canada Post's senior vice-president of Communications and Stakeholder Relations, Robert E. Waite, points out, help firms protect themselves legally:

> I think the difference today from 10 or 20 years ago is that people are far more litigious and aware of lawsuits. We don't just worry about getting a news release out there. We look at it from a legal aspect. We are careful about timing and scrutiny. The news release is a way of getting some potential coverage but it should often be reviewed by your legal experts before it goes out the door.[1]

Having a lawyer review the document before it is released allows the legal expert to provide input on wording that could raise legal questions, depending on the seriousness of the crisis. For instance, in acknowledging a passenger train rollover, officials for the transportation company operating the train would want to ensure that any message distributed to the public shows sympathy for victims of the crash while not inadvertently implicating the company in the cause of the accident. No organization wants its expression of sympathy to be misinterpreted as an admission of guilt when no admission is warranted.

A news release must demonstrate that during a crisis the organization:

- Understands the situation and how it affects the organization and its stakeholders;
- Has a grasp of the *perception* that people have of the crisis: from the organization's perspective and that of its publics;
- Has control over the crisis;
- Is taking action.

Telling a Story in News Releases

When I made the transition from news reporter to corporate communicator, my director was Fred Cederberg, a veteran newspaperman who had entered the civil service after many years in the media business. Fred instructed me to write as I did when I was a reporter. Doing so, Fred insisted, was the best way to ensure that the story the newspaper printed was the closest to the one we wanted to tell. I learned that it should also be written in a way that would put the best face possible on an organization.

Traditional newspaper reporting always offers the two-sides-of-the-story approach. By contrast, the news release presents an argument, idea or initiative from the perspective of the organization. It is essentially positive and proactive in its content and says: "This is what we're going to do, and this is why it will be good for our stakeholders and the public." To get the message to those publics, communicators write for their initial audience, the reporters, and this means that communicators write in a way that will make it easy for reporters to absorb the information being provided. Reporters are given an opportunity to see the information in the same way it would be written in a newspaper — in a straightforward, newsy style. By taking this approach, communicators are helping the reporters get to the essentials faster, and in a form that helps them visualize the shape of a story. Their work has been made easier: the facts they need are neatly laid out, which can take pressure off them as they near one or more deadlines. This improves the chance of seeing the story in the media, with the points communicators want to make.

COMMUNICATORS AND JOURNALISTS

In the book *Weapons of Mass Persuasion*, author Paul Rutherford states that there are 20,000 more public relations professionals than journalists in the United States, and 40 per cent of newspaper copy consists of items that are essentially written not by journalists but by public relations writers.[2]

Why do journalists do it? Sometimes it's just too easy to take a reasonably well-written news release and regurgitate the facts as presented. Let's keep in mind that in a media-savvy culture, this is not seen as a positive thing at all: it screams of rampant one-sided reporting on corporations, choreographed news conferences and the co-opting of a willing press corps. Although these are regrettable factors, in truth, the practice of recycling copy more often reflects an overworked, overstressed journalism industry, where reporters are forced to become increasingly quick studies and expected to manage multiple stories and deadlines at once. Few journalists can easily work 14-hour days, and when one story is finished, another story — and its deadline — looms.

News releases are often the starting point for a reporter creating a story. While it is accepted that editors usually won't run a news release as is, the release does provide the facts and information that journalists will arrange to give readers a sense of context. It establishes the series of events against a backdrop of how this crisis is affecting all parties involved and what the organization is doing to make things better.

HOW REPORTERS CREATE A STORY

To capture the public's attention, the media rely on a couple of common elements. It has long been recognized in the media that a good story will draw readers, viewers and listeners. As discussed in Chapter 7, a journalist's job is to find the hook, that special angle on an event, that will draw a reader, viewer or listener into the story. The hook is used in a story's first paragraph or, sometimes, as a headline.

To build a good story, writers include a well-defined beginning (or lead, sometimes spelled "lede") that sets up the story in an exciting way, with supporting facts filling out the middle and the end of the story, all written in crisp, clear language that delivers information quickly and concisely. Reporters use the *inverted pyramid* style, which positions the most important information at the top of the story and less important or supplemental information at the bottom, for two reasons. First, journalists favour the inverted pyramid style because it gets the gist of the story into the first part of the story. The key facts are presented first; readers who move onto the next story without finishing the first have a reasonably good sense of what the story is about before they shift their attention away from it. Second, space in newspapers is at a premium: editors looking to fit as many stories as possible on a page cut stories from the bottom up; hence, a story that has less useful information in its last couple of paragraphs won't suffer, in terms of facts and newsworthiness, if pared down. In broadcast journalism, with time at a premium — some newscasts have 15- or 30-second news items — the most important facts need to be presented at the front end of the item.

News releases that are written using the techniques of the news story, with the hook at the front, followed by the supporting factual elements of who, what, when, where and why, are appealing to the media's sensibilities and values. Even ending with an assertive description of *where we go from here* is employing a story technique, digesting and presenting the result or resolution of the story. In this way, communicators are able to present an intriguing news hook that will make reporters take notice — and no matter how seasoned or cynical the journalist, his or her interest will be piqued by a genuinely interesting hook — and also a story that more or less writes itself for the journalist.

STORY ELEMENTS IN A NEWS RELEASE

- A headline that attracts;
- A lead that grabs the reader — a hook that will entice the reader to keep reading;
- A supporting quote from a spokesperson that supports the lead;
- Information that links back to the preceding paragraphs in a way that makes sense;
- Language that creates an effective picture of what the organization is doing.

- Delivers key messages (also called core messages) that are worth repeating through the body of the news release;
- Shows that the organization is accepting responsibility. (Remember though that accepting responsibility is not the same as accepting blame.)
- Demonstrates that action is being taken;
- Avoids negative words, or words that serve to reinforce that the organization did something wrong.

Good communicators use the story elements listed above to structure their messages and accomplish the goals of their news release, intriguing the reporter rather than merely plastering information onto a page for them. These practices ensure that the information communicators wish to provide has a chance to make it into the story the reporter writes.

The catch is that journalists are taught to balance a story: if there is a positive, there must be a negative.

If a company announces in a news release that it is shifting production from Canada to Mexico to improve its productivity and reduce costs to customers, a journalist will report this, quoting the company. But the journalist will also dig for additional information. He or she might find that the company was really trying to prevent unionization, was trying to shift attention away from shoddy workplace practices or was running from allegations that it was polluting the environment.

Answering the Tough Questions in a News Release

To prepare a news release, communicators ask themselves questions: How do we want our organization's publics and stakeholders to see the organization? How do we want it to be portrayed in the media? They then write the news release based on the answers to those questions. They ensure that the news release contains what they want to say, in a style and format that satisfies the organization's senior people.

Communicators also need to ask more difficult questions — the ones that journalists will ask to add balance to the story, to tease out the less positive aspects. A communicator working for the company that relocates to Mexico will write a news release that says exactly that: "We are moving operations to reduce costs and improve efficiencies." But they will make the tough questions about union-busting, shoddy workplace practices or environmental damage part of the news release, too. They won't shy away from these questions when preparing material for distribution to the media, but they will remember that they are representing a company, not writing a news story. This means presenting the company's actions in a positive light.

Organizations approach crises in different ways. Some respond to the crisis by backtracking and repeating details, approaching the crisis by repeatedly acknowledging what has happened. Others work from the position that enough has already been written or said about the crisis, and what now needs to be addressed are the steps the organization is taking to move forward. Common sense and judgment have to be used.

Here's an example. ABC Company makes wagons for kids. Because of a defective cotter pin that holds the back wheels in place, there have been five instances of children falling off their wagon because the pin sheared off and the wagon went out of control. One child, Johnny Giguere, broke an arm, but in the other cases (and these are the only cases that have been reported to the company) the children have suffered only minor bumps. ABC's customer service department has handled the complaints, but the company wants to recall the wagon. However, Johnny Giguere's parents are talking about a lawsuit, which the company's lawyers agree can likely be settled out of court. A news release is drafted, but the question is: Should the company mention that five children suffered injuries? Or should it simply say that the product is being recalled because of a defective part?

If the news release mentions that several children have been hurt, will spreading this information among the company's publics open a floodgate of lawsuits? Simply mentioning this information lets people know that they are not the only ones who have been affected by the defective product, and it may prompt them to take legal action.

Most company representatives would prefer to say that the product is being recalled because of a defective part and will not focus on injuries, although if asked by customers or media, competent communicators will know it's in their company's best interest to tell the truth. But what if a journalist writes a story about the kid with the broken arm? In this case, ABC stands to look as though it is trying to hide this information, along with the knowledge of the danger inherent in the wagons. Is ABC obliged to acknowledge this situation in a news release, or is it better handled in a media interview?

The news release can simply state that the wagon is being recalled because of a defective cotter pin. In a media interview, ABC may or may not be asked about Johnny Giguere's broken arm. If ABC is asked how the company found out about the defective pin, the communicator may choose between saying either that the company learned of the defect from customer complaints or that the company learned of the defect when minor injuries from using the wagon were reported. Communicators must simply use their judgment, while maintaining a commitment to the truth. The reporter may try to set up the communicator (it's wise to remember that resourceful reporters *will* find the information they are looking for): "Well, it came to *my* attention that little Johnny Giguere broke his arm. What do you say to that?" The last thing a communicator wants is to be squirming in front of a reporter while scrambling to come up with an answer. In this case, the communicator must acknowledge what has happened: "Yes, we are aware of what happened. It is important for us to have products that are completely safe, and we are taking this opportunity to correct the situation."

The decision of how much information to provide in a news release is based on customer sensitivity to the issue and how the company feels about what has already been said in the media — what does it need to do to reduce the damage to its image or reputation? Communicators don't necessarily have to acknowledge everything about the crisis in a news release, rehashing each painful detail, if they can handle these questions through direct dealings with the media.

When a company has done a careful analysis of how various publics, especially the media, is treating an issue, it may decide that it needs to loudly and fully present all the negative information about a product or events in the news release. It may feel that only by so doing can it avert a crisis that could result from the information coming from another source. An analogy of this kind of wholesale publishing of negative elements is found in the forestry industry: in a prescribed burn, sections of forest are deliberately burned to prevent outbreaks of unmanageable wildfires. Alternately, a company might feel that full disclosure of the extent of harm is necessary to safeguard consumers.

In either case, when writing news releases that disclose negative elements, it's essential for communicators not to use weasel words — words that are used to soften, misdirect or avoid the effect of criticism of an organization (in other words, "weasel out" of its responsibility) in dealing with crises. Journalists are in the business of words, and they can see through weasel words more easily than other stakeholders and the public. The news release must be direct and concise, and it must deal directly and in a forthright manner with the crisis at hand.

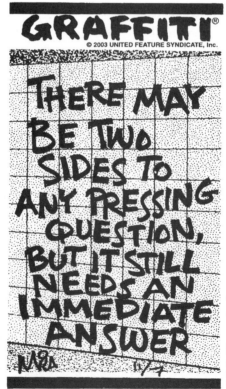

Case Study: Natrel and the Contaminated Milk Crisis

Most people's image of cow's milk is nutritious, delicious and safe — unless the one-litre carton of milk you purchased was filled with cleaning fluid, making you nauseated. Natrel, the maker of Sealtest dairy products and juices, found itself in a difficult situation when, at the beginning of February 2005, it had to issue a recall notice because cartons of chocolate milk packaged in the company's plant at Don Mills, Ontario, were tainted. A cleaning chemical used to rinse the cartons contaminated close to 12,000 single-litre cartons of Sealtest 1 per cent chocolate milk. One person who drank the milk ended up in hospital and Natrel received several complaints.

Newspapers carried banner front-page headlines: "Caution: it may not be what you think; recall issued for tainted chocolate milk" (*Toronto Star*, February 2, 2005). The front-page photo in the *Toronto Star* showed a variety-store owner pouring clear liquid into a glass.

CORPORATE GLANCE: NATREL

A processor and marketer of dairy products, Natrel is a division of Agropur Cooperative, itself 100 per cent Canadian owned and operated. Located in Granby, Quebec, Agropur has $1.9 billion in annual sales and a membership of 4,400 dairy farmers.

With head offices in Longueuil, Quebec, Natrel operates eight manufacturing plants: four in Quebec, three in Ontario and one in British Columbia. It was formed in 1990 and has net annual sales approaching $1 billion. Natrel employs more than 1,500 workers and markets such well-known brands as Sealtest, Québon, Natrel Fine-filtered, Natrel Ultra'Milk and Natrel Omega-3.[3]

How did Natrel respond? Quickly and effectively enough that the story stayed in the media for only three days and then disappeared. The one sticking point was in the accusation by some media that the company could have come clean earlier than it did, suggesting that it knew about the problem for a couple of days before doing anything about it. In fact, Natrel was ensuring that it had all its facts straight before distributing information to the media, a valid reason for delaying, especially since Natrel had a sense that the situation was not a life-threatening one. Behind the scenes, Natrel was working to determine the seriousness of the issue and having the tainted milk cartons analyzed.

Organizations have to ask themselves, "Should we go to our stakeholders and the media before we have our facts straight?" The answer varies: some will wait until they have finished the investigation while others will offer a holding statement. A holding statement is a means of simply saying, through a news release, "We understand that a problem has occurred and we are taking steps to investigate the matter. We are taking the matter seriously and will report back to the media as soon as we have an answer." Organizations run certain risks if they delay in speaking to their publics (speculation and rumour inevitably fill any gap), and yet there is also a need to not disclose sensitive information until it has been fully researched and vetted by appropriate personnel in the organization. Even if an organization delays in providing information and takes some criticism, if it can provide a solid explanation or plan that is supported by solid research, the chances of ending the crisis there are very good. If, on the other hand, the company rushes a response to its publics that turns out to lack grounding or fails to provide a solution, a crisis will likely result, one that will be much more difficult to extinguish with ensuing messages.

NATREL'S TAINTED MILK CRISIS
WHAT THE MEDIA SAID

CTV.CA, FEBRUARY 1, 2005: "Sealtest recalls contaminated 1% chocolate milk: Chocolate milk lovers in Ontario are being told to watch what they drink, after a Toronto man gulped down a potentially contaminated carton of milk and ended up in hospital."

CTV.CA, FEBRUARY 2, 2005: "Human error tainted chocolate milk, Natrel says: The contamination of one-litre cartons of Sealtest chocolate milk was the result of human error, the milk's manufacturer, Natrel, confirmed in a statement."

CBC.CA, FEBRUARY 2, 2005: "Recall affects thousands of milk cartons: Nearly 12,000 cartons of chocolate milk were recalled from Ontario stores [yesterday] after the discovery that some of them had been contaminated with an industrial cleaner."

WHAT NATREL SAID
"During sanitization, some food-grade sanitizer was accidentally left over in the production lines at the time of filling. The ingredients in this sanitizer are similar to those found in household vinegar and soap, and represent only 0.5 per cent of the cleaning solution, the rest being water. The sanitizer in question is not toxic and should not represent any health hazard."[4]

When the media came calling, the company was prepared with a news release that identified both the product and its expiry date. (The same copy as in the news release was also posted on Natrel's website, under the headline "Response for customers and consumers regarding Sealtest brand 1% 1 litre FE 07 chocolate milk.") The news release was clear, simple and official:

A Statement by NATREL Regarding Sealtest
Brand 1% 1 Litre FE 07 Chocolate Milk

Toronto, February 1/Canada Newswire — Natrel has withdrawn all Sealtest 1 litre 1% Chocolate Milk with the FE07 and 1478 codes. No other codes, sizes or products are affected.

The contamination was the result of human error at Natrel's Don Mills plant. During sanitation, some food-grade sanitizer was accidentally left over in the production lines at the time of filling.

The ingredients in this sanitizer are similar to those found in household vinegar and soap and represent only 0.5 per cent of the cleaning solution, the rest being water. The sanitizer in question is not toxic and should not represent any health hazard. Consumers may return the affected product to the point of purchase or dispose of the product immediately. A report by CANTOX on the toxicity of the substance accompanies this statement.

Natrel takes this incident very seriously and regrets the inconvenience and concern this may have caused our customers and consumers. The safety and integrity of our products is of paramount importance. Management is undergoing an immediate review of the processes and procedures currently in place to ensure that such an incident does not occur again.

Natrel has been working closely with the Canadian Food Inspection Agency to ensure that the affected product has been removed from the shelves, and will continue to fully cooperate with the Agency to review its production procedures and, ultimately, prevent such incidents from happening again.[5]

The following backgrounder accompanied the news release to reinforce Natrel's response and key messages.

```
-------------------------------------------------------------------

                            MEMORANDUM

To:     Doug Little, Natrel
From:   Karen Levine, CANTOX
Date:   February 1, 2005
Re:     Contamination

CANTOX Health Sciences International has been asked to evaluate
and comment on the potential health impacts associated with
potential contamination of a dairy product (i.e., chocolate
milk) with a sanitizing solution that is used to clean and main-
tain beverage and food processing equipment.
    Based on the information provided to CANTOX thus far by the man-
ufacturer of the sanitizer and by the beverage processing plant in
question, we predict that there will be no significant ill-health
effects from the ingestion of the contaminated product.
    Under a worst-case scenario, the contaminated product is
believed to contain 99.5 per cent water, and 0.5 per cent of a
"soap and vinegar"-like cleanser that is comprised of several
ingredients, all of which have been shown to be not acutely
toxic.[6]

-------------------------------------------------------------------
```

The communicators handling the Natrel crisis would likely have asked
themselves these questions when putting together the news release:

1. How toxic was the cleanser that was used? Was there a serious injury as a
   result of the tainted milk?
2. How do we get the message across to our publics that the cleanser was
   not toxic and was no cause for panic?
3. Do we or don't we take responsibility for what happened? Was it human
   error?
4. In the event that human error took place, what do we say about our commitment to health and safety standards?
5. When did this error take place?
6. What happened that created the problem?
7. What are we doing to correct the problem?
8. Is this problem limited to just the one type of milk? How likely is it that
   other products were tainted?

9. What message can we deliver about our relationship with our customers?
10. What expert testimony can we bring in to support us and to verify the harmlessness of the cleanser?
11. Who is our spokesperson? Which identifiable company figure, which figurehead, will position the company's messages and take responsibility for what is said?
12. What steps will the company take next?

In the days that followed the onset of the crisis and the February 1 news release, Natrel made itself available to the news media. With a front-page story in many newspapers, the company recognized that it would be harmful to try to distance itself from the story. Instead, Natrel made it clear that the tainted milk was an isolated incident, that it had taken decisive action to determine its cause and that it was following up with a plan to ensure that a similar incident wouldn't happen again. Spokesperson Lynne Hamilton provided the details of the company's actions; this approach was strengthened by the company's news release as well as the toxicology report.

On February 2, the media reported on the recall of the tainted milk and quoted Shashi Kulkarhi, an officer with the Canadian Food Inspection Agency, as saying that ingesting the cleanser could have adverse health consequences. This statement, coming from an official of a high-profile public agency, was cause for concern. On February 3 the *Toronto Star* interviewed Steven Street, the man who drank the tainted milk; he complained that he was still feeling ill. However, the story also quoted Jack Uetrecht, a University of Toronto pharmacy professor, who said that the tainted milk's effect would be little more than a gut ache.

USE OF EXPERTS

The company relied on the strength of third-party expert endorsement to reinforce its message. That came in the form of Natrel's backgrounder, a memorandum from CANTOX Health Sciences International to Natrel, attesting to its findings that the contaminated products would not cause significant ill-health effects.

For the company, the situation was clearly hampered by negative third-party commentary from the Canadian Food Inspection Agency's Kulkarhi; his comment that the cleanser in the tainted milk had "a potential for adverse health consequences, which may include death" set off alarm bells in the media. That kind of commentary is great fodder: media love any threat to life that may be revealed in the course of researching a news story. How would the company get the message out that the tainted milk was essentially harmless? How would it avoid having a battle of expert against expert? A company doesn't want its essential key messages lost in a battle of professors, with media feeding on each and every sound bite. An extended, dramatic battle in the media in which a company is eventually vindicated is, in terms of a company's reputation, only a pyrrhic victory.

For Natrel, the answer was in shoring up the strength of its expert testimony. On February 2, it issued a five-page news release with the weighty headline "Natrel releases the complete toxicology report performed on the Sealtest brand 1% chocolate milk that was contaminated with sanitizer. The full report from CANTOX Health Sciences International is below." The toxicology report was intended to deliver complete scientific information backing up CANTOX's finding that the tainted milk was harmless. The report's lead indicated that CANTOX had "more than 20 years, experience in evaluating the safety-in-use of a variety of products including foods, drugs, pesticides, and industrial, commercial and consumer chemicals." In concise technical language, CANTOX made it clear that the sanitizer would have few ill effects, emphasizing that it was made mostly of water, vinegar and hydrogen peroxide.

Natrel's five-page toxicology report is an example of a weighty piece of information that was targeted not to customers but to the media. The report was too information-laden for the average person to consume, but not necessarily too dense to distribute to health reporters, who have the experience and expertise to decipher scientific information. For Natrel — hard hit by what it considered unfounded allegations that it had failed to explain the situation early enough, suggesting that it was trying to cover up sloppy food management practices — the lengthy news release was a means of ensuring that all the scientific data were out in the media's hands. Natrel sought to include as much concise information as possible, covering *every single angle* that could arise in a news story. Overkill? Not when the media are getting quotes from the Canadian Food Inspection Agency saying that the tainted milk could cause death.

> In the battle of experts, the organization that can offer either the most clearly defined argument or the most indisputable research will win.

In this case, Natrel, through CANTOX, had the last word on the issue; convincing enough that the media began to let the story drop. Although on February 3 media were reporting that the person who became ill from ingesting the tainted milk was considering a lawsuit, the treatment of the story was beginning to favour Natrel. Clearly, the company's expert endorsement had helped the media and public accept that the cleaning solution was non-toxic, because the media stopped reporting the sensational side of the story. Instead, the *Toronto Star* quoted the University of Toronto professor of pharmacy as saying that the tainted milk would "do a number on your gut, but I wouldn't be worried long term. The effects would be immediate and should resolve themselves within 24 hours or so."

The issue was resolved after this point, having spent approximately three days in the media and the court of public opinion. The story fell off the media's radar because they had exhausted the story's possibilities. There was enough scientific expertise and explanation to satisfy the media about the tainted milk. And the media stories of a possibly serious illness caused to a Natrel customer by a trusted, high-profile company tapered off. Natrel had demonstrated strong corporate responsibility in addressing the situation by ensuring that a toxicology report was provided and by giving assurances that its customers would continue to be provided with a safe product. The company was able to rebuild trust in its products with an assertive, information-packed, short-term media campaign.

WHY NATREL'S STRATEGY WORKED

Natrel's approach to the tainted-milk crisis worked because the company acted quickly to address the problem. The company took responsibility for the mishap and produced news release materials explaining the fine points behind the tainted milk— the toxicology report. This was essential in providing reassurance to the public through the media that the error was a once-in-a-lifetime occurrence and that steps would be taken to ensure it didn't happen again. The company made promises it could keep, and these were relayed in its news release, including a promise of a full review of company procedures.

Natrel also stayed in front of the media and didn't rush to attempt to close down the crisis. The company stayed responsive and answered media inquiries as they came in, and it stuck to its key message that the cleaning agent was non-toxic; it engaged the use of arm's-length, third-party scientific expertise to prove this. In a positive way, the company was also vindicated after the *Toronto Star* sought out its own expert (the University of Toronto professor) to verify that the company's claims were true. Through a strongly worded, effective news release, Natrel used the right tools to restore balance to its image, and it was able to deliver these messages in a way that convinced the media that it was a fair, balanced and focused company dedicated to providing the highest-quality products possible to consumers.[7]

THINK TANK

1. What other examples have you seen in the media of food products being tainted? How did the company handle the situation?
2. Would you have done anything different from Natrel? What if there was a call for other types of compensation from the company?
3. Can you think of situations in which the use of outside authorities to support a company's key messages wouldn't work?

Expert Testimony

Expert testimony is an excellent way to strengthen a company's message during a crisis. Clearly, it offers the company the opportunity to gain greater credibility and profile. Albert Einstein once said that "the whole of science is nothing more than a refinement of everyday thinking." Science pervades our day-to-day approach to life and the issues we face. Depending on the industry sector, doctors, scientists, and legal experts all have a measure of cachet with the public. That expert testimony is also a stamp of approval of what the company is doing to solve its crisis.

In a situation in which communicators rely on scientific expertise, they will want to avoid pitched battles between experts. Even in matters of science, it is reasonable to assume that for every expert who says one thing, there is another who thinks the converse and is willing to offer opposing testimony.

Science is not a haphazard endeavour. Rather, it's a systematized method for gathering knowledge through observation and experimentation. By its nature, science is meant to be unbiased and to "see what it can see." It is not a mercenary tool to use to exculpate a company from wrongdoing by gathering only those facts that will show the company's innocence. That said, historically we've seen that scientists are as adept at finding ways to prove their science as politicians are at rephrasing promises to the public. Even practitioners of the hard sciences may disagree among themselves. However, that doesn't stop some organizations from looking to scientists, or to any other experts for that matter, for support for practices that are indeed harmful. The cigarette companies, for example, mustered many scientists to support their assertion that the ill effects of smoking were not as serious as most studies had proven them to be; in fact, this approach sparked the creation of the term *tobacco science* to describe, according to Word Spy, a website devoted to new words and phrases, "a science that is skewed or biased, especially toward a particular industry."[8]

Communicators serve their company best by managing the long-term reputation of the company, something only accomplished by working *with* the truth, not slanting it or manufacturing it. Communicators engage the scientists either because they know that their company's practices are acceptable, or because they are ready to work with the consequences of discovering that the company has failed in some way in its practices. Either way, by employing an expert, a smart company lessens the chances of its publics or media panicking in the face of an information gap, a gap which, depending on the severity of the crisis, may be filled with speculation far worse than the company's actual misdeeds or negligence. In other words, experts are not employed to spin facts or argue innocence in the face of contradictory evidence. They are employed to show publics that the company is taking control of the situation and is being open about the facts.

When experts disagree, communicators can win their case by presenting the facts well and by following the rules of leadership: use strong key messages and adopt an open and proactive approach to finding solutions rather than simply reacting to what someone else's scientist says. An open and proactive approach means anticipating testimony that weighs against that testimony on which the company relies. Communicators make the weighing of this expert testimony part of their key messages and also something their experts will investigate and will prepare them to address to their publics.

VARIETIES OF EXPERTISE

There are many types of experts; not all are in the sciences. A person with extensive experience in the company's industry or in a related field, usually but not necessarily with an academic background, can be approached to provide expert testimony to support the company's position. For instance, in legal issues involving the operation of an automobile, a licensed mechanic with many years of experience may be considered an expert. You'll see in the next case study that police chiefs, political figures and animal control officers are also considered experts, in that they have a knowledge and understanding of a field that is outside the day-to-day sphere of most people.

TYPES OF EXPERTS

SCIENTISTS. They provide the hard results from a test.

POLITICAL FIGURES. Traditionally they are held to the standard of values of the Everyman. Ideally, they represent and reflect in their communications many of the thoughts and emotions present in the communities they represent, however large or small. People gravitate to political figures, seeing them as representative of the communities they serve.

FIELD EXPERTS. Those who may not have academic credentials but have a wealth of day-to-day experience in a specific area.

FIRST-HAND EXPERIENCERS. They have an unfiltered experience of a life-threatening or life-changing situation; for example, a victim of a crime or of negligence. These authorities can inspire great sympathy from publics and are sought out for the raw emotional power of their testimony.

FINDING AND WORKING WITH EXPERTS

To find the right expert help, communicators will use information drawn from news releases and news stories, or from established relationships with organizations or disciplines in which the expertise is to be found. The goal is of course to gain the help of the foremost expert in the field that applies to the company's issue or crisis. Most organizations will have established, long before a crisis, and based on its core operations, a list of competent outside experts that can be called upon when crisis hits. In fact, doing the necessary research to establish this list and keep it updated is an important part of crisis planning.

Many crises, however, will involve areas of expertise that fall outside a company's core operations, and therefore research will be required to find suitable experts. In this case, communicators should first work with communicators in other companies that have relationships with experts in the area of concern. Failing this, communicators must do their own legwork by contacting organizations that:

- Regulate the pertinent field or academic discipline;
- Approve grants to fund study in the field;

- Confer honours for excellence in practice or study;
- Publish new research in the area or organize symposia or conferences.

Communicators contact experts to solicit both advice and support for the direction their company will take during a crisis. Finding an expert to provide an opinion can be time-consuming. Even after a willing expert is located, communicators will want to do their homework and ensure that the expert they hire has credentials that will carry weight with the media and the company's stakeholders. This can be done by canvassing more broadly with the organizations described above.

Most authorities and experts will be pleased to be approached for their opinion; being called upon to provide an expert opinion often helps them reinforce their own standpoints or perspectives within the academic or professional communities they belong to and within the larger cultural communities as well. Put another way, being asked to participate in matters of importance to the wider community enhances an expert's profile as an expert. Despite the reputation enhancement that serving in a crisis offers, experts generally charge a fee for their services.

This is an important point, because questions may arise from such a transaction. Critics within your publics may see paying an expert for an opinion as the same as paying an expert to *arrive at* an opinion favourable to the company. Nevertheless, it is normal for companies to engage an expert to provide an assessment or critique of their workplace initiatives. If the matter is handled in an upfront, professional manner, it will appear less like the company is paying someone to agree with it and more like it is simply seeking the educated opinion of a respected third party.

Communicators should give experts all necessary briefings, even though most are usually already familiar with the issue at hand. Experts are also provided with drafts of the news release well in advance so that they may see where their own quote and data fit in.

DECIDING ISSUES WITH EXPERT SUPPORT

Expert testimony can be very important when issues are not cut and dried and may not be settled by an appeal to science. Questions of policy often rest on matters of the soft sciences, in which the battles between experts may be unavoidable. Here's a case in point. Beginning in the fall of 2004, Ontario Attorney General Michael Bryant, under Premier Dalton McGuinty, decided to introduce legislation banning pit bulls in Ontario. The generic, non-breed-specific dogs had been creating trouble for years, biting people and other dogs, and Bryant was determined to ban them.

Case Study: Banning Pit Bulls in Ontario

Was the presence of pit bulls in Ontario a crisis? Judging by the response of the public — letters pouring in to the Attorney General's office, discussions on radio talk shows with near hysterical people calling for a ban, petitions, newspapers running photographs of scarred children the day after being bitten — it qualified as a crisis, though it was primarily an urban issue and tended to be isolated to the Greater Toronto Area. It didn't matter that other dogs such as the Labrador retriever (holding a sterling reputation behaviourwise) and the German shepherd were also on record as high-occurrence biters — pit bulls, with their reputation as the breed of choice for bikers, white supremacists and criminals, were the target.

On October 15, 2004, the Ontario government issued a news release with the headline "McGuinty government to introduce pit bull ban."

Following is the complete news release:

MCGUINTY GOVERNMENT TO INTRODUCE PIT BULL BAN

Legislation To Ban Dangerous Breed,
Increase Dog Owners' Responsibility

TORONTO — The McGuinty government is making our communities safer and responding to the concerns expressed by thousands of Ontarians by introducing legislation this fall to ban pit bulls in the province, Attorney General Michael Bryant announced today.

"People want to be protected from the menace of these dangerous dogs," said Bryant. "Some of these dogs are nothing but a loaded weapon waiting to go off and so we are taking action to make our communities safer."

Bryant will introduce legislation this fall to amend the Dog Owners' Liability Act. The legislation, if passed, would:
- Ban pit bulls
- Muzzle existing pit bulls, impose other province-wide restrictions to improve public safety, and allow municipalities to impose appropriate controls
- Increase fines up to a maximum of $10,000 and allow for jail sentences of up to six months for owners of any dangerous dog that bites, attacks, or poses a threat to public safety.

If passed, the legislation would allow for a transition period for existing pit bulls. During this time, owners would be required to comply with strict new requirements for continued ownership.

Bryant said the proposed ban is meant to be supportive of municipal governments, and that this proposed bill respects the municipality's authority under the Municipal Act. This comprehensive approach would avoid a patchwork of bans.

"I support the province's swift action," said David Miller, Mayor of Toronto. "This problem is not exclusive to any single municipality, it is a province-wide issue and therefore the best solution is a province-wide strategy to keep Ontarians safe from dangerous dogs."

"My officers have encountered a number of dangerous situations involving pit bulls," said Julian Fantino, Chief of Toronto Police Service. "This proposed ban will help my officers and police services across Ontario keep our community safe from dangerous dogs."

"The ban of pit bulls that Kitchener has had for the past seven years is helping to keep our community safer from a breed that has demonstrated undesirable, aggressive behaviour," said Carl Zehr, Mayor of Kitchener. "I believe that every Ontarian deserves this level of safety and am pleased that the provincial government will introduce legislation that will, if passed, ban pit bulls province-wide."

"Our experience in Winnipeg has been one of success," said Tim Dack, Chief Operating Officer of the Animal Services Agency of the City of Winnipeg. "We have seen the number of pit bull incidents decline dramatically since introducing a pit bull ban 14 years ago. I applaud the Government of Ontario for their decision to ban pit bulls and deal with this urgent public safety issue."

"I feel safer knowing that the Ontario government has taken steps to protect us from the extreme danger posed by pit bulls," said Diana Fischer, a victim of a pit bull attack. "The particular problem with pit bulls is the inability to stop them once they have started to attack, the viciousness of their attack and the seriousness of the injuries they inflict. I know this based on my experience as a trainer - through which I've dealt with hundreds of dogs - and my experience being attacked by a pit bull who was trying to kill my own dogs."

"I commend the McGuinty government for moving forward quickly on this very important initiative," said Rod Morrison, Mayor of Wawa. "Protecting the public from the menace of pit bulls and toughening up on owners of dangerous dogs that attack is in the best interest of all people, in every town, city and community across Ontario."

"With today's announcement, we are proposing serious action to respond to the concerns of people worried about their personal safety," said Bryant. "Our government is committed to protecting all Ontarians from these highly unpredictable dogs."[9]

ANALYSIS

The tone and language of the government's press release are certainly right for what it wanted to accomplish and the lead paragraph spells it out: *The McGuinty government is making our communities safer and responding to the concerns expressed by thousands of Ontarians by introducing legislation this fall to ban pit bulls in the province.*

Notice the words used in the lead: *communities safer... responding to the concerns* ... These statements strike an emotional chord and help underscore the link created between an organization and its publics. The key message is clear: "*You* are afraid and threatened. *We* are here to help."

The news release continues with a quote from Bryant: *People want to be protected from the menace of these dangerous dogs. Some of these dogs are nothing but **a loaded weapon waiting to go off** and so we are taking action to make our **communities safer**.*

In this second paragraph, the government repeats the community safety message. It thereby reinforces to the public that the government is acting in the public interest directly, to prevent harm to all citizens. As an appeal, this satisfies the public's expectation that it should and will be protected from harm. Any message that addresses expectations of stakeholders is therefore always a strong one, even to opponents, because the organization in question is, whether the critics approve or not, honouring a commitment to a stakeholder group. In a society and marketplace in which many publics feel disconnected and disempowered, messages emphasizing honouring commitments are powerful. The statement that adds the sharpest emotional appeal to this message of fulfilling an obligation to protect the public is the one in which the pit bulls are referred to as "a loaded weapon waiting to go off." The role the government is emphasizing in its messages, and the one through which it stands to gain the most support in this crisis, is that of protector. Protection of its citizens is arguably government's first mandate, and it is the one most connected with stakeholder fear. Thus, rhetorically, the key messages that emphasize both stakeholder fear and added protection are bound to be effective.

This may be seen as fear-mongering or politicking on the part of the government (to get people onside, the government may have desired to stoke their fears a bit). And indeed, some members of the public would perceive this strong rhetorical stance as cheap leveraging of a message. But it would be seen by others purely as an attempt to take as much control as possible of a situation, under conditions that may appear to be out of control. But using fear-based tactics has risks — communicators risk being accused of not telling the whole truth (such as the background information on statistics on other high-incidence biting breeds), and they walk a fine line between telling people the straight facts or putting their own spin on the issue in order to build support from publics. Journalists are sensitive to spin — they see it every day. Stakeholders react positively to spin if it reinforces what they believe to be true. But usually, spin will simply anger most people and make them less likely to lend support; or it may (if the facts are not correct) expose the communicator (and by extension, the organization) as having failed to do adequate research.

The government increased the impact of its messages by drawing on high-profile figures for support, including mayors of Canadian towns that had already banished pit bulls. The government avoided the use of dog experts with views that did not support the ban (and there were many, including veterinarians and others who generated websites dedicated to the issue) in order to present a uniform line of thinking that underscored the government's essential key messages on the subject. Its messages were focused on reinforcing an approach to the matter that would be accepted, even applauded, by an anxious public.

The communicators for the Attorney General weren't writing a news story; they were preparing a document that would present their information, ideas and action plan in a positive way. The news release was designed to present these facts only, letting opponents of their plan present facts that supported *their* claim.

The Attorney General also used *sympathy* — the testimony of a victim, and a dog trainer at that — to drive home its message. A victim's testimony provides a different kind of authority than the typical expert or authority figure, but what it loses in academic or political clout it gains in emotional appeal.

DID THE GOVERNMENT GO OVERBOARD WITH EXPERTISE?

The government certainly ran into several major opinion roadblocks in the ensuing months. Opposition came from dog owners (and not just pit bull owners) and others who believed that the legislation was discriminatory and draconian. Experts including veterinarians and humane society officials waded in to oppose the ban, on the basis that it was the dog owner — not the dog — who was responsible for the biting problem. Public support wavered for months.

The polarity caused by the crisis and by parallel municipal action in different areas of the province set the tone for extreme action. In Windsor, for instance, where pit bulls were banned October 1, 2004 (and where 74 pit bulls were euthanized in a three-month period), a group called Advocates for the Underdog created a pit bull "underground railroad" to spirit pit bulls out of Windsor. Headlines from the second week in January, 2005, created a picture of pit bull as victim, certainly not an image favourable to the McGuinty government.

EUTHANIZING PIT BULLS: THE HEADLINES

"Banned pit bulls ride to freedom" — *NATIONAL POST*
"'Underground railroad' saves dozens of pit bulls" — *OTTAWA CITIZEN*
"Covert operation rescues pit bulls" — *WINDSOR STAR*

For Bryant, it was a case of facing a fragmented public increasingly asking, "Who's right?" This would likely have continued had not the stoic, decisive and high-profile Toronto Police chief Julian Fantino come back into the debate in the early days of 2005 and offered a strong thumbs-up for the ban, reinforcing his quote from the October news release. In the media, Fantino widely testified to the dangers of pit bulls, particularly the threat to his frontline officers trying to do their jobs. His support for the ban was largely considered a public relations coup for the McGuinty government.

Most opponents of the bill said that the ban was vague and unscientific. This was the stance taken by groups such as the American Staffordshire Club of Canada, which stated that the act's "vague wording" would bring the

Staffordshire, a recognized breed, under fire because its appearance and physical characteristics were similar to the government's definition of a pit bull. The club said on its website: "This Act's vague and undefined language promotes a climate of fear towards all dogs and their owners and provides police with significantly expanded powers of search and seizure, in both public settings and private homes."

Yet, for the McGuinty government, expert testimony clearly worked. By March of 2005, the government had enough public support, strengthened by expert testimony, to bring its bill to the House. And it passed, as announced in a news release headlined "New law bans pit bulls, increases dog owners' responsibility."

The news release's lead continued to draw on the protection issue and, in an attempt to be more inclusive, was broadened to include not only pit bulls but "any dog posing a danger."

The first paragraph reads:

> Ontarians will be better protected from all dangerous dogs following passage of a law that bans pit bulls and toughens penalties for the owners of any dog that poses a danger to the public, Attorney General Michael Bryant announced today. "Ontario becomes the first province or state in North America to have a law that protects all its citizens from pit bulls," said Bryant. "We are also holding all dog owners more accountable for the actions of any breed.[10]

The law, set for August 29, 2005, would allow pit bulls already in Ontario to stay, provided they were sterilized as well as leashed and muzzled when in public. Pit bull puppies born within three months of the ban would be allowed to live under those restrictions. But any dog born after that time would be considered illegal and would have to be destroyed, sent out of the province or donated to a research facility. As well, as mentioned in the original news release, fines could reach $10,000 (possibly including a six-month jail term) for a dog owner whose animal was guilty of biting or attacking a person or generally being a menace to public safety.

When the Dog Owners' Liability Act took effect, critics reacted immediately;

one lawyer filed a notice of application with the Supreme Court of Ontario on behalf of a client, citing the act as an infringement on the Canadian Charter of Rights and Freedoms. At the time of publication of this book, that issue was still before the courts; interestingly, a one-year scan conducted of news items pertaining to pit bulls found 194 stories dedicated to the topic (including stories of more pit bull attacks during the spring of 2006) — apparently there was no waning of interest in this issue.[11]

THINK TANK

1. Do you think the government overdid it in appealing to fear? When and how should organizations appeal to fear or concern in their communications?
2. Can you think of other examples where an organization might have played on the public's or consumers' fear to promote its position? Does this approach work?
3. What position would you take as a communicator if you worked for the Ontario government?
4. What position would you take if you were working for an organization that represents breeders of pit bulls?

Environmental Scans

Research is an essential part of a communicator's job, but it's not something that is easily done when a crisis hits. Extensive research into a crisis often takes a lot of time, which communicators may not feel they have when publics are panicking and the crisis is accelerating. Communicators are generalists, and so research into issues monitoring and crisis planning generally entails working with experts. As mentioned earlier, communicators need to make contact with experts in their industry long before a crisis occurs; they need to get to know them well and, ideally, have positive working relationships with them. An organization's experts might include industry leaders, university professors, representatives of professional associations, and experienced professionals.

A communicator's relationship building should move naturally from getting to know these professionals to meeting with them on a regular basis, sharing information (only information that is in the public domain, of course) and maintaining regular contact; usually a phone call or email every two to three months or so will suffice in keeping both communicator and expert in the loop. In addition, experts should be on the distribution list for publications targeted to the organization's external publics. In these ways, communicators integrate expertise into their company's ordinary communications function.

Another key aspect of research that falls properly within the issues monitoring process, which was explored in Chapter 3, is actually more pertinent to the discussion in this chapter. It is by and large through networking with experts, communications colleagues, and industry associations and peers that the communicator's early warning system, the environmental scan, is conducted. Environmental scans are a company's broad study of change in the wider social environment in which a company operates. Communicators should always approach an environmental scan by asking, "How will these issues and trends affect my organization and how important is this information to my company's direction?"

While communicators could conduct environmental scans in an irregular or ad-hoc manner, or even on an annual basis, the best approach is to conduct them on a continuous basis, every two months if possible, by adding information to a database specifically designated to keep track of issues and trends. Communicators can review all available media to gain an accurate picture of the changing business environment (which will also be done daily as part of the organization's issues identification process), but they will also want to broaden the scope to include marketing studies, scientific reports, government publications, analyses of consumer habits, and product and market studies. They should focus on several key elements:

- *The Economy.* How will changes in the economy affect the organization?
- *Legal issues.* Are there changes to laws or bylaws that will affect the organization?
- *Regulations.* Are government regulations under review, changing or about to be more strictly enforced or monitored?

- **Technology.** Is the technology related to the industry changing in ways that will affect the organization?
- **Labour.** Are there labour issues abroad that may affect the organization or its employees?
- **Natural environment.** Are there environmental issues that need to be kept track of, in terms of the organization's production processes or other elements that may affect the environment?
- **Social and cultural issues.** What are the buying or behavioural habits of clients or customers and the public? What effect will a booming economy or rapidly striating income levels have on the organization?
- **Supply chain.** Are the organization's suppliers changing their business practices? How will this affect the organization?[12]

SWOT ANALYSIS

Trends and changes can be charted and compared with factors within the communicator's company: growth, profits, labour issues, new products or technology, as well as more subjective factors such as the company's overall effectiveness in communicating with media and stakeholders. Communicators may wish to employ a SWOT (strengths, weaknesses, opportunities and threats) analysis to define how important these emerging issues are to their organization. SWOT was developed by researcher Albert Humphrey at Stanford University in the 1960s and is often used to look at both internal factors (what do communicators have within their organization that can help or hinder?) and external factors (what forces outside the organization can affect its success?).[12] Here's an example of how a new technology introduced by a competing company might be examined in terms of SWOT:

Strengths: How well is the organization doing right now? What advantages does it currently have? Can it continue to compete in the face of this new technology?

Weaknesses: What is the organization's weakness that is a potential threat? What criticisms is the organization likely to hear from its customers?

Opportunities: Are there new markets that the organization can tackle? What opportunities does it have to maintain its competitive edge? What other trends are presenting themselves that it can take advantage of?

Threats: How serious is this issue to the organization? What impact will this new technology have on business? How long before the organization has to adopt this technology or change its own?

KEY TASKS OF ENVIRONMENTAL SCANS

Brainstorm. Collecting ideas and then winnowing them down to several strong action-oriented initiatives will help communicators define the company's goals. Discuss ideas and news with colleagues. Discuss the industry associations and levels of expertise that the company needs to be connected to, from business and industry associations to universities to trade associations.

PR associations. Becoming part of a public relations association allows communicators to network with other professionals, whether or not they are in the same industry; the essentials of communications cross all boundaries.

Government. Major announcements and initiatives of all levels of government need to be followed. At the provincial and federal levels, broad-based announcements may affect the industry and communicators need to be aware of them. Set up meetings with local government officials. This includes government bureaucrats, especially those dealing with planning as well as business development, along with the mayor and local politicians. Ensure they have a familiarity with the organization's business. Communicators will wish to be regularly in touch with civil servants who work in the ministries or divisions of the ministries whose functions are most likely to impact their industry.

Focus on local issues. As the adage goes, "Think globally, act locally." Communicators must look at their communications role as positioning their organization in a global way, but must also take action at the local level. Being tuned in to what is happening locally is important: being part of a local community is essential to business and to the communicators who manage their companies' public profiles. Joining the local chamber of commerce or business association is a great way to stay informed of changes in the business community and to stay abreast of the opinion leaders in the community.

Links to academia. Communicators should establish contacts with local colleges and universities. Seek out opportunities for the organization to provide technical expertise, facilities or guidance to college or university programs related to the company's field.

Network. When communicators network with contacts, they should heed the words of marketing guru Peter Urs Bender, who writes in *Secrets of Power Marketing,* "Networking is communicating (not necessarily telling *your* story). Listen more than you talk." It's essential for communicators to let people know their story, but they also have to listen to what others have to say, gauge the significance of that message, relate it to the organization and see it in the context of the industry as a whole.

Internet resources. Communicators can use the Internet to compile up-to-date information on the industry, and to keep the file updated. These resources shouldn't be relied on exclusively but instead used to provide background and context. The most important sources of information are peers and industry experts.

Industry associations. Communicators should be aware of the local, regional and national industry associations for their organization. For instance, a company in the automotive parts industry might have memberships in groups such as the Automotive Parts Manufacturers' Association. Beyond knowing of the organization and reading its newsletters, communicators should make an effort to link in with its members and administration to learn its current views on the industry and any directions the industry is taking.

Stakeholder groups such as industry associations often synthesize a wide variety of information for their members, giving them access to basic, up-to-date news quickly. But this doesn't preclude communicators from working hard at the local level to follow trends and developments.

Be aware of crises elsewhere. Looking at a broad range of examples of crisis management as well as those specific to the industry is an important task in an environmental scan. Connect with other communicators who have been through a crisis and ask them, "How did you handle that situation?" Communicators are usually more than happy to share information and provide advice on what worked and what didn't in a crisis situation.

Conclusion

Communicators, like journalists, need to tell convincing stories, and what makes these stories convincing is using the same techniques of story building that journalists use. News releases provide information for the company best when they are balanced between their purpose (to present key messages to all of the company's publics) and their function (to present stories in a compelling way to journalists, the first audience to come in contact with the material). Communicators can also provide convincing and compelling information by being in regular contact with industry experts, whose knowledge, wisdom and skill can inform their approach to issues and crisis, and by drawing on these experts effectively when their support is needed in a crisis.

In approaching this task, communicators need to constantly be thinking of how their publics will react to the information presented to them. They need to ask what emotional impact this issue will have with their publics and ensure that their key messages are targeted to effectively addressing that impact. They need to ensure that the language used is appropriate to the matter at hand — they want to acknowledge and address emotional concerns but in a way that convinces their publics that they are taking charge. Playing on the emotions of publics in a rhetorical way is not only unfair to them, it could create a great deal of criticism both during and after the crisis.

In this chapter, we also talked about expert testimony, a tool that is used to underscore the messages delivered by communicators, frequently in tandem with a news release, strengthening and supporting the organization's position during a crisis and often explaining complex details in laypersons' terms. Expert testimony aligns the communicator's message with commentary from high-profile stakeholders, scientists or opinion leaders and is often the underpinning for the strategic direction the organization is taking to resolve a crisis.

Finally, communicators need to constantly be monitoring their environment: talking to experts and industry peers, scanning marketing studies, reading periodicals and gathering as much information as they can — and then charting the trends and directions that their business environment is taking in order to more properly prepare for issues and crisis management in the future.

10

Tools III
The Question-and-Answer Document and Media Interviews

We've seen how an organization uses the news release to set out its position — to make it clear to its audiences where it stands on an issue. But what about the questions that will inevitably come from its stakeholders, the public and the media after a crisis breaks? How do communicators deal with the immediate, confrontational and sometimes accusatory questions? This may be one of the most challenging aspects of crisis communications — anticipating what the publics will ask and creating appropriate answers to those questions.

In dangerous situations, professionals work with a safety net, a release valve and a backup, whether they're circus performers, police officers, firefighters or military personnel. The same is true of communicators, whose organizations' reputations are on the line. The question-and-answer document, or Q&A, is the document that allows communicators to speak from a safe set of messages in the face of challenging questions.

In this chapter we examine:

- The process of anticipating the organization's publics' emotional responses to the facts of the crisis;
- How communicators posit potential scenarios and the questions that they will provoke;

- How communicators research and write appropriate and effective answers to these questions;

These three elements lead to the creation of the Q&A.

In this chapter we also examine how communicators handle those tough questions in an interview, and why it's essential they have their research done and are prepared to think (and speak) on their feet. Ultimately, their work with the Q&A turns challenges into opportunities, allowing them to take their publics to where they want them to be: in a position to see the organization as a proactive, progressive entity that can get past its difficulties and set a course for a positive future.

The Q&A

HOW Q&As SERVE VARIOUS PUBLICS

A Q&A is sent from a communicator to the manager and director, and it may also be shared with senior personnel. For internal stakeholders, the Q&A allows them to understand what their organization is doing. Too often, employees — especially in large organizations — are privy *only* to information through the grapevine. A Q&A, sent via email or hard copy, gives employees the most immediate information they need to understand the crisis and their company's actions in handling it. It sets out the company's goals in moving through the crisis and resolving it. It also forestalls employees providing information to the public, either inadvertently or deliberately, that may be incorrect.

For external stakeholders, the Q&A creates a comfort level, letting them know that the company is maintaining a sense of stability and direction, even in challenging times. For the media, it gets down to the questions that they would be asking very soon, in news conferences, via email or over the phone. An effective Q&A gives the media a shortcut to the quotable material that they will use in their news stories.

THE CRISIS Q&A VERSUS FAQ, OR FREQUENTLY ASKED QUESTIONS

Communicators are expected to have strong writing and research skills and an ability to organize information, develop key messages and create strategies. In addition, communicators also have a most valuable role to play in being able to take a big step back and ask, "What will the public, the stakeholders, and the media ask about this issue?"

This is how communicators approach the Q&A, which on the company website may appear in the form of an FAQ, or frequently asked questions. During a crisis, a public-access Q&A (one that is sent to the media and stakeholders and posted on the website) may look different from a standard, day-to-day Q&A, the kind that spells out details of the company's products or initiatives. The crisis Q&A will be clearly headlined as pertaining specifically to the crisis: "An update on XYZ Corporation's actions in response to flooding at its Moose Jaw, Saskatchewan, plant," for example. The title will make it clear that the Q&A is dealing specifically with the crisis issue at hand.

GENERATING THE Q&A

In its initial form, the Q&A is an internal document and may be shared only by people within the organization, to prepare them for the questions to come. Communicators may also create a document that can be issued along with the news release, capturing anticipated questions from the public or the media.

The Q&A undergoes a rigorous approvals process precisely because it is designed for use during a crisis, a period in which any misstep can aggravate harm to a company's reputation. Communicators' research in creating an effective Q&A should begin long before a crisis hits. They may think of a crisis scenario and then begin gathering information that forms the basis for answering the "what ifs" that would flow from it. This creates a template that they can file and have on hand. Up-to-date company information, key messages that are already pre-approved, and boilerplate data (stock historical information about the company that has already been researched and approved) is necessary. Then, when the crisis hits, they can go to work generating a Q&A that explains the five Ws and clearly spells out for their publics the actions the company is taking to resolve the crisis.

> In creating a Q&A, no question is too outrageous or too touchy to consider. Communicators must be prepared to be asked — and to answer — the difficult questions that may come.

THE PLACE OF EMOTIONS IN THE MESSAGES

The five-Ws approach is valuable not only because it's a practical way of getting all the important issues dealt with on record. Focusing on the tough questions can and should be seen as a way of focusing on the emotional aspects of the crisis for all of the company's publics. It also brings information across in a way that tells stakeholders and the public that those in the company are human too. This is what any reasonable person will expect — that an organization is not just a soulless entity but is staffed with caring individuals who can relate to others during a crisis. The Q&A's emotional tone tells the company's publics that it is acknowledging the human element in any crisis — whether it's hurricane survivors struggling to make it to the next day or computer technicians who make a mistake during a system upgrade and foul up the accounts of thousands of bank clients.

Communicators can't simply say after a devastating blast at their manufacturing plant, "The loss of several lives was unfortunate." Many people still remember the anger directed at the U.S. government when it tried to call the deaths of American soldiers acceptable "collateral losses."

Avoid the "Fashion Show" and the "Grocery List" Approaches

When communicators write material and then move it through the approval process, they must steer clear of presenting a "fashion show" or succumbing to a "grocery list" for clients or bosses who will review and approve the material. This holds true whether clients are external (they have hired the communicators to handle the communications role) or internal (the communicators are working within a hierarchical organization and their approvals list includes managers, directors and vice-presidents).

The Fashion Show

A "fashion show" is a demonstration of a number of approaches to a communications document. It occurs when a client or senior manager says, "Just give me a few samples to review. I'll decide which one I like." The fashion show is the result of unfocused thinking or of a client or boss who doesn't really know what he or she wants or needs. It can result in the creation of products that deviate far from the original intent of the one communicators are trying to create. It can also mean frustration for the communicators — particularly if they are dealing with a crisis that needs to be addressed quickly.

When communicators sit down with external clients or with senior personnel in the organization, they must have them spell out what they expect the piece to say. Senior staff may need help developing a reasonably strong sense of who their publics are and what needs to be said to effectively address the issue. Communicators must get them thinking about their key messages and how those key messages loop back into the original goal of the written material — and how the key messages will address the crisis.

The Grocery List

The "grocery list" approach can be summed up as: "I want this, and this and this . . . and this too, because *they are all important. You just can't leave anything out.*" That is, external clients or senior staff lay out a long list of information and messages that they want crammed into a communications piece. In dealing with this approach, communicators need to remind their client of the need to stay focused on the topic. Grocery listing leads to cumbersome, muddled, heavy text that will confuse the company's publics. If more detail is needed than what is provided in the Q&A, it can be supplemented with other documents, such as a one-page release followed by a bullet-point backgrounder. The company as well as its publics will be much better served if the Q&A stays focused on messages that the company *needs* to present.

Communicators must prepare their spokespeople before they talk to the media and stakeholders. Let's look at an example of the Royal Bank of Canada crisis discussed in Chapter 2. Here are some of the questions communicators working for RBC might expect to be asked, along with some possible answers. Notice the focus on the five Ws. These form the core of the Q&A, approaching the topic in the same no-nonsense, who-what-when-where-why (and how) manner the media and the general public will.

Q. *What happened with the computer system?*
A. The bank was implementing a computer upgrade and what should have been a routine programming upgrade did not work. Incorrect keystrokes as well as a failure on our part to conduct quality-assurance tests led to the problem. As a result, transactions that were made on May 31 and June 1 were not reflected in our clients' account balances. We recognize the consternation this caused our clients and we are focused on correcting each transaction manually.

Here it is important for the bank to be upfront about the problem. The bank explained exactly what happened and says that the bank was concerned about the effect of the problem on its clients and that it was working to get the problem fixed. The bank acknowledged the crisis and promised that action was being taken.

Q. *How many customers were affected?*
A. Approximately 2.5 million customers were affected.

The bank would not shy away from the hard numbers. It would be direct and honest with customers and with the media.

Q. *Why wasn't this glitch caught and corrected early on?*
A. We caught the glitch early on and expected that it would be fixed by the end of the business day. However, the challenge of fixing each account manually created further problems. We are providing updates on our website and customers may contact our customer service employees for an explanation of why the problem occurred and how we are working through it. We appreciate the fact that clients are not seeing their accounts updated; however, at the same time it's essential that our customers know that their bank accounts are not threatened. Their money is safe.

Again, the bank is direct and open, admitting to the fact that there were expectations that were not met. However, the spokesperson would also follow with information designed to ensure that the information flow was continuous, with website updates. As well, an important message was delivered: clients' money was still safe.

Q. *When will the problem be fixed?*
A. The problem is being worked on now by our IT service team. We expect it to be fixed in the next several days, but it should be understood that service delivery will continue, as always. Our commitment to our customers remains unchanged. It's also essential for our customers to know that their money is safe and that we are working to get the system back in order. We have issued a news release outlining the steps we are taking and information is also available through our customer service representatives, on the bank's website and in person at any bank branch.

Here, there is a promise that action is being taken and that service is continuing. The answer also repeats the message that information is being rapidly updated and provided to the public and the media.

Q. *What kind of compensation, if any, is the bank offering customers?*
A. First of all, we are ensuring that money is available to clients affected by this situation. To accommodate our clients, we are extending hours at many of our bank branches. We are also making a commitment to refund banking service charges, fees, overdraft interest or associated past due fees that may have been incurred due to the disruption. If RBC clients see that a charge has not been reversed, we encourage them to bring it to our attention.

The bank is making a commitment that it will follow through on: clients can still get money by visiting a bank branch and will have service charges refunded automatically. (The bank would later offer a "Make It Right" program to handle other claims.) The bank put people first – an essential ingredient in handling a crisis.

Q. *Is this the first time this has happened at RBC?*
A. We have had minor accounting problems in the past — many large institutions have experienced problems with their computer systems — but a number of factors, all human factors, lay behind the problem. We have

worked to isolate the reasons for the problem and have taken action to ensure that this will not happen again. At the same time, we are confident in the technology that we use and are certain that this problem will be solved to our customers' satisfaction, to whom we owe our thanks for their patience and understanding. We value our customers and are taking the time necessary to ensure that this issue is tackled and dealt with effectively.

The bank is acknowledging that this isn't an isolated problem and that problems sometimes occur in large and complicated computerized accounting systems. The bank is also acknowledging the inconvenience this problem caused for its customers, creating an emotional link to this stakeholder group, one that focuses on a common ground – a shared challenge that both parties have to face, with the bank taking full responsibility.

Q. *Why didn't the company's protocols work?*
A. There were several factors that combined to create this problem. If we had implemented the upgrade on a Friday instead of a Monday we might have been able to correct it over the weekend, a less busy time for the bank. There were also issues around the failure of quality assurance tests. Fortunately, and most importantly, we were able to keep our customers' accounts safe and have been able to fix the problem, taking a step-by-step approach that may be time-consuming but is essential to protecting our clients' accounts. Frankly, this has also been a learning experience — as a result, we are implementing more effective checks and balances on system upgrades for the future to ensure that this problem doesn't happen again.

The bank is demonstrating that it is taking ownership of the problem, has been active in finding a solution and has made a promise that it is delivering on.

Q. *Why were senior staff members not available immediately after the crisis hit?*
A. We had senior staff on hand during the crisis. Our CEO was out of the country at the time that this issue arose, but this did not affect the bank's ability to immediately take action to correct the errors that were made. At all times, our customers' accounts were safe, information and updates were readily available and we worked to ensure that we would return to regular service as soon as possible.

The bank is not deflecting the question, merely indicating that, even if the CEO was out of the country, proactive steps were being taken to tackle the crisis. It demonstrated a commitment to being a responsible and proactive business, ensuring the security of its clients' assets.

Q. *Who are some of the clients that were affected?*
A. Affected clients ranged from large corporations to retired persons, office workers and tradespeople to small business owners and doctors — all valued clients who deserve the best customer service possible. We are pleased that even during this challenging time, we are able to continue to deliver quality customer service. It's a promise that will continue after this issue is resolved.

Again, the bank talks about putting people first and ensuring that it will live up to its promise of maintaining its overarching commitment to serving its customers.

Media Interviews

In a media interview or news conference during a crisis, it's essential to be prepared, to be an active listener, to be ahead of the reporters' questions. Basic professional practices are more important than ever, but there are additional techniques communicators must be aware of when dealing with media during a high-stakes and high-pressure situation. A communicator uses the same approach to interviews as he or she does in generating the questions used in a Q&A: anticipating all the questions using briefing notes, and doing a fresh analysis of the specifics of the crisis.

BEST PRACTICES FOR INTERVIEWS

Professionalism and respect for the audience. It is essential for communicators to apply the golden rule to their dealings with their publics, to "treat others as you would want them to treat you." Nothing goes over worse with an audience than telegraphing a condescending or patronizing attitude, avoiding their questions or trying to dodge their inquiries. Communicators need to show the same respect they would expect were the roles reversed.

Be open, listen and act. Communicators must be candid with reporters and be themselves. Reporters know that all people make mistakes and that communicators may not have an answer for every question. But if you make a commitment to get an answer, make a note of it and follow up.

Never lose your cool. Most journalists don't, but some do take a certain pleasure in making people squirm, fidget or lose their cool. Losing your composure may suggest that you are hiding information. Try to remaining professional and calm no matter what the question.

Be ready. Ensure that you have researched your answers and are ready to go before the media. Never speculate, guess at an answer or speak off the record.

Be accommodating. Understand if a reporter is late or must postpone an interview. Arrange to speak with the reporter at another time. Communicators should treat the interview as a vital connection and take responsibility for ensuring it is rescheduled.

Effective communication. Being an effective communicator means providing answers in language that people understand and in a way that is simple, concise and to the point. Long drawn-out explanations will serve only to demonstrate that the communicator doesn't have a grasp on what is being asked, or it may suggest that he or she is trying to avoid providing an answer. Communicators must listen actively to their questioners and recognize the need to frame their answers in a way that responds directly to the questions.

Be quotable. This means being focused enough on the subject to speak in good, strong sound bites that encompass the key messages you expect to see in the news story. Construct short sentences in plain language (see below), using the active voice. These short sentences will get your message into the media, clearly and without confusion.

Use plain language. Don't use language that sends reporters, your colleagues or others to the dictionary. Find simple, clear and concise language to explain your organization's position.

Learn to use effective body language. Too many times we see spokespeople who come across as fidgety, bored, aggressive or uncertain — even if the words they use are precise and correct. Experts say that up to 80 per cent of communication is non-verbal. According to research by the U.S. Army, people only remember about 7 per cent of what a communicator says — crisis or no crisis. As such, the impact of statements will often be carried by non-verbal communication, your body language — everything from smiling and your standing or sitting position to affectations such as chin stroking and hand gestures. A number of books have been published specifically on the subject of "tells," or minor physical actions or inactions that reveal truths about the speaker, from the speaker's honesty and comfort to his or her interest level in the conversation. While it may not be necessary for communicators to exhaustively study body language, they need to recognize that it is an important factor in delivering a message. Efforts to understand and put conscious effort into using your deportment to enhance your connection with your audience will pay rich dividends.

When talking face to face with the media or being interviewed on camera, be natural and confident but not arrogant or aggressive. Speak clearly and stand straight, even during a radio interview (it's amazing how posture affects the sound of your voice). Practise using your hands to accent your points. Spokespersons without public-speaking training should practise in front of a small audience that is supportive but still critical enough to point out flaws in their speaking and provide feedback on how their body language works or fails to help them build rapport.

Be an active listener. Don't treat questions as prompts for one of your prepared answers. Instead, interpret them in terms of what they mean to the overall direction of the news conference and what they mean to your organization. Communicators need to think on their feet and be able to respond to the meaning or subtleties of reporters' statements or questions in a way that demonstrates they care about what is being asked, and what way it is being asked.

Put the human dimension of the crisis first. Don't become a talking head. Media (and the public they serve) appreciate a sense of humanity in the way an organization approaches a very real, human issue. Statements focusing on the human element include:

- "We feel very badly about the injuries to our workers and we are doing all we can for them right now";
- "Ensuring the safety of people in our organization is our number one priority";

- "Our organization is committed to responding to this crisis quickly and efficiently and we are doing so."

Know the media outlet, the audience and the interviewer. Know what position the media outlet that is going to interview you takes toward your organization: hostile, friendly, neutral? Also know something of the audience of the media outlet, whether news show, magazine or newspaper: Does that particular media outlet appeal to a particular demographic or political stripe? Are its listeners, readers or viewers university students, stay-at-home parents, tradespeople, white-collar workers, business executives, conservationists? You may find that some of your messaging appeals to a particular audience and not to others — modify the messaging to suit a particular demographic as needed.

If it's a television or radio show that's interviewing you, consider phoning the show's producer and asking for general details — who will do the interview, what kinds of questions will be asked, how much time will be allotted for the interview? Take a look at the media outlet's website and put a face to a name (talk show hosts often have their pictures posted on the website); this will give you a certain comfort level when you meet the interviewer. Read what the show says about itself on the website and, if there is time, watch or listen to it, to get a sense of its overall theme and direction.

Anticipate the questions and know the answers. Write down anticipated questions and then develop key messages that reflect an understanding of those questions. Again, use language that is simple, direct and colourful — language with impact.

Focus on the goals. Good communicators will be prepared before going into a news conference or interview, knowing well their key messages, and with the ability to respond to all questions. Communicators should not be afraid to say they don't have an answer to a question, but they must be able to commit to finding an answer and getting back to the reporter later.

Know your key messages. You don't have to memorize them, just be able to explain them and use them to elaborate on the organization's position.

Bring difficult questions back to the key messages. Acknowledge the reporter's question and be prepared to answer it, even if this means indicating that you don't have an answer at that time. If you don't have the answer, offer to get an answer. Never leave a questioned unanswered, and don't reply with a simple yes or no. Be natural but bring the question back to your key messages: again, key messages should always form the core of what you are saying to reporters.

Compose yourself before answering a question. Be factual, proactive and brief, and keep your answers to about 15 to 30 seconds long. Stick to the information that you know and can deliver within the allotted time frame, whether the interview is 5, 10 or 15 minutes long. Don't worry about dead air and don't feel compelled to fill it. The interviewer's job is to keep the interview moving — the communicator's job is to represent the organization and answer questions. Avoid being drawn into speculating — your job is not to answer "what ifs"; it's to tell the audience what your organization is doing.

HANDLING DANGEROUS QUESTIONS

Hypothetical and speculative questions. As mentioned earlier, some reporters will ask a hypothetical "what if" question to get communicators to speculate on the outcome of the crisis or to find a weakness in the message being conveyed; this will move communicators off the path of their intended message. When handling questions about your company's position in a crisis, you are often under time constraints — you may have 20 minutes or a half hour to handle a news conference, or you may be limited to 5 minutes of radio or television time. That time is crucial in terms of getting the right messages out to your publics. Moving off track means that you are not able to spend time on the messages you want to deliver. You need to redirect discussion to the topics that you want to discuss. Speculation gets communicators into uncharted waters — and may result in them setting policies the company doesn't want or establishing directions that the company does not necessarily want to take. You might say to a speculative question: "That's a good question. I don't have an answer for that. But what I can tell you is this ..." and move to your key messages.

Speculative but fair or reasonable questions to which communicators don't have an immediate answer may also be dealt with by simply offering to get the reporter an answer later. If communicators make this promise, they need to call the reporter back with an answer. It is essential to never answer even wildly speculative or unfair questions with "no comment." A "no comment" is a non-answer, and although it may be true that the communicator has no comment or cannot comment on a particular question, it tends to make the communicator and the company appear evasive. It's better to be assertive but not confrontational — an approach that, with practice, communicators become comfortable using. It also presumes that the communicator is well informed and well prepared.

© Scott Adams/Dist. by United Feature Syndicate, Inc.

Assertive communicators listen actively — and politely — to reporters but also indicate firmly that they need to clarify the matter at hand, and while the reporter's questions might be interesting, the communicator is most concerned with ensuring that the media understand the facts clearly, rather than the potentials and "what ifs." For instance, a communicator representing a hospital in which an outbreak of virus occurs will want to deal with the issue of getting appropriate care for those immediately affected by the virus, protecting health care workers and safeguarding other patients and visitors. The communicator's job is not to speculate in response to questions such as, "What happens if the virus gets out of the hospital?"; it's to deal with the facts of the immediate situation, such as what measures are in place to contain the virus.

Most reporters will not belabour a point by asking the same question over and over again. They also have a deadline to work to, and not getting an answer to a speculative question means that by asking the same question again they are wasting their own time, too. Most reporters will simply move on to the next question.

A fine example of sticking to one's key messages in the face of speculative questions occurred in July 2006, when actor Mel Gibson was arrested for drunk driving in Los Angeles. Celebrities are often the target of speculation and rumour at the best of times; at the worst of times, they can create a feeding frenzy for reporters. And those connected with them are also subject to the same treatment. In this situation, Gibson allegedly spat out anti-Semitic slurs at the police officer arresting him. According to the media, the remarks were detailed in the arrest report, and they questioned whether the authorities covered up the fact that Gibson had made the comments; that is, there was no public disclosure of his remarks.

The Office of Independent Review, an arm's-length agency that monitors the Los Angeles County Sheriff's Department, initiated a review of the incident; Gibson issued an apology the next day, calling his comments during the arrest "out of control [and] despicable," according to the Associated Press. But media put their toughest questions to Los Angeles County sheriff Lee Baca, asking why there was a cover-up. "There is no cover-up," Lee told the *Los Angeles Times*. "Our job is not to [focus] on what he said. It's to establish his blood-alcohol level when he was driving and proceed with the case. Trying someone on rumour and innuendo is no way to run an investigation, at least one with integrity." Lee stuck to the right key message — "We did our job; let us continue to do it" — and refused to be drawn into the grey area of speculation.

Bridging. Bridging is a technique that communicators and spokespersons use to move from a question's starting point to the message they want to present and discuss. They avoid rising to the bait of the hypothetical question; instead, they create a bridge back to the key message by confronting the question in a direct manner and integrating it into the path back to the key message. Assuming that a reporter's question is moving the communicator from familiar to unfamiliar territory, a bridge brings the communicator back to safe territory. One way to bridge is to simply acknowledge the reporter's statement or question, clearly indicate that you do not agree with what is being said and state the reason why, and then move back to the key messages. Sheriff Lee Baca's comments about the arrest of Mel Gibson are a good example of this.

The sheriff was asked: "Did your office cover up Mel Gibson's comments?" The answer is direct but a bridge nonetheless: *"There was no cover up."* The sheriff then provides an explanation: *"Our job was not to [focus] on what he said."* That statement bridges Sheriff Baca back to the key message, which was that the police were supposed to *deal with Gibson's drunk driving charge,* not with what Gibson said during his arrest.

The sheriff is able to discount the reporter's question by working it into the response and finishing the statement with a strong comment that closes the issue: *"Trying someone on rumour and innuendo is no way to run an investigation ..."* Certainly, the rumour mill might continue to churn after the microphones are shut off, notepads are closed and the reporters leave the press conference, but the position of the Sheriff's Office is well established.

Let's consider an example, in this case a chemical spill at a manufacturing plant that has operated at the same location for 30 years, employing more than 500 workers. The key messages are —

1. No one was hurt;
2. The spill was contained and staff members were evacuated;
3. Safety precautions were taken;
4. Authorities were called and the spill was cleaned up;
5. A full investigation of the cause is underway.

The effective communicator opens the interview with a clear and concise statement that includes the company's major key message: "We are, first and foremost, pleased to report that no one was hurt."

REPORTER: *What happened?*
COMMUNICATOR: We had a chemical spill in our manufacturing area. No one was hurt and all staff members were evacuated. Safety precautions were taken and the spill was cleaned up.

REPORTER: *What if someone had been hurt? Couldn't dangerous, toxic gases formed by the chemicals have killed somebody?*
COMMUNICATOR: Let me be clear. No one was hurt. And the chemicals in question did not form any gases whatsoever.

This is the bridge. Note that the communicator does not repeat the reporter's inflammatory words *dangerous* and *toxic*. Instead, he or she takes part of what the reporter said and uses it to defuse the question and move on to what the communicator wants to say.

An ineffective bridge would reinforce the perception of the dangerous nature of the chemicals in the plant ("Yes, our chemicals are dangerous and toxic, but we do take safety precautions with them"). Such a bridge could lead to more questions that turn the interview into a discussion of the dangers inherent in the plant, leading to questions such as, "So how dangerous *are* the chemicals?" Whether the chemicals are dangerous or not, the communicator is not there to talk about toxicity — he or she is there to talk about the action the company took, and its success in resolving the matter. An effective bridge deals with the concerns expressed but doesn't dwell on them.

COMMUNICATOR: Again, no one was hurt, and this was because of our safety procedures. We contacted the local police and fire departments as well as the Ministry of Labour and the Ministry of the Environment immediately. This is part of our overall safety program. It's a precautionary procedure that is followed by all members of our manufacturing team. We acted quickly and decisively to contain the spill and get it cleaned up.

The communicator (or company spokesperson) doesn't even have to acknowledge that human error was obviously involved: it is understood that the accident happened as a result of human error. If someone asks, "What caused the spill?" the communicator can respond with, "It was the result of human error." He or she can then move to a discussion of safety and the fact that the spill was contained and cleaned up.

REPORTER: *Isn't this a dangerous place to have a business, though? Aren't there a lot of people in the vicinity who could have been hurt?*

COMMUNICATOR: *No. In fact, it is a good place to be in business. We have a very strong safety record. Our operations are in line with federal and provincial safety standards, and the plant is regularly inspected. We also host regular media tours to demonstrate the safety and efficiency of our operations. And it's important to note that for 30 years we have been good corporate citizens. We are active members of the business community and the community at large, making a significant contribution to the health and economic well-being of this city, through job creation, sponsorship of local events and support for many festivals and charities.*

The reporter's question provides an opportunity for the communicator to mention the company's activities, its key products and markets, and investments that have been made in the company's operations that will benefit not just the company but the community. It gives the communicator a chance to talk about the company as a member of the community, building rapport and putting a human face on the company's operations. It moves the focus away from the potential view of the company as a dangerous place and instead creates an image of the company as a sound place of business and a contributor to the community. But communicators don't want to make their talk all "sunshine and smiles" by ignoring the reason the media contacted them in the first place.

False facts/assumptions/unsubstantiated information. Still working with the example of the chemical spill, if the reporter says, "I understand the Ministry of the Environment will be issuing a fine to your company for this accident?" he or she is testing to see if the communicator will bite at a question for which there is little or no basis. Here too, the hope is that the communicator will speculate or offer information not previously delivered. Reporters like a scoop and will sometimes toss out a line to see if a spokesperson surrenders a speculative answer.

The answer to such a question or ploy should make clear, *without repeating the information the reporter posed*, what the company is doing. If the communicator repeats the information, it may appear in the news story. Instead, the answer should be decisive: "That's incorrect. The Ministry of Labour and the Ministry of the Environment have sent a team to inspect our facility, and we are working with that ministry to investigate this accident. This is standard procedure. We are providing as much information as possible about the situation and will continue to work closely with government officials through the course of the investigation." The communicator emphasizes that the company is working *with* established authorities to control the situation.

Leading question. A question, often in the form of an accusation, that tries to lead the communicator to a speculative answer is called a "leading question." Here's an example: "Last year, your company president was quoted as saying that the company was going to implement new safety procedures. Are you telling us that you still haven't got a safety procedure in place?" Such questions often come out of the blue and usually refer to an authority figure, in this case the company president. But what if that president is no longer with the company or is not at the news conference or interview? As mentioned earlier, reporters want to get the scoop on their rivals; if they can make a communicator stumble or can create a sense of anxiety as the communicator fumbles for the right answer, they may be able to draw out information that can be used as an effective hook for their story. This tactic has value for them in that it can make the story appear more exciting: "Chemical spill dangers a concern: company lacks safety procedures." It also takes the story in a direction the company may not want it to go.

The worst thing communicators could do is play into the reporter's hands by responding: "Really? Our president said that?" and so appear unaware of company procedures. Instead, they have to stick to the key messages. They acknowledge the situation, be clear and concise, and talk about the company's safety plans. This shifts the emphasis back to what the communicator wants to say, rather than giving the reporter what he or she wants to hear: "We have a very strong and comprehensive safety program in place, one that is certified in accordance with federal and provincial safety regulations. Human error is a part of life, but the fact is that after the spill we were able to employ our safety training procedures, evacuating the plant with no injuries and implementing the cleanup in a matter of minutes. This demonstrates the strength of our safety program."[1]

Conclusion

In the documentary *The Fog of War,* former U.S. secretary of Defense Robert S. McNamara (who also served as president of Ford Motor Co. and president of the World Bank) spoke of his experience as a major corporate leader as well as an advisor to and confidant of American presidents. He said that when answering questions posed by the media, one shouldn't look to answer the question that *has been asked* but, rather, focus on answering the question that *one would have wanted to hear.*[2] In other words, communicators are looking to answer the question that they can answer fully and completely — the one that fits their agenda — even if it hasn't been posed.

Bafflegab? No. McNamara's point is not that one should obscure the truth but that, in telling the truth, communicators are still serving their company and must always be seeking to put its key messages first.

But let's think about how this may or may not work for an organization. How long will such a tactic work in front of determined media or knowledgeable stakeholders? Unless the communicator has complete control over the media session and can cut off discussion (it may be argued that high-ranking corporate or political officials can control the news conference, essentially being able to turn off the flow of questions), the strategy will likely have a brief shelf life. McNamara's principle that communicators need to stay focused on the key messages is one they should rely on: it doesn't do a communicator any good to not handle questions in a direct way. With the number of fast fact-finding outlets available to reporters, it doesn't take them much legwork to establish an approach to a story that may seem far-fetched to a communicator but makes sense to them, and the range of questions they may pose is nearly limitless. The communicator's job, then, is to be mindful of what may be around the corner, do the necessary homework, answer questions truthfully and be aware of the need to stay focused on the company's overall direction. The communicator needs to go "outside" and see the organization the way others view it, and to use the knowledge gained in doing so to assist in creating effective messaging and an appropriate direction for the organization.

11

Tools IV
Creating Dialogues and Gathering Information: Websites and Blogs

Information gathering and exchange is a communicator's business. During a crisis, this business is magnified and intensified. In this chapter we look at how communicators must accomplish these tasks in two online arenas: first, the website, home turf for the company; and second, blogs, a no man's land of public opinion that offers both risks and opportunities to the savvy communicator during a crisis.

Two Tools for Opening a Dialogue with Publics

A company website is a controlled medium and thus inherently friendly. It is a primary point of contact with a communicator's publics — and is at least as important as the communicator's office. A website will receive many more hits during a crisis than a communicator will phone calls, and also may be used far more frequently than the customer service department by members of various publics. A website has the advantage over other channels of communication (such as advertising, media and letters) in that it is relatively inexpensive and can be quickly customized, updated and restructured to meet the emerging needs of communicators and publics during a crisis. And, unlike other media channels, the company website is conducive to carrying all key messages in *exactly the intended way*, with all necessary supporting information. Finally, it can be set up to allow two-way communication in numerous ways, from the high interactivity of an email address for queries to less interactive options, such as forms with preset fields into which people may sort their concerns or comments, or questionnaires with only a multiple-choice format for feedback.

As a means of communicating, blogs are not nearly as safe or predictable as websites — communicators control the information they post on a website; they don't know what might show up on a blog. Blogs are an online forum, maintained by the company's website administrator, in which members of the various publics can join debates on issues that may concern the company, either before or during a crisis.

The advantage of blogs is their element of two-way communication: communicators will know immediately how their communications are being received by a large community of stakeholders, and by the general public. This knowledge can give communicators and executives a heads-up on how the community is thinking and can help generate ideas for effective approaches to the crisis as it evolves. The risk of participating in a blog during a crisis is that well-meaning communicators may add fuel to the fire of the debate, especially if they have misjudged their publics' points of view or sentiments on the issue. Communicators may have to think on the fly, quickly preparing or vetting messages for spokespeople. But blogs can enable a company to establish a friendly, receptive and extremely interactive face for several publics. Further, a free public forum has the strategic and tactical advantage of allowing members of a company's publics to tell all members of the blog community exactly how they feel. This information channel thus allows for a multitude of voices and concerns to be expressed, unlike the media outlet, which speaks with a single voice. The downside of this channel is the energy that must go into sifting through the posts and determining which messages are important.

In this chapter, we examine the following tasks:

- Using websites to best advantage in crisis;
- Streamlining information flow into website channels;
- Monitoring blogs during a crisis, from outbreak to resolution;
- Setting communications goals for blogging.

The Website

The website is an essential communications tool for updating both internal and external stakeholders. As much as people once turned on their radios for immediate details of a crisis and then turned on their television sets to 24-7 news channels, they now rely increasingly on the Internet for information.

Just how busy is the Internet? By early 2005, the archive site Google Groups had recorded an estimated 845 million messages posted to news or discussion groups. Estimates from other sources put the number of Internet users at 900 million; according to a survey by Internet group Netcraft, there were almost 65 million websites as of June 2005.

Websites have a dual function as a communications vehicle:

1. They present an organization's messages to all publics, incorporating all the advantages of both hot and cool media within an environment the organization controls;
2. They can create a channel of communication from the various publics to the organization — a channel that can be constrained in any way the communicators choose.

The website, when fully exploited as a communications tool, is a powerful means of communicating during a crisis. It allows for rapid publication of key messages, news releases, Q&As, and backgrounders and it provides an effective and customizable conduit for feedback from publics.

THE ELECTRONIC AGE: STAKEHOLDERS, THE GENERAL PUBLIC AND THE INTERNET

Mitchell Kapor, founder of Lotus Development Corporation, once said that "getting information off the Internet is like taking a drink from a fire hydrant" — lots of information (too much sometimes), and instead of slaking one's thirst, it can threaten a web surfer with a pretty quick drowning. And yet, organizations' publics are learning to turn down the fire hydrant tap, reducing that flood of information to a useable stream or trickle. It's also understood that stakeholders and the general public are used to instant information on demand. This means that when a crisis hits, teams must communicate quickly. The speed at which communicators deliver correct information is vital: it is essential to give stakeholders and the general public the company's version of the unfolding crisis before the media hear of it and stirs a panic. Today, reaction and response can often be measured in hours, minutes, or even seconds; stakeholders and the general public can see change happening not at the speed of the morning newspaper hitting their doorsteps the day after a crisis, but 10, 15 or 20 minutes after the crisis hits. In March 2005, when a man set himself on fire in a van outside the Ontario Legislature, people could watch a streamed video of the event — the man screaming and pouring gasoline on himself, and police and firefighters smashing the van's side windows, rolling him out and beating out the flames — on the website of 24-hour local news channel CP24, operated by Toronto's City TV, a mere 20 to 30 minutes after the event happened. This quick coverage enabled people to form, alter and embellish their opinions about the police officers, firefighters and emergency medical workers on the scene: Did they do a good job? Were they fast and efficient in their response? Did emergency medical personnel respond quickly enough?

If a crisis hits an organization, chances are that the communicators will find themselves dealing with instant coverage too — and the instant judgment that foments so quickly in whatever cool media is fastest in reaching the public. (Hot and cool media are discussed in Chapter 7.) Websites allow communicators to get their company's position out to its publics quickly, as today many people go first to a website for news. The website gives the company a crucial first point of contact that establishes a comfort zone for its publics and sets the stage for whatever information comes out of the organization afterward. Even in the face of negative news, the company can let its publics know where it stands, what it has done to deal with the crisis and what it is planning to do in the immediate future to resolve the issue. The media will also go to the website for information; good, strong quotes, as well as an explanation of the company's actions, will form the basis of many fact-driven news stories, helping dispel speculative media stories or rumour-driven articles.

PRIORITIZING THE COMPANY WEBSITE

It's important for communicators who manage websites to recognize that information gets stale fast. There are so many sources of constantly updated information, and web surfers looking for the most current information will jump from site to site to get it. If the most current information available is found somewhere other than the company's website, especially during a crisis, it suggests to the company's publics that others, rather than the company itself, are the most authoritative source of information about the crisis. This will certainly create an information gap with a company's publics that will give the impression that the company is not being proactive; at the extreme end, it could take the form of mistrust, contempt or suspicion of an attempt at spin or outright cover-up. And yet, for several years, especially in the early 1990s when websites were just starting to be recognized as an important tool, organizations threw scant resources at website creation and maintenance. Organizations often hired summer students as the webmasters, their job being to update standard corporate information that frequently remained unchanged for a year or longer. Clearly, this is now inadequate for the information needs of most organizations' publics during normal operations; during a crisis, the website must be a priority.

In addition to information gathering and exchange, a communicator often serves as a customer service representative for the organization. To that end, keeping people up-to-date with the latest information is an important part of their job. Only since the late 1990s have organizations begun to take their websites seriously, not only keeping track of quantifiable data such as number of visits to the site, but also examining the quality of the communications process — looking seriously at *what people want* and what they need, and responding in kind. Communicators are recognizing that with increased Internet use, the website is a valued resource for up-to-the-minute information, especially during a crisis. As soon as a new element is added during a crisis — a plant shutdown ends, normal business resumes, a product recall is successful, the organization has achieved a particular milestone in its crisis resolution — this information should be passed along to its publics via the company website.

Remember that the news release, plus appropriate backgrounders, fact sheets and FAQs, should be posted to the company's website, with new material added when necessary. These materials will give visitors — media, stakeholders and the general public — an immediate and clear picture of what the organization is doing.

In most cases, a website demands constant attention to serve the organization well even during normal periods; in a crisis, constant updates are essential, and numerous updates during a crisis are a strong sign of a company taking control and staying focused on solutions and on its publics. Indeed, stakeholders and members of the general public are likely to call or send letters in large numbers demanding website updates if they're not finding them. For this reason, the company's web team *must* be part of the crisis communications team, and they must be prepared to create new web pages and update existing ones rapidly as the crisis evolves.

Case Study:
Man Found Dead on Centennial College Campus

In January 2004, Toronto's Centennial College experienced a crisis when a man was found shot dead in a car at the daycare centre of its main campus in Scarborough, a geographically large community in the city's east end. In its January 9, 2004, edition, the *Toronto Star* ran the headline: "Man, 26, found shot dead in car at college residence." While Centennial College officials were quick to assure the public that neither the victim nor the shooter, who had fled the scene, were in any way connected to the college (this based on information from the police), the college became the focus of concern within the community.

The Scarborough campus, like that of many post-secondary institutes, is large, with many pathways and treed areas — pleasant and safe during the day but presenting opportunities for crime at night. In addition, the Scarborough community had long been a subject of concerns about street and gang-related crime. College officials, therefore, had the daunting task of reassuring students that their school was still a safe place and that the college was taking action toward that end.

College officials came forward with a statement outlining the college's position: that it was working with the police and taking steps to ensure the continued safety of its students. Much of the information provided to the public was done through the college's website: it posted the most current information available in a news release and statement. The website outlined security measures already in place, such as a door-to-car escort service available to students who attended night classes or stayed late on campus. The college also sent a letter via email to all internal stakeholders (students and staff) and held information sessions for the public, bringing together members of the community to talk about their concerns over violence in the community and safety at the Centennial campus. The public information sessions were advertised on the website as well as through the media. The result was that the college turned a crisis into an opportunity for getting out a message that it supported safety in the community.[1]

Case Study:
Dawson College's 2006 Shooting

Centennial College's approach was mirrored by Montreal's Dawson College in the fall of 2006. Dawson College established a linked section to its regular website after a September 13, 2006, incident in which a gunman entered the college and began randomly shooting at students, resulting in several injuries and the death of student Anastasia De Sousa. In the weeks following that shooting, the college established "A Time to Heal," a section on its website featuring information on counselling; a message from the college's head, director general Richard Filion; an FAQ and a feedback page. All the information proved effective in allowing students an opportunity to grieve, share their feelings and gain support as they came to terms with the shooting.

The website bolstered a strong corporate communications approach that included making the school's top administrators available on the evening of the tragedy and the two days following the shooting, to consult with the media and students. The shooting took place on a Wednesday; by that Friday, September 15, employees returned to the school. The following Monday, September 18, the school reopened to students. In addition to having the director general on hand to welcome students, psychiatrists, psychologists, therapists and grief counsellors were available on-site to both staff and students. A media event was created around the re-entry of students to the college, yet the focus for the college remained on ensuring that students' needs were met as they coped with the tragedy. A week later, a non-denominational healing ceremony was held at a downtown Montreal church. All these activities were underscored by comprehensive information that was regularly updated on the college's website.[2]

ADVANTAGES OF WEBSITE COMMUNICATIONS DURING A CRISIS

By now it's clear that websites offer communicators distinct advantages over other forms of communication during a crisis: instant access and readily available information, and an ability to control the content that is placed on the website.

Compartmentalized information. Communicators can package information specifically for or even limit access to specific audiences: clients, customers, business partners, suppliers, the media and the general public. (Most companies have an intranet site for employees, which cannot be accessed by people outside the organization.) Passwords allow access to any restricted pages the website may have.

Rich information and context. Communicators have the option to present in-depth information using both hot and cool media, including photographs and virtual tours of the crisis site. The website can offer details that answer the questions that reporters might ask. Chapter 9's discussion of

Natrel and its posting of a full toxicology report to its website is an example of a company providing as complete a picture as possible to its publics. A website helps provide a company's publics with context for the company's actions during a crisis — the company no longer becomes a beleaguered organization or a prevaricating corporate villain; instead, the website offers a chance for publics to see the company as an upstanding corporate citizen and a cornerstone of the community.

Twenty-four-hour-a-day information. A website allows communicators to update information at any time; they can provide breaking information as it happens, allowing them to set the pace for informing the public. This kind of control is an asset when dealing with media that also continually update their websites. By being first out the door, communicators become the source of the information, not just part of the news story.

Interactive information services. By setting up online communications that enable stakeholders to send the company their questions, concerns and opinions (e.g., via email or through web forums, often called bulletin boards, where interactivity is the focus and participants can post opinions on an issue), communicators can effectively gauge the reactions of stakeholders and the general public to the crisis, and to the steps the company is taking to resolve it. In the examples of the Centennial College incident and the Dawson College shooting, the interactive information services provided by the colleges gave website users a sense of greater accessibility to the schools about the crises. This served to offer the communities an opportunity to better understand the colleges' positions and the steps being taken to handle the heightened anxiety.

PRESENTING CRISIS UPDATES ON THE WEBSITE

Whether or not the company is in a crisis, the homepage of its website should be business as usual. However, there should be an easily accessible and well-marked link to information on the crisis, perhaps under the header "Update"; for example: "Update on XYZ Corporation's product recall." Contact information for the person or department that the various publics should contact with questions or concerns about the crisis can be provided at this linked web page.

CRISIS SCENARIOS AND WEB COMMUNICATIONS

There are several situations for which communicators can effectively use the company website to gain stakeholder support and bring its publics into the information loop.

Natural disasters. During earthquakes, hurricanes or floods, websites can provide stakeholders with links to emergency service sites. Provide information on the status of the organization and what steps are being taken during the natural disaster. Offer stakeholders and the general public an opportunity to post messages to the company, particularly if they work at the company or have friends or relatives who work there and the organization is caught in the middle of the disaster.

Human resources issues (such as labour relations). Websites can be used to provide updates on the status of labour relations discussions, strikes, arbitration, and so on.

Criminal activity. Anything from a reputation-damaging white-collar crime, an allegation of negligence, an act of terrorism, or a theft of material from the company's plant may cause a crisis for a company. Communicators may offer concerned stakeholders a chance to get answers to their questions as they try to deal with the information overload that often accompanies the reporting of criminal activity relating to an organization. It can also give stakeholders a heightened comfort level through the provision of updates on the steps the company is taking to deal with the immediate threat.

Consumer product recall. Some companies post a web page on which all customer service complaints can be logged about a recalled product. The page can be set up so that an automatic-response email is immediately sent back to the visitor making the complaint with an update on the status of the product.

Media link. For any crisis, information tailored to journalists who are crafting stories for the company's other publics can be offered specifically to the media. The latest news release can be immediately posted. The media link might be titled simply: "Media information on XYZ Corporation's product recall." On this web page, the contact details for the person or department providing information about the crisis to the media and media relations will be different from that on the homepage; that is, visitors to the homepage might be asked to contact a customer service representative with their questions.

Dark Sites

Since media often gather information and write a story, particularly in the early stages of the crisis, strictly from the information they glean from a company's website, communicators might consider creating a company dark site (also called a "stealth site"). A dark site is a website that is ready to launch as soon as — and *only* once — a crisis hits. Dark sites are designed to handle very high volumes of traffic without crashing.

The dark site carries prepackaged key messages targeting specific scenarios that have been identified by the organization. A mining company, for instance, will have messaging on what action is being taken after a mining disaster. They are web-based workups of briefing notes or crisis plans, ready to be rapidly revised to address the specifics of the crisis that presents itself.

Dark sites are being lauded by media-training companies as tools that assist in getting the jump on response times in a crisis. They are designed to shorten the time lag in gathering information and getting a response out the door that is often filled by negative media stories or a perception that the organization handling the crisis is trying to hide the truth. The dark site provides members of the crisis team instant access to the facts that have been gathered ahead of time and provides the same set of key messages to everyone responsible for handling media inquiries. As well, accessibility to the news media means that the organization's comments and position are on the public record very soon after a crisis erupts.

Dark sites work very well, as long as the information they contain is accurate and the scenarios they are designed to address correspond to the ones that actually occur. A dark site should never be launched by panicky communicators who, under pressure to provide key messages or a plan of action quickly, may misjudge how applicable the site is to the specific crisis.

TIPS FOR PREPARING DARK SITES

Here are eight points communicators must keep in mind when creating a dark site:

1. Identify any and all issues that may turn into crises for the company.
2. Use briefing notes or a crisis plan to create a separate site for each crisis. Each dark site should be a separate site that will be linked to the home page of the company website. Each dark site shares duplicate information; for example, background information and company history.
3. Ensure that essential information pertaining to the particular crisis the dark site addresses is as complete as possible, to eliminate the need for excessive revision when a crisis breaks.
4. Ensure that company information relating to its activities in managing and bringing closure to the crisis is as accurate and up-to-date as possible.
5. Include contact names and phone numbers for the key contacts within the organization, including spokespeople and public information providers during the crisis.
6. Clearly identify the crisis. (This identification will be modified accordingly before the dark site is launched as a link to the company website.)
7. Clearly outline the steps being taken to resolve the crisis.
8. Have information links in place, including a feedback link for handling inquiries and comments from the company's customer base.[3]

Blogs

Like websites, blogs (a word derived from the term *web logs)* have been touted as an efficient means of communicating with stakeholders and members of the general public.

A blog is maintained by an organization's website administrator. Entries on the blog include a title, body copy (text), a permanent link to or URL (uniform resource locator) of that body copy, and a post date (the time and date the entry was posted). The blog entry often includes comments, categories or tags (short forms used to link together major topics) that the entry discusses, and links (called "trackbacks" or "pingbacks") that connect the entry to other sites that make reference to the posting. It's important for communicators to know, too, that blogs aren't strictly an in-house exercise: many Web-hosting companies provide tools for generating blogs, allowing external stakeholders and members of the general public to create a blog about any organization they wish.

In January 2005, *Forbes* magazine estimated that approximately 23,000 new blogs are created every day. In December 2005, the *Toronto Star* estimated that there are 20 million blogs on the Internet.[4]

Web log promoter CorporateBlogging.Info, an organization based in Malmö, Sweden, that offers information and advice to hundreds of organizations, as well as information on how to blog, notes that blogs are a great place to exchange ideas. Indeed they are. For an organization, corporate blogs can ensure a steady influx of public reaction to how the company is handling a crisis.

In the same way that communicators can use their company website to communicate with stakeholders and keep them updated, they can use a blog as a tool to provide two-way communication to stakeholders. A blog is often written by (or ghostwritten for) a company's senior executive — often the CEO or president of the organization. A blog is an exercise in directly positioning the company's senior executive team as a public persona that goes beyond the corporate — the blog is a personal, often heartfelt, journal.

But a caution is essential: a blog is not for the faint of heart. During a crisis, it is as likely that someone is lambasting the company for bad management as it is that someone is supportive of the company's actions. So before communicators suggest that senior executives start a blog, communicators must ask themselves how committed — and tough — they and their spokespeople are. Are they committed enough to log on every day, even during a crisis, to write their entries? Do they have the time to review the daily entry, if that entry is written for them? Are they up to speed on the company's latest developments and can they speak with authority on these issues? And are they tough enough to maintain that commitment when they're faced with angry bloggers who believe the organization is failing to act in an ethical way?

© Stephan Pastis/Dist. by United Feature Syndicate, Inc.

THE CHALLENGE OF BLOGGING

When working with blogs, communicators must remember that they don't know who the audience is or what that audience is thinking until they provide feedback. All a communicator can do is put information "out there" and then see what comes back. The comments might range from the serious to the silly. A blog is a great way of tossing out the question "What do you think?" and then getting a measure of what the company's publics are thinking. But, to use a well-worn analogy, blogging is a lot like fishing: you can use the same bait and your catch be a salmon or it could be a crappie — you just don't know what you will get. For instance, TSN (The Sports Network) offers a blog for viewers of sporting events; after a Canadian Football League game, the TSN website's blog is loaded with viewer commentary, some of it insightful, some less so. But the quality is not the point: for the network it simply means "Hey, people are watching, they're listening and they're reacting. We're having an impact on them." The blog also works well for the network by helping it build its information base — it tells them who is using the website and what they are saying about the broadcasts.

If an organization has committed to blogging, it's essential that a communicator provide updates for the company blog during a crisis — it's one more daily duty to be added to the list. And, as mentioned, communicators must have the support and often the participation of their executive people to either write down daily thoughts for posting or to at least approve what has been written. The blogger should be willing to spend a portion of the day, a half hour perhaps, on seeing that the blog is updated, the incoming comments scanned and, in some cases, responded to.

SAHARA, THE BARBARY LION: A HYPOTHETICAL EXAMPLE

Here's a hypothetical situation. A small family-owned zoo has a long-standing practice of renting its bushy-maned, 200-kilogram rare Barbary lion, named Sahara, to film productions. The robust lion, native to North Africa, fell victim to human incursion into its territory. The majority of Barbary lions are kept in zoos and wildlife parks. Sahara was donated to the zoo when he outgrew his previous home. Born and raised in captivity, Sahara is tame, having been handled by an animal trainer who is accredited by a national organization for zoos and aquariums. In addition to film, the lion makes appearances at schools as well as charity and corporate events to promote the importance of conservation and of protecting the world's vanishing wild species. However, a local animal rights group has taken exception to the use of the lion in film productions and promotional events, stating in a news release: "Lions are meant to live freely. They should not be subject to living under such conditions and forced to learn 'circus tricks' to ensure their survival. Sahara is a rare Barbary lion, now extinct in the wild. The animal deserves to be used effectively to propagate its species." The news release goes on to say that the lion should be donated to a conservation society that will use it in a breeding program and hopefully reintegrate it into a conservation area in Morocco.

From the perspective of the local zoo, the animal rights group is clearly off base, yet the group is gaining ground with the public, getting media attention and spreading erroneous information. The facts are clear to the zoo: the lion was born in captivity; he was hand-raised by humans; he is accustomed to being kept almost as a pet (and the zoo owner always mentions at events that while some lions may be tame, they nevertheless have the potential to harm other animals or people if threatened). Sahara cannot be reintegrated into the wild, even in an enclosed conservation site; attempts to do so could result in Sahara being severely harmed or killed, because Sahara would not know how to function as part of the lion pride. There is, however, an international Barbary lion breeding program that the zoo is attempting to become involved with. Because the lion is not yet mature, he is not ready for the program and his potential as an effective breeder is still unknown. However, the zoo does know that the lion is doing a great deal of good in the community by teaching children about respect for wildlife, both at the zoo and through school visits.

The zoo issues a news release, holds a press conference and creates a blog on which the zoo owner posts daily information about the zoo and, especially, Sahara. The owner talks about the support he has received from a national organization of zoological gardens as well as from environmental groups, and he encourages people, especially schoolchildren, who have met Sahara to write in with their thoughts about Sahara and what he offers to people.

The Benefits of the blog. The blog the zoo owner created has several benefits, among them:

- It gives a major stakeholder base, schoolchildren, a chance to interact with the zoo officials, including the zoo owner;
- It allows the zoo to disseminate accurate, unblemished information about the Barbary lion and about Sahara in particular;
- It offers the members of the public a chance to get to know more about Sahara and the zoo, and to feel that their opinion counts;
- It creates a cascade of information and feeling; blog participants post their thoughts, and are in turn able to see the posts of other writers. This forms the basis for generating, nurturing and maintaining a positive response to Sahara's situation.

Why is the blog a better approach for the zoo than trying to reach the public through the media? The blog removes a major filter — the media — thus allowing an unconstrained, undiluted, often highly emotional exchange of information between the public and the zoo. It serves as an effective barometer for how the public *really feels*, and the zoo does not have to rely on media reports or commentary to form a picture of public opinion about its handling of Sahara. It can see it clearly by reviewing the blog.

In the weeks after the blog is created, the majority of comments are positive — the public clearly wants the zoo to keep Sahara and realizes his value to the community — and the blog helps the zoo position itself as a promoter of strong community and conservationist values. After several weeks, the zoo provides the results of the blog to the media as part of a media event. It also issues a news release, in which the key messages recount not only the numbers of people who posted on the blog but highlight the many positive comments made. Over time, the animal rights group stops its protests, and the local media move on to other topics. The zoo owner decides to keep the blog operating after the crisis has passed, as a means of maintaining effective two-way communication with the zoo's publics.

BLOGS: OPPORTUNITY OR THREAT?

Blogs are usually seen as beneficial or hazardous, rarely neutral, according to Michael O'Connor Clarke, vice-president of business development of

Marqui, a company that works with its clients to automate and simplify their marketing activities. For Clarke, the blogosphere, the interconnected community of web logs and bloggers, is a great place to build transparency between companies and their stakeholders, as well as the general public. American billionaire Mark Cuban; Mark LaNeve, vice-president, GM North America Vehicle Sales, Service and Marketing; and other business leaders all update their blogs daily. Companies have sprung up that monitor blogs for a range of corporate customers, sifting through the messages and online diaries to find information and then feeding that information to their clients on a daily basis.

> "Let's just say there are two views: blogs as 'opportunity' and blogs as 'threat.' There's a fairly simple point that's being missed in the ongoing debate [over the value of blogs and blogging to companies]: any corporation has a lot of conversations going on at any point in time; if you supply a service or a product, any two customers are talking about you at any one time. The great thing about blogs is that you can ... actually interact with the customers who are talking about you. Let's assume there are a million different conversations going on about your business and your market — any good corporate communications person, if given a choice between being a part or not being a part of a conversation, will choose engagement."[6]
> — Michael O'Connor Clarke, vice-president of business development, Marqui

Daniel Lyons, a writer for the business magazine *Forbes*, sees blogs as a major threat to corporations: get on the wrong side of a group of angry bloggers and your business could be threatened. In "Attack of the Blogs," Lyons cites the experience of Circle Group Holdings, whose founder, Gregory Halpern, was the target of a blogging attack that tagged him as a fraud and crippled his company's reputation. He also mentions the example of Kryptonite, a company that makes bicycle locks that are supposed to provide "the toughest security for moderate to high crime areas." In 2004, bloggers posted messages detailing how the lock could be opened with a regular ballpoint pen.[7] Needless to say, the company was left with egg on its face — and a multitude of unhappy customers.

Although both claims about blogs are valid, successful communicators would rather hear what's being said about their companies so they can act on that discussion than wait for unpleasant surprises. It's an organic approach to business that can help communicators feed information back into the organization, using what they read in blogs to generate new ideas and new approaches to stakeholder relations.

TIPS FOR EFFECTIVE BLOGGING

Communicators should keep the following points in mind when blogging (or advising their senior personnel):

Debate. Communicators can use a blog to effectively debate the negative points that have been raised about the company. A point-counterpoint argument works well to acknowledge but then refute the darts that have been tossed at the company.

Choose whom to respond to. Bloggers who are high profile (heads of companies, stakeholder organizations and politicians) or those who have made a flagrant or dramatic point about the company should be responded to. Those who make silly, sophomoric or clearly ineffectual commentary should not be. The corporate blogger needs to pick his or her engagements carefully, speaking to what the company wants to speak to.

Gauge the effect of the blogging. The effectiveness of the company blog can be judged by examining both the quantity of responses to its postings and the quality of understanding of the issues: Are people understanding the message? How are they responding to it? Are they being won over by the communicator's pithy arguments or positioning of the company's actions? Or do the responses indicate the need for the company to rethink its approach to the issue?

Decide on tone: formal or informal? Although the blog is headed by a prominent company official, the tone, in most cases, should be conversational — it should have the feel of people sitting in a coffee shop talking about issues of concern to them, not the arch and superior tone of a company executive saying, "This is how it is." The company official needs to take a loosen-the-tie, roll-up-the-shirtsleeves approach, asking, "What do you think about this?"

Deliver key messages informally. Key messages are often carefully written for maximum sound bite and economy, but on a blog, these messages need to be communicated in a far more natural style. They should be presented as supplemental to the open discussion, though they of course are still the company's key messages. For example, if a company is being blogged about its track record of involvement in the community, a spokesperson might write, "I'm often asked about what our company does for the community. In the last few years, we looked at our goal of helping build a better community presence and took it up a notch. Over the past 10 years, we've supported fundraisers such as the Terry Fox Run, raising more than $2 million, and it's why we're getting involved in several new ventures this year."[8]

Conclusion

There was a time when companies communicated with their publics through phone calls, snail mail, a face-to-face meeting or a press conference. Those days are gone. Today, it is essential for communicators to be innovative in the way they talk (and listen) to their publics. The use of websites and blogs, as daunting as they may seem to many, in particular offer communicators a chance to get up-close-and-personal with stakeholders and the public. These forms of interaction also remove a filter — the media — from the corporate communications equation, giving communicators fresh, unprocessed views of how their company is doing. They offer communicators the opportunity to draw on raw, unblemished data straight from the source, rather than interpreting views and positions transmitted through the channel of sound-bite television or radio, or carefully written, edited and often slanted newspaper reports. The challenge of seizing the potential of this powerful new communications channel is making certain that the organization and its leaders have the resources to take a hard look at what the organization's publics have to say. The results will need to be scrutinized against current messaging and practices, and decisions will need to be made as to how important the impressions of stakeholders and members of the general public are, what they mean to the organization immediately and in the future and just how significantly they should be applied against the organization's ongoing direction.

Clearly, an effective organization will be measured by its message (and the way it gets that message across), its relationship to its publics and its ability to react in a positive and direct way during a crisis.

Key Concepts

BLOG: An online diary of sorts, a blog is an excellent means of creating and nurturing two-way communication, offering direct feedback to stakeholders and the general public on issues and allowing companies an opportunity to respond, change and take a new direction if necessary. It gives a company's top executive an opportunity to put a friendly face on the organization in an atmosphere of congenial discussion.

DARK SITE: A website that is prepared in advance, ready to be linked to the company website as soon as (but *only* when) crisis breaks.

INTERNET: the Internet, or World Wide Web, is used by almost a billion people worldwide — companies ignore its reach, impact and significance at their peril. In a web-savvy world, websites are often the first place people go for news.

WEBSITE: A company website can provide two-way interaction between the organization and its publics; it ensures a consistency of message and offers around-the-clock opportunities to update information. Websites enable communicators to compartmentalize information, make it current by allowing 24-hour-a-day updates, provide detailed information and offer the organization's publics a chance for feedback.

Part IV: Interview and Exercises

Bob Cohen,
Bob Cohen Communications

Bob Cohen has had a long career in corporate communications. A graduate of McGill University (bachelor of science) and Carleton University (bachelor of journalism), he is also a graduate of several management training programs. Cohen got started in the communications business on the journalism side, with Southam Inc., where he held positions at the national and local level, including health and science correspondent, parliamentary correspondent and Toronto bureau chief; he served as news director with Citytv before moving into a 15-year corporate communications career with the Ontario government. In provincial government communications, he served in senior capacities, handling a range of issues, including crisis communications.

As a consultant, he counsels clients in government and the private sector on ways to effectively handle their communications challenges. For years he was at the helm of organizations that planned, wrote and distributed thousands of news releases, often during times of crisis.

ON WHAT CONSTITUTES A CRISIS

"In communications terms, a crisis is when a story about an enterprise is on page one of the local or national newspaper — it could be above or below the fold [traditionally, above the fold means the major, attention-grabbing headline and the first thing readers see when they look at the newspaper], but no matter where the story appears — on the first page or in the first few pages — it means the organization has got a problem, and that's a crisis. A narrowband issue affecting some stakeholders may not become a crisis — that may be an issue that can be dealt with directly, by contacting those stakeholders. A crisis takes hold when it's, for instance, a product such as Tylenol, a commodity that's sold to millions of people, and something goes terribly wrong."

ON THE ORGANIZATIONAL STRUCTURE AND CRISIS

"The organizational setting is essential. First, communicators need to understand that the way the company is seen in the news media will have a seminal and critical impact on its success. And second, build into the organization the structures to ensure it's not going to have a crisis, but if a crisis *does* come up, that it can be dealt with in a methodical way. The bottom line is that structures are all fine and good, but crisis communications is really all about values and forthrightness. If a company doesn't have the right people, the best organizational chart is not going to be worth a damn, and if it does have the right people, that chart won't matter."

ON LEADERSHIP DURING A CRISIS

"Leadership during a crisis has to come from the top — whether from a company president, a CEO, a premier, a prime minister, what have you. The way the leaders position themselves in terms of the crisis is essential. The only way to deal with a crisis is to be forthright and straight up — leaders have to be able to approach the issue with confidence. That will go a long way in terms of establishing credibility. The last thing you do is bury your head in the sand.

"There must be awareness from the top. The people at the top must be honest enough to say, 'I don't know what's going on' or 'I don't have enough information,' then sit down with their staff, including the communications team, and fix the problem."

ON ANSWERING QUESTIONS

"Communicators have to be prepared to say that they can't answer questions *at that time* — but that they will find the answer. And they have to be able to speak in plain language. Some stakeholders may know the bafflegab of the industry, and communicators can speak to them in that language when they call. But crises are largely about public trust, public confidence and public understanding. Communicators have got to be fair and translate technical language as they go. And they have to be able to demonstrate that the organization is taking action."

ON HANDLING A CRISIS FOR THE ONTARIO MINISTRY OF LABOUR

"I was director of communications for eight years with the Ministry of Labour, in the 1980s, at a time when the government was constantly getting beaten up on labour issues. There were several labour union strikes, and in particular a couple of serious garbage strikes in Toronto — garbage was piling up everywhere. The provincial Ministry of Labour was involved marginally, at the discussion table with the City and its workers. And although it was not the bailiwick of the provincial government, as the director of communications, I told the deputy minister that, even given our small role in the crisis, we needed to hold a daily media conference. So the ministry told the media, 'We will meet in the provincial legislature media studio every day at 3 p.m., and we will tell you what is happening right up to that minute.'

"There were afternoons when the media showed up and we told them that there wasn't anything to tell them that day. But that was fine, for what we did was provide a conduit for information between the Ministry of Labour and the media. The daily media conference had a very salutary effect — it stopped an awful lot of running around. It provided an opportunity for us to get the news of the day out, to get information into the hands of reporters. The daily conferences operated on the notion that people always wonder if they are getting the straight goods. Assuring people that you have the public's interest at heart will go a long way."

Exercise: The Toy Car Crisis

CORPORATE GLANCE: PONJO TOYS

LOCATION: Vancouver, British Columbia.

THE PRODUCTS: A range of children's toys, from dolls and action figures to toy cars, interactive computer games and board games — 37 models of toys in all.

THE COMPANY: Employs 56 skilled workers in its plant and an additional 15 in the front office. The company, which exports to several countries, including Australia, the United States and Brazil, has annual sales of $35 million.

HISTORY: The company has been in business for 25 years. The founder, Florence Marston, named it after her son Paul, whose nickname was "Ponjo."

DETAILS: Ponjo Toys has an excellent track record for toy safety. The Canadian Standards Association certifies Ponjo's products, and the company clearly marks each package with the appropriate age range for each toy and provides a caution that children should be supervised when playing with it.

SENIOR PERSONNEL: Florence Marston, founder and CEO
Peter Ferreiro, communications director

THE CRISIS

It's a Monday morning and a child is in critical condition after choking on the wheel of a toy car produced by Ponjo Toys. The two-year-old was playing with his older brother's car and managed to get the wheel off it. His mother discovered him, blue and lifeless, at 8:10 a.m. Emergency medical services was called; the child arrived at Children's & Women's Health Centre of British Columbia at 8:30 a.m.

At 11:30 a.m., the crisis hits the company: you have just gotten word from both the police and from a hospital administrator that a toddler choked on a Ponjo toy part. A check of the serial number reveals that the toy was a Sandstorm 500 Sport Truck, a toy sport utility vehicle built the previous year and rated for ages eight and older. The truck passed the company's stringent safety testing to federal standards. CEO Marston has called for the immediate recall of the toy and says the company will offer money back to customers who bring this particular model to a company-approved retailer.

Two members of the local media have already called, looking for interviews. Ponjo's communications director, Peter Ferreiro, has asked you to write a clear, concise news release and Q&A outlining the company's position on this crisis. The company will need the release ready in 45 minutes.

YOUR TASK

Write the news release and Q&A. Keep in mind that the news release should demonstrate compassion for the family involved, as well as a proactive approach by the company in addressing the crisis. Give your draft release and Q&A to a classmate or colleague for review and feedback.

V Case Study Exercises

12 | Practice Scenarios

If water derives lucidity from stillness, how much more the faculties of the mind! The mind of the sage, being in repose, becomes
the mirror of the universe, the speculum of all creation.

— CHUANG TZU

We can take a few words of sage advice from ancient Chinese philosopher Chuang Tzu, for it's appropriate that we give ourselves time to reflect on
what we've read, and to clear our minds and take a common-sense approach
to practical exercises.

In this chapter, we look at several case studies as the starting point for tackling similar problems in the practice scenarios that follow them (the first prac-
tic scenario stands alone). Drawn from real-life, recent crisis communications
scenarios, the hypothetical scenarios that follow are designed to give you an
opportunity to discuss, debate, decide, develop and deliver:

> *Discuss* the crisis and tackle it from the perspective of the organization
> you would be representing in the case study. Brainstorm the case, make
> notes and confer with colleagues or fellow students.

Debate the case with a view to seeing the crisis from as many angles as possible.

Decide how you will handle this crisis. Think about the approach you will take with your publics. Decide who will be on your crisis management team.

Develop a communications plan, key messages and communications products.

Deliver your key messages and products. Do a practice run and use an audience of colleagues, fellow students and others to gain feedback. Then review and ask yourself what worked, what didn't?

Practice Scenario 1:
Tasers, the Shock Felt Around the World

The topic: Tasers are becoming the weapon of choice for many police services; they will stop a suspect cold without causing death — at least in most cases. Troubling evidence has been mounting in recent years that, albeit occasionally, people are dying as a result of tasers (an acronym for Tom A. Swift's Electric Rifle, from the kids' stories about adventurer Tom Swift) use by the police. At the same time, police services are calling for more tasers, because of their allegedly non-lethal nature.

Shaped like a large gun, a taser delivers an electrical charge (50,000 volts) from a distance of four to five metres, through a wire that attaches itself to clothing or skin after the user fires it. The charge disrupts the body's nervous system, causing muscles to seize and instantly immobilizing the suspect. But the statistics for taser-related deaths are troubling.

The proponents: Often criticized for killing suspects during attempts to place them under arrest, police departments are interested in better ways to apprehend dangerous suspects without the risk of death.

In November 2004, Toronto newspapers reported that then Toronto Police Chief Julian Fantino asked the police service board to approve the acquisition of 500 tasers for his officers at a cost of $1 million. In a report to the board, he said,

"It is considered by many experts to be the best less-lethal weapon currently available to law enforcement and has been credited with ... saving hundreds of lives."[1] This came at a time when a *New York Times* report claimed that, since 2001, 50 people in the United States had died after being stunned by tasers.

The forces using them: According to TASER International Inc., tasers are used by the RCMP, as well as by municipal forces in Edmonton, Vancouver and Ottawa-Carleton and several correctional service departments across the country. In total, 62 police and correctional services departments in Canada use tasers and 5,400 in the United States. More than 1,100 tasers are in use in Canada and 100,000 in the United States.

The detractors: Organizations such as Amnesty International have called for discontinuing the use of tasers. CBC News quoted Amnesty secretary general Alex Neve as saying, "Obviously police should be using non-lethal alternatives. But the standards say those non-lethal alternatives should be fully investigated. We need to have a study; we need to understand what those risks are."[2] Police organizations are also beginning to question their use.

The company's position: *Maclean's* magazine quoted Steve Tuttle, vice-president of communications at Arizona-based TASER International Inc., as saying that "such doubts [about the taser] are groundless," citing the more than 50,000 incident-free uses in the field as proof the devices are safe. "Our technology is explicitly designed not to cause fatalities," he says. "We've still not been listed as a direct cause of death."[3]

OTHER NEWS NOTES

In August 2004, a 29-year-old man in Brampton, Ontario, became the fifth person in Canada to die after being subdued by a taser. He was said to be high on drugs at the time.

Also in August 2004, a 43-year-old Kingston man, high on cocaine, was subdued by police with a taser and later died in hospital after suffering a seizure. As *Maclean's* reported, Ontario's deputy chief coroner reported the cause of death as a drug overdose, but "was not yet ready to dismiss Tasers as a factor." Following the death, the Canadian Association of Chiefs of Police called for a full review of taser use.

In an October 2004 report, CBC News reported: "Canadian police say Tasers have saved 4,000 lives since police forces started using them in this country in 1999. Still, Staff Sgt. Peter Sherstan, of the RCMP's Emergency Response Team in Edmonton, says Tasers should not be considered non-lethal. 'The RCMP's position is that Tasers are a less-lethal alternative,' Sherstan told CBC Radio. 'There are still risks.'"[4]

In January 2005, the *Toronto Star* reported that the U.S. Securities and Exchange Commission (SEC), a federal agency that enforces securities laws and regulates the securities industry, was "looking into claims about the weapon's safety." This was the result of a major US$1.5 million sale by TASER International to a distributor: allegations of stock price manipulation levelled at the company led to the investigation, which was closed by December of that year, with the company cleared of any wrongdoing. According to the *Star*, TASER International president Tom Smith said the company had "nothing to hide and are fully co-operating with [the SEC]." Smith said the SEC inquiry is not looking into the safety of the device, only whether the company's claims match the findings of their safety studies.[5]

In May 2005, in Moncton, New Brunswick, a 34-year-old man collapsed and died after the RCMP used a taser to subdue him in a bar. It brought the number of taser-related deaths in Canada to nine.[6]

CRISIS FLASHPOINT

You are the communications director for a regional policing operation in the District of Topsall, British Columbia. The police chief is Sam Langford. The force has used tasers for three years and the district's 175 officers have been fully trained in their use.

Two nights ago, one of the officers on duty, Michelle Brighton, used a taser to subdue a large (six feet two inches and 275 pounds), angry, out-of-control 38-year-old male who was threatening people at a house party in Kewna, a town in the district.

The man's name was Hugh Bourne. He had been drinking excessively but it is not known whether he had drugs in his system. Shortly after being subdued, he went into cardiac arrest and died. His body was flown to Vancouver General Hospital for an autopsy, which is expected in about five days. Bourne's was the only death associated with a taser since the district began using them. The taser had been used in 27 previous cases without incident.

THE CRISIS

Despite his bad temper, Hugh was generally well liked in the town. Bourne was also the son of Martin Bourne, the mayor of Kewna. Mayor Bourne, who sits on the District of Topsall's Police Services Board, was a vocal opponent of the district acquiring tasers. He's even more adamant now that his son is dead. Kewna also has a very vocal Amnesty International unit, which has been calling for the police department to discontinue their use of tasers.

The local newspaper, the *Kewna Express,* ran a story on the incident and included a very incendiary quote from the mayor: "I told the chief five years ago that we shouldn't have tasers in this district. They were a waste of money and the risks were just too high. And now, for me on a personal level, this is a hell of a way to have my point proven, with the death of my own son."

The *Kewna Express* also ran an editorial stating that the takedown of Hugh Bourne was the third incident in which police were criticized for using excessive force (the two previous incidents involved the use of nightsticks to subdue drunken troublemakers outside the local bar). Citizens are becoming agitated over what they deem to be police brutality.

YOUR TASK

1. Begin by answering a series of questions: who does this affect, how will the public react, and what do we need to anticipate in terms of response to our position?
2. Develop a communications plan to handle the media questions that have been coming from media, not just local but national (CBC and CTV) and

international. Consider the positions of the media, the general public, the mayor, and Amnesty International.

3. Create key messages for Police Chief Langford. Note that a local RCMP sergeant, Ron Telkven, has called to lend his support. Sergeant Telkven is an acknowledged expert in the use of tasers.

4. Create a Q&A in anticipation of the questions that you will receive from the media.

QUICK HIT FROM A GREAT MIND

"To know your enemy, you must become your enemy ... Keep your friends close and your enemies closer ... knowing the enemy enables you to take the offensive, knowing yourself enables you to stand on the defensive. Attack is the secret of defence; defence is the planning of an attack."

— Sun Tzu

The lesson here for communicators is to pay close attention to what the publics say and to learn how they think. This gives the communicator the ability to take the initiative in approaching them during a crisis.

Case Study 2: When the Lights Go Out

At 4:11 p.m. on August 14, 2003, the lights went out. So did everything else connected to the electricity grid. It was the beginning of a crisis for Ontario and Quebec and a big part of North America's eastern seaboard, affecting millions of people and resulting in deaths in some areas. Eventually, the problem was traced to transformer problems and energy flow through a transformer in Ohio but, for several days, people either lived on edge or took to the streets, relaxing outside their homes, watching the stars or simply enjoying a respite from work.

For everyone from politicians to bankers to service utilities workers, though, the situation was a crisis. Depending on whom you spoke to, politicians either handled or mishandled the situation. For Ontario's then premier Ernie Eves, it was a chance to take a stab at Rudolph Giuliani–style leadership (discussed in Chapter 8). As the *Toronto Star* reported on August 20, "Public-opinion polling is quietly being conducted to gauge Premier Ernie Eves' performance through the blackout crisis, but the [Ontario] Conservative party denies it is behind any survey." Eves would encourage greater energy conservation in the future, but his party was criticized for being unready to handle the crisis.

COPING WITH THE CRISIS

It took two days for power to be restored in most areas affected by the outage. According to Statistics Canada, the blackout resulted in 19 million lost work hours in Ontario and Quebec, with 2.4 million workers affected. In the aftermath, the *Toronto Star* reported that, in Canada, insurance claims resulting from the blackout totalled $4.9 million.

There were widespread media reports that Canada's Office of Critical Infrastructure Protection and Emergency Preparedness (OCIPEP) — which held the federal reins for handling the crisis — wasn't up to job, lacking staffing and necessary phone lines to deal with the plethora of media calls coming in. It was allegedly especially lacking at the top, as the *Guelph Mercury* reported on September 6, 2003: "When the power went off and the federal government was fumbling for answers in the dark, the man at the epicentre of Canada's emergency operations [James Harlick, assistant deputy minister at OCIPEP] was canoeing and out of contact."

In the aftermath, as the *Christian Science Monitor* would report, people became more conservation-minded. There was a need for greater investment in the electricity-delivery infrastructure in the United States, and government bodies and many large private sector firms found that their crisis communications plans actually worked during the blackout — and worked reasonably well.[7]

How well Canadian companies learned from previous crises was put to the test during the blackout. Robert Waite, now senior vice-president, Communications and Stakeholder Relations for Canada Post, and formerly Canadian Imperial Bank of Commerce's senior vice-president, Communications and Public Affairs, had an opportunity to address the issue at a conference on crisis communications later that year. He said that CIBC's "Business Continuity Management framework for management of the business impact of major disruptions" was in place within minutes of the occurrence of the power outage. Auxiliary power was activated; actions included updating the employee emergency hotline to keep people informed; and the company opened its alternate site recovery centre in Hamilton and began a series of messages to emphasize the safety and security of its operations.

"Beyond considerations of employee safety and security and adherence to government directives regarding transportation and employees' reporting to work, our focus [was] on continuation of CIBC's most critical functions and minimization of the impact of the outage on customer service levels in all sectors," said Waite.[8]

Still, the crisis sent people into panic mode. Newspaper reporters were out in full force; the blackout would generate thousands of news stories over the course of the next three months.[9]

THE 2003 BLACKOUT: WHAT THE MEDIA SAID

TORONTO STAR, August 17:
THE HEADLINE: "Pollsters quietly judging Eves' performance in crisis."
THE LEAD: "Two years ago, electricity robbed Lewis Wheelan of his two legs and his right arm. On Friday, the lack of it may have taken his life."
The story was about a man, recovering from life-threatening injuries, who needed constant air conditioning to keep his skin grafts from overheating. The power outage may have caused his body to overheat, causing death.

MACLEAN'S, August 25:
THE HEADLINE: "Power politics and the Ontario Conservatives."
THE LEAD: "Where were you when the lights went out? Ontario Premier Ernie Eves was on his way to his own nomination meeting in picturesque Caledon East, the prelude to an election call — and now likely a victory — that seems always to be eluding his grasp [Eves would go on to lose the election that fall] ... for hard-luck Ernie. Thursday's big blackout was the political equivalent of being stuck in an elevator nowhere near an accommodating floor. But that's what you get for playing loose with a system that needs more than crossed fingers to keep the juice flowing."

COMPUTERWORLD, September 23, 2003:
THE HEADLINE: "Blackout experience yields divergent backup strategies."
THE LEAD: "Human nature being what it is, IT managers' responses to the alarm bells set off by last month's massive blackout have a lot to do with whether or not they were affected by it. According to a survey of 500 IT managers released last week by data center user group AFCOM [the Association for Computer Operations Management], IT managers in the blackout area are tending to focus on fixing their own problems, such as improving backup power."

Practice Scenario 2: TextCorp

You handle communications for Montreal-based TextCorp, a 50-employee service provider of encrypted information for clients across Canada. The information is time-sensitive, deals with privileged company information and is used by clients to make decisions about their investments. TextCorp's top three clients include the investment division of the Actinolite Credit Union, which handles millions of dollars in assets each week, the Eastern Seaboard Library Workers Union, with more than 1,500 members, and Comety Investments, a company that manages the portfolios of 850 clients, with investments valued at $1.2 billion.

A power outage has occurred in the city. You have no way of knowing how wide-ranging the outage is, but you do know that 5,000 clients are not going to be receiving the information your organization has promised them in the next two hours. Actinolite will be missing vital information on its investment in a major oil refinery operation, the library union has assets that it is trying to move to new accounts and Comety Investments has $80 million in client funds that are being reinvested. All are waiting for the encrypted information in order to fulfill their respective deals.

TextCorp has a backup power system, but as bad luck would have it, the backup generator blew after running for five minutes — not enough time to get all the encrypted transactional information through to clients. The generator was up and running again within a half hour, but IT feels that information should be sent to the company's second site as a safeguard — to store the information at a site that still had power before attempts were made to send out the information to customers. TextCorp is essentially working in the dark. Power is limited to the main building only and the second site, which is within walking distance; the company has a third location with five employees in Pointe-Claire, about 18 kilometres to the west. The Pointe-Claire site has already received calls from Comety Investments asking for a status report on its files. Comety knows about the power outage, having been advised of the situation at TextCorp.

According to radio reports, more than three-quarters of the city is in darkness. Employees are sending information to the second site, and the company is sending several employees out of the city core, to the Pointe-Claire site with appropriate files, in order to send out the encrypted information from there. TextCorp knows, through contact with that office, that the Pointe-Claire site is unaffected by the blackout. The problem is that those employees are stuck in traffic and will not reach the Pointe-Claire site for at least two hours.

The president of the company, Raminder Singh, has asked you to tackle the task of communicating with clients and the media. Singh and vice-president Nancy Childs will need to have the facts quickly and will need to know their roles. Prepare answers for the following questions:

- What's first on your list of things to do?
- What products will you need to create?
- Who are the most important people to contact?
- What is the timeline for tackling this crisis?
- What will you say to internal and external stakeholders and the media?

QUICK HIT FROM A GREAT MIND

"Flow with whatever may happen and let your mind be free. Stay centered by accepting whatever you are doing. This is the ultimate."

— CHUANG TZU

These words don't so much imply that we let go as that we should keep our minds open, focusing on the task at hand and being receptive to ideas that flow to us and through us. Communicators can brainstorm, make notes, talk with colleagues — always using and reusing the thoughts that come to them. Ultimately, they can create innovative ways to deal with an impending or immediate crisis.

Case Study: Handling the Executive Gaffe

One usually expects a highly educated person — such as the head of a leading university — to have the qualities we associate with leadership: intelligence, decorum, tact and diplomacy. So, in a set of remarks delivered in January 2005, Harvard University president Lawrence Summers's suggestion of why women were not heading for high-level science jobs came as a surprise: he claimed it was because of biological differences between women and men, rather than systematic discrimination.

According to Summers, these differences result in men's science test scores being at the high and low end of the scale, with women's marks clustered in the middle. Summers faced several challenges because of his gaffe, from student associations, faculty, critics and the public, with many calling for him to step down as president. The Associated Press reported that "in explaining why fewer women scientists rise to the top, Summers said he was inclined to favour family pressure and biology as explanations over discrimination and social factors." The transcript of Summers's remarks that clarified his viewpoint — that biologic differences somehow were at the root of mediocrity — was widely panned.[10]

IVY LEAGUE POTBOILER AS HARVARD PRESIDENT LANDS IN HOT WATER: WHAT THE MEDIA SAID

MACLEAN'S, world edition, January 31, 2005: "Harvard University president Lawrence Summers set off an academic firestorm across the U.S. when he suggested in a speech that women may not have the same innate ability as men in math and science ... Summers stood by his remarks for a few days, and then apologized. He also offered US$25 million to hire more women and other academic minorities."

AMERICAN SPECTATOR, May 2005: "Summers, in his remarks on the state of women in math and science faculties at the most elite universities, challenged the sacred cows of the oppression lobby and suffered the consequences of his political incorrectness."

SCIENTIFIC AMERICAN, May 2005: "Harvard University president Lawrence Summers struck a nerve early this year when he [tried to] explain why fewer women than men flourish in scientific careers ... What does the research say? Evidence linking inequities in anatomy to intellectual ability is hard to come by."

Suppose you are responsible for developing communications strategies coming from the Harvard University president's office. Think about the major points of contention in the crisis and prepare answers for these questions:

1. What did the president of Harvard miss in making his remarks?
2. What next steps would you take in your communications strategies?

Practice Scenario 3: Pearson Manufacturing

Let's examine gaffes that high-level executives may make, gaffes that demonstrate a lack of understanding of the organization's publics or the subject at hand. You are the manager of corporate communications at an integrated manufacturer of auto parts in the small city of River Glen, Ontario, located two hours northeast of Toronto. The town has a population of 75,000. The company, Pearson Manufacturing, serves major automakers and has been in business for 52 years. It employs 700 people: 30 in the front office and the balance on the shop floor. It has been featured in several automotive magazines, is fully ISO certified and has made strides in incorporating the most modern design and manufacturing technology into its operations.

Your company has come under criticism from a coalition of university student associations, women's rights groups and civil rights activists for an alleged practice of not hiring many minorities, recent immigrants (in particular, those who are also minorities) or women, either in the front office or on the shop floor. In fact, unofficial polls show that this is true; minorities account for only three per cent of the company's workforce, there are no immigrants employed by the company, and women fill only 10 per cent of the positions. There are no minorities or women among supervisory or management staff. A recent federal census put the minority population of River Glen at 10 per cent, and the female population at 52 per cent. As well, a survey by a large metropolitan newspaper indicated that River Glen's minority population is growing strongly, by 5 per cent per year since 2001.

Your company has come under fire in the past by these same groups; only one, the River Glen College Student Association, is based in the city; the others — Next Generation Civil Rights, Pan-Canadian Women's Rights, The Organization for Corporate Change, and Grassroots Change Now! — are based in larger centres across the country, including Toronto and Ottawa. Eight years ago, a former company president made a commitment that the company would embark on a plan to hire more women and minorities, but a change in presidents effectively put those plans on the back burner. The community college, River Glen College, has approached the company to work on a plan to boost its workforce in these areas through a placement program in several of the college's technology programs. The college's idea was to attract skilled immigrants (often but not always represented by minorities), give them additional training through college programs and allow them to fulfill workplace training requirements at Pearson Manufacturing in order to gain their certification. This plan is "in the process," according to Pearson Manufacturing's human resources director, Sherry Feld, but there are no other details as of yet. Data from Statistics Canada show that the community is home to many new Canadians with technical skills; the local newspaper, the *River Glen Advocate,* has also published stories about minority Canadians with training in the skilled trades trying to find a place to live and thrive in River Glen. Many have received training in their countries of origin and additional certification through apprenticeship programs or colleges in Toronto or Montreal. Immigrant placement agencies have also sought to place skilled tradespersons with Pearson and with other manufacturers in town.

The *Advocate* recently asked Pearson's president, Larry Johnston, why the company didn't hire more women and minorities. Here is what he said to the reporter:

I want to hire more minorities and women, I really do, but we need people with good hands-on Canadian skills. We need to rely on people who have had their training here in this country, who can bring a set of skills to the workplace that we know we can rely on. And frankly, I don't see a lot of women coming out of programs with the kinds of skills we can use. As well, we speak English in this workplace — what if I have a worker using a $15-million piece of equipment, and he doesn't understand the instructions?

Immediately, the company was under fire from the community college, the newspaper (in an editorial calling for the company to move into the twenty-first century) and human rights organizations, including the Coalition for Human Rights; even the local auto parts manufacturing association called to express concerns. The CBC and CTV also called — although this may be only a local story, one for their regional outlets, there was a rumour that it might go national. The company owners, who represent the fifth generation of their family in River Glen, try to keep a low profile and are also upset. They are uncomfortable in front of the camera and prefer to see their company as a family-owned, family-values-focused cash cow, rather than one that aggressively confronts and adapts to change. Meetings between the owners and Johnston reveal that they don't want to "rock the boat" and they believe that this matter, given time, will "settle out on its own."

YOUR TASK

1. Develop a crisis communications plan to take the company out of the immediate crisis.
2. Consider these questions as you develop the crisis communications plan:
   - What measures are necessary immediately? What will you do over the short and long term?
   - What key messages will you develop for the president? Are there messages for the human resources director? Who should handle the questions that come in from the company's various publics?
   - What plans do you have for closing information gaps with your publics?
3. Create a Q&A to handle media questions.

Case Study: The Baseball Steroid Controversy

Famed baseball slugger José Canseco pens a book, *Juiced,* about his (and others') exploits with steroids, providing, well, *juicy* gossip, anger, drama and suspense for fans. In his book, Canseco claims that steroid use is common in the sport; his book triggered a U.S. Congressional House Committee on Government Reform hearing into the subject on March 17, 2005.

Called to testify, Canseco and others, including Mark McGwire, Sammy Sosa and Rafael Palmeiro took to the stand to speak their minds. The hearing room was littered with people whose lives were connected to the scandal, including a couple whose 24-year-old son died of a self-inflicted gunshot wound — his parents say his suicide was the result of steroid abuse. Also in the room was a couple whose 17-year-old hanged himself as a result of depression stemming from steroid use.

The focus was not just on the whys of steroid abuse among young athletes (e.g., to become bigger, faster and stronger) but on penalties necessary to curb the abuse and set an example.

Major League Baseball commissioner Bud Selig was given the task of tackling the problem. In a letter dated April 25 to the players' union, he proposed a three-strike penalty:

1. A 50-game suspension for a first-time offender;
2. A 100-game suspension for a second positive test;
3. A permanent ban from baseball for a third positive test.

As well, new rules would penalize the use of amphetamines.

As Hal Bodley reported in *USA Today*: "'Steroid users cheat the game,' Selig says in his letter. 'After three offenses, they have no place in it.'"

The *Toronto Star*'s Garth Woolsey, in a May 2, 2005, column, said of Selig's proposal:

It cannot be an accident, a foul tip, this orchestrated timing of the "leak" of Selig's proposal to the players' union. Bud and the boys must be feeling the heat. The U.S. Congress last week heaped praise upon the NFL for its relatively tough stance on steroids. Earlier, of course, the D.C. committee had been scathing in its treatment of [the] MLB. Perhaps anticipating that the law-makers are getting ever more deadly serious, Selig appears to be trying to head them off at the pass with his three-strike policy, outlined in the memo he has sent to [Major League Baseball] union boss Donald Fehr.

A May 12 article in the *Hamilton Spectator* stated: "Baseball owners unanimously endorsed commissioner Bud Selig's proposal for toughened steroid testing."

And to emphasize the wide-scale impact of steroids, a May 14 article in the *Toronto Star*, titled "Life in Needle Park," discussed the rampant use of steroids among young baseball players in the Dominican Republic: "A lonely grave in a cemetery plot filled with garbage and stench looms as the next battleground in the war over performance-enhancing drugs in baseball."

By May 19, the U.S. Congress had brought forth a recommendation of a two-year suspension for a first-time steroid offender (with major financial penalties for the leagues that didn't comply with the order), a move big-league sports bosses such as NHL commissioner Gary Bettman and NBA commissioner David Stern said were too severe. The implication by Bettman and Stern was that their leagues could police themselves. Selig was the sole commissioner who was relatively warm on the idea — but then he had already beaten Congress to the punch with his own set of guidelines.[11]

Practice Scenario 4: Continental Lacrosse League

Let's move the crisis north of the border. You are a communications director with an unpleasant task. As the public relations head of the Continental Lacrosse League, based in Winnipeg, you have been informed that a player, Ashley Hill, from the league's Saskatchewan Rogues team, admitted to steroid abuse. Hill had been arrested for going on a drunken rampage in a local restaurant, beating up two patrons and destroying furnishings. After being released from jail on bail and awaiting trial, he opened up to several newspapers as well as CBC Television.

"Steroids are all over the league," he was quoted as saying. "For most players, you need to beef up and the beating we take demands that we can recover quickly from muscle damage. Steroids are the only way to ensure that you have a healthy career."

After Hill's admission, five other players in the 10-team league — from the British Columbia Salmon, the Moncton Belugas and the Halifax Atlantic Storm — have admitted to steroid abuse; some are even saying that there has been a quiet conspiracy among players to share information about obtaining steroids and injection techniques. Taking a page from José Canseco, Hill is talking about writing a book about his experiences.

All of this is news to you — there hasn't been much talk about steroid abuse in lacrosse ranks. Your league — it's only three years old — is still getting on its feet and is struggling to capture a strong audience; it can ill afford negative publicity. For instance, it has a program called Lacrosse in the Schools that supports introducing the sport to schoolchildren at 27 boards of education across the country.

Each team in the league has a media relations officer: all have contacted you for direction on this issue. The federal government has expressed interest as well, with Sport Canada and Health Canada both placing phone calls to your organization, suggesting that there might be an inquiry into steroid abuse in the lacrosse league.

On the positive side for your organization, there has been talk of a fledgling program for drug testing that will be implemented in the next season, seven months away. And although events are still unfolding, there are also plans to bring Hill and others to a board of inquiry, formed from a panel of university athletic experts connected to the league in an advisory capacity as well as of former league athletes. The board will decide on punishment and establish guidelines for the future.

YOUR TASK

The lacrosse league president, Lonnie Montford, is in no mood to talk; instead, he took off "on vacation" for two weeks. Media are calling your office for comment. They especially want to know what is happening with Hill — will he be suspended? What will you say to the federal government? What information do you need to provide to the other teams' media relations officers? Prepare a Q&A to handle this crisis.

"When the shoe fits, the foot is forgotten.
When the belt fits, the belly is forgotten.
When the heart is right, 'for' and 'against' are forgotten."

— CHUANG TZU

When communicators have the right information, the right approach and the right tactics, the specific steps of the crisis plan will often seem to disappear into one seamless action. After all their planning and preparations training has been ingrained into them and their team, communicators will move instinctively: they will know what's right to do at each stage. These instincts take time to develop, and much practice. Never fear making a mistake on the way to building these instincts.

Case Study: A Heritage Moment

What price does one put on a community's heritage? In Lunenburg, Nova Scotia, the decision was easy for Clearwater Seafoods, which put a big part of the town up for sale. Obviously, the price of heritage is whatever the seller can command.

The property was along the waterfront — wharves, storehouses, docks — all part of the town that had a proud seafaring tradition; all elements of a community listed as a World Heritage site 1995, the United Nations calling it "the best surviving example of a planned British colonial settlement in North America."

Clearwater was moving because its operations had shifted away from the town once it acquired a new fleet of ships; the scallop processing that the town provided was now redundant. The property was for sale for just under $10 million.

A *Toronto Star* story emphasized the pending loss of an historical district, including comments from the saddened residents who feared that the town would turn into a tourist trap but held out hope that a wealthy individual who valued the district might step in and save the waterfront. The problem was that many of the buildings were falling apart; they would need a big investment from whoever invested in the town.[12]

Clearwater Seafoods came across as the villain in the piece; company president Colin MacDonald was quoted as saying that it

doesn't take much intelligence to see that change is going to happen. That is the reality. The waterfront in Lunenburg will change, just as it has in Halifax and Toronto and many other cities. The people of Lunenburg will have to figure out how they want that to happen.[13]

What are your immediate impressions? How is the company going to be seen by public and stakeholders in the wake of Mr. MacDonald's comments? Come up with some ideas about what the company could do to improve relations with the community, even if Clearwater were still adamant about selling the property.

Practice scenario 5: Tarnauer Extraction

This example is of an issue that either may become a full-blown crisis or may remain simply an issue that the organization must deal with.

You live and work in the city of Saskatoon, Saskatchewan. You work for a family-owned mining company, Tarnauer Extraction, a company that has been mining uranium, potash and coal from various locations in the province for 75 years. The company is anxious to sell the land around a depleted mine in southern Saskatchewan, near Grasslands National Park, not far from the U.S. border.

However, federal and provincial naturalists have found a rare colour variation of the already endangered black-footed ferret; the ferret is a member of the weasel family and is yellowish-brown in colour, with distinctive black markings on the feet and tail and a black mask across the face. This newly discovered variation is grey; scientists believe it may qualify as a separate subspecies. The black-footed ferret is a darling of the media and naturalists — it's cute and cuddly, it feeds on rodents such as the prairie dog and it was driven to near extinction by human incursion and development. It has a place next to the spotted salamander, peregrine falcon, bald eagle, prairie buffalo and other animals that have been driven to the brink of extinction, especially by agriculture and pesticides. It is believed that the property owned by Tarnauer is the only place on earth where this grey black-footed ferret, the colony estimated at less than 30 animals, survives.

The story broke only two days ago and you are still scrambling to pull together information. The problem is that the board of directors of Tarnauer is insistent on getting the land on the sales block. The company president, Arnold Tarnauer, has admitted behind closed doors that the company is in a financial pinch and needs the money to cover offshore extraction work; this is not public knowledge. However, the company is by no means going broke — it still has several medium- to high-profile projects underway, and it is sensitive to public and media perception.

Sadly, in the boardroom there doesn't seem to be much sensitivity to the issue of the grey black-footed ferret — and this is becoming a crisis that has animal rights groups and conservation organizations picketing the front doors of Tarnauer in small but vocal groups. These organizations want the land set aside for the future preservation of the ferret. While they are not privy to news of an impending land sale, rumours are circulating that the company will sell the land, and conservationists are concerned that the habitat might be threatened. It has attracted national media coverage and coverage from U.S. media outlets in North and South Dakota. On the plus side, several private sector-supported organizations have approached the company, saying they want to purchase the property and use it as a nature preserve. However, the company owners are leaning toward an offer from ParryCorp Development, an organization that, if its bid for the land is successful, will build a retirement community on the property. ParryCorp is planning to offer ten times the amount that Tarnauer would likely see from any of the private-sector organizations seeking to buy the land.

YOUR TASK

1. Begin by considering the following questions:
   - Is this a crisis? When would it become one, and what factors would contribute to it being considered a crisis?
   - Which stakeholders should the company contact?

- Are there any supportive organizations that might provide strong third-party endorsement for ensuring that the land is protected for the ferret?
- Who is a critical member of the crisis communications team?
- What position do you think Tarnauer needs to take? Save the ferrets? Or sell to ParryCorp? What will be the long-term implications of either decision?

2. Devise a pitch to convince Arnold Tarnauer that this is an issue that, handled carefully, can serve to enhance rather than diminish his company's reputation.
3. Devise a crisis plan with all supporting actions that assumes that the company must sell the land, despite the discovery of the ferret and the potential crisis vis-à-vis reputation damage to the company.
4. Devise another plan for a compromise solution in which the land is not sold but partnerships are sought to compensate the company in some way.

Case Study: Finger Food

Some readers may be old enough to remember the Second City TV comedy show, where "typical" Canadian brothers Bob and Doug Mckenzie (played by Rick Moranis and Dave Thomas) sit around drinking beer, frying back bacon and talk about putting a mouse in a bottle of beer — "that way you can take it back to the beer store and complain, and, like, you can get a free two-four, eh?"

It's the kind of notion that makes for the modern urban legend. Stories like this pop up all the time — the dead rat in the bucket of fried chicken, the body parts in the hamburger, the girl who eats a cockroach-infested burrito and ends up with cockroach eggs in her gums ... so it shouldn't really have come as a shock when a Las Vegas woman sued Wendy's after finding a finger in her bowl of chili at a Wendy's restaurant in California in March 2005.

For Wendy's, it was a public relations crisis, despite the fact that the fast-food franchise operator was ultimately vindicated when the 39-year-old woman in question was charged with larceny a month later. It turned out she had placed the digit (which belonged to an acquaintance of her family) into the chili, ostensibly to embarrass the company into paying her millions of dollars in damages; it also turned out that she had a history of litigious activity and false claims.

The media were able to find some humour in the issue, as the *Moncton Times & Transcript* reported on March 25, 2005, in an article titled "Finger found in Wendy's chili":

> A woman bit into a partial finger served in a bowl of chili at a California Wendy's restaurant, leading authorities to use a fingerprint database yesterday to determine who lost the digit … all employees' digits were accounted for, officials said, adding the well-cooked finger may have come from a food-processing plant that supplies the company.
>
> (Reprinted with permission of Brunswick News Inc.)

Wendy's handled it well. According to an article in *Maclean's*,

> [to] its credit, the chain has done much to get to the bottom of this PR disaster. It has checked its staff and suppliers for missing digits; it has had them take lie detector tests; it has explained how its chili is mixed with a spatula specifically to work out the big chunks. It is even offering free Frosties in certain areas where business has fallen by half — and a $100,000 reward for information on the finger.[14]

The woman was charged with fraud on April 22, 2005, and the source of the finger was found in May, as Canadian Press reported in a May 13 article titled "Finger woman said she found in Wendy's chili came from husband's co-worker":

> The mysterious finger a woman claimed to have found in a bowl of Wendy's chili came from an associate of her husband's who lost the finger in an industrial accident, police said Friday. "The jig is up. The puzzle pieces are beginning to fall into place, and the truth is being exposed," [Police Chief Rob Davis said].[15]

Practice Scenario 6: Birchbark Brewing

You work in the public relations department of a craft brewery, Birchbark Brewing. Birchbark produces a range of ales and lagers for the Canadian market. The company is based in Woodstock, New Brunswick, and employs 150 workers. It exports its beer to the northeastern United States, Ontario and Quebec.

Someone must have been watching Bob and Doug Mckenzie, for a customer has complained of finding a mouse in his beer bottle. No case of 24 is being asked for here; instead the customer, now being called "mouse man" by many media outlets, is asking for a cool $1 million.

Local and national media have shown an interest in the story and have made several calls; in fact, you first read about the situation in the media, picking up one of the national newspapers on a Saturday morning and seeing the headline "Distraught beer drinker finds mouse in beer" in a bottom corner of the front page. The story text was wrapped around a photograph of the beer bottle and the dead mouse, magnified by the bottle's green glass. In another story in a local paper, a former health inspector is quoted as saying that there was a "mouse problem" at Birchbark a few years ago. You know this is unsubstantiated and that the plant operation is kept exceedingly clean. You also suspect, as your own contacts in the police department assure you, that mouse man's claim is likely a practical joke. But you can't take any chances.

Your president, Laurence Manseau, asks you to lead the team in tackling this issue. He wants to avoid "negotiating through the media" (using the media to broadcast the company's position, then waiting to see what the opposition says, in print or on television, before responding), wanting Birchbark to be as proactive as possible in its approach to the crisis.

It has been three days since the crisis began. Within 24 hours of the first story's appearance, you issue a media release that quotes Manseau:

> Birchbark is investigating this issue and will provide regular updates as more information becomes available. The police have also been contacted and are conducting an investigation into these allegations. We are

confident that our local police services will get to the source of this issue. Meantime, we are covering all the bases here at Birchbark.

On the heels of the story, the company has received a letter from mouse man's lawyer, spelling out his demands.

Birchbark's beer sales have dropped 25 per cent since the mouse in the beer was reported; you are also looking at ways to handle a rumour that anyone who can prove they bought beer on the same day as mouse man will be offered not one but *three* cases of free beer. The idea behind the rumour is that the company is allegedly trying to drive up interest in the product and that indeed the beer is mouse-free. However, Manseau feels that from mouse man's story, the attention it has attracted and the rumours of free beer, if handled deftly, could serve to enhance the company's reputation after the crisis is over.

YOUR TASK

1. Discuss the crisis with your colleagues and the company president. What information do Birchbark customers and the media need? What is the best course of action to take in handling it? Are there specific stakeholders that you need to reach when you tackle the crisis?
2. Consider these questions: What is the first to-do on your list? Who is the most important person in this scenario? What strategies can you use to not only recover the reputation of your brand but enhance its reputation overall?
3. Outline the possible outcomes. What tactics can Birchbark employ if mouse man wins his case?
4. Determine how you will handle this crisis: What do you need to think about in terms of media response? What will you say to Birchbark's stakeholders? In addition to the company president and you, who would do well as part of the crisis management team?
5. Create a communications plan and key messages for the crisis management team.
6. Deliver the company's key messages and products, having taken a hard

look at the messages first and figuring out what will work for Birchbark. Assess your success based on the response of consumers and the media to your approach (classmates should act as both media and consumers).

Case Study:
The Governor General Offers Tea and an Apology

It appeared to be a routine school visit. A group of 60 high school students were touring Rideau Hall, the Ottawa residence of Canada's then Governor General, Adrienne Clarkson, on February 15, 2005. Jeremy Patfield, a 15-year-old student from Whitby, Ontario, saw the Governor General while on tour and, according to news reports, asked the tour guide, "Is that the woman that spends the money on the Queen when she comes?"

Bad question, bad timing; the tour was immediately cut short and Patfield was threatened with a three-day suspension. However, the question *really* came at an inopportune time for the Governor General, who had been widely criticized for spending extravagantly while in office on travel and other expenses.

The student was simply echoing the sentiments of the Canadian public. The media were inundated over the next couple of days with calls and letters supporting the student and criticizing the Governor General, despite the fact that she wasn't the one who stopped the group's tour — the fault lay with an overzealous tour guide. Patfield's suspension was later lifted after a meeting with school board officials, his school's principal and his parents.

Surprisingly to many, the Governor General placed a personal call to the student, inviting him to tea at Rideau Hall. The media appeared to be surprised by Clarkson's actions, as Governors General do not usually invite members of the public to tea, and it's rare for the Governor General to open the doors of Rideau Hall as a means of ending a crisis. Governors General, while sometimes warm and welcoming in the past, have often been seen as being somewhat distant from the Canadian public, though Clarkson and her successor, Michaëlle Jean, appeared to be effecting a change in this traditional view of the role.

A February 18 Associated Press story carried by newspapers across the country drove home the point, spelling out the Governor General's act of contrition:

It's not every day the Governor General calls to apologize. But that's what happened to the 15-year-old high school student whose question about government spending resulted in his class's tour being cut short. "You can imagine ... I'm doubly embarrassed because someone asked a question — in my home — and doesn't get the answer. So I really wanted to make that right," Adrienne Clarkson told the Canadian Press minutes after she called Jeremy Patfield to apologize.

The *Toronto Star*'s February 18 story, headlined "Teapot ends the tempest," stated:

Jeremy Patfield says he'll ask Governor General Adrienne Clarkson about her spending habits in person when he takes tea with her at Rideau Hall in Ottawa. The Whitby teen — who likes his with three spoonfuls of sugar and a splash of milk — got the personal invitation from Clarkson yesterday and an apology for a mix-up that saw his school class tossed from a tour of her vice-regal residence this week.

STUDENT SUSPENSION: THE HEADLINES
(All based on a February 18, 2005, Associated Press story carried by numerous newspapers)

"Clarkson apologizes to student" — *FREDERICTON GLEANER*
"Suspension lifted after student's remark on Clarkson spending" — *CORNER BROOK WESTERN STAR*
"Ontario student avoids suspension for asking Governor General question" — *MOOSE JAW TIMES HERALD*

A February 21 editorial in the *Kitchener-Waterloo Record* was succinct in its support:

While parents often admonish their children to "say sorry," the art of apologizing is one that adults often avoid. The natural human tendency is to blame someone else, to deny there was a problem or to avoid the issue completely. One has only to consider testimony before countless commissions and boards of inquiry to realize that few public officials are ever responsible for the misjudgments, errors or disasters that occur. Yet last week ... the Governor General of Canada made [a] very public (apology).

(Reprinted with permission by *The Record* of Waterloo Region.)

Practice Scenario 7: Lexco Corporation

You work for Lexco Corporation, a large and diverse company that manufactures and distributes a range of computer technology-related items, mainly software and some hard-drive components. It is located in Port Martin, not far from Welland, Ontario. The head of the 15-year-old company is Hubert Lexton, who created it while a student at the University of Waterloo; the company employs 75 highly trained personnel and is linked to the University of Waterloo's computer engineering program. It is also a model corporate citizen, earning top marks from the local chamber of commerce for its business efforts — and accolades for its contribution to many community charities. Hubert Lexton is seen as a bit of a respected eccentric, looked at in awe by many people in the town both because he decided to make the picturesque Port Martin his home and because he is a significant employer with a world-class reputation. Lexton often wanders through Port Martin's small downtown core in a battered porkpie hat, brown corduroys and sweater vest, BlackBerry in one hand, notepad in the other, dreaming up marketable new ideas for his company.

Lexco's 700-hectare property includes a nature preserve that borders Lake Erie in southwestern Ontario, and the company has invested in rebuilding this natural area for future generations, in cooperation with the University of Guelph's ecological studies unit and nearby Niagara College. Niagara College's arborist and landscaping students have helped plant many of the native species. The media have lauded the company for its work; the preserve has a marshy area and stands of old-growth trees as well as frog ponds and platforms for osprey nests — and it's a home to much local wildlife.

Unfortunately, two days ago, five children (aged 10 to 14), were "threatened" by a security guard at the nature preserve. They were riding their BMX bikes over fragile plants, possibly destroying some of the delicate wildflowers. While the preserve has more than five kilometres of hiking paths and encourages the public to visit the area, the company has a clear policy of no bikes on the preserve — and security personnel are mandated to enforce this rule. Clearly, the company's security guard was only trying to enforce policy, but an interview with him suggests that he was being a bit heavy-handed. The children went home with their story of what happened and their parents called the media, which came down on the company in a surprisingly negative way; media as far away as Montreal and Toronto are suggesting that the company was, quite frankly, being mean and nasty to nature-loving kids. The local chamber of commerce has called to ask what happened, and a Welland-based eco-tourism company, PondTours, is worried that the company will no longer welcome its tour buses to the company's site.

Lexton himself is perplexed — the criticism goes against his image of being both genial and welcoming to the townspeople, as well as to tourists who want to wander the preserve's hiking paths. In discussion, Lexton is adamant that he wants to repair the damage to the company's reputation. Lexton doesn't want to fire the security guard but does want to find a solution — and fast, as he is concerned about the company's public image.

YOUR TASK

1. Develop a plan to handle this crisis and bring it to a close as quickly as possible.

Conclusion

As we've seen in this chapter and throughout the book, strong communicators will work to deliver sound and effective advice to senior personnel in their organization. They will think in a strategic way, while having the practical, tactical hands-on skills to research, organize and write various communications products that enhance and maintain a positive reputation for the organization. They also use the tools they have at their disposal and look to new developments in electronic technology to get their message out. Good communicators have access to, and build comprehensive business relationships with, their publics: their internal and external stakeholders, the media and the general public. They always think ahead, always ask the "what if" questions. They prepare their company's spokespeople with key messages that will help move them, no matter what the topic, from an issues mode back to the organization's normal day-to-day operations. And if a crisis hits, the communicator will be ready, with a crisis communications plan and a set of strategic steps that will bring the crisis to a close. As the philosopher Chuang Tzu said: "Stay centered by accepting whatever you are doing. This is the ultimate." In other words, don't stray from the path of managing your crisis. Hold to your principles, your skills, your knowledge and experience, and follow through.

Notes

CHAPTER 1: MODERN CRISIS COMMUNICATIONS

1. Lianne George, "Forget SARS, West Nile, Ebola and Avian Flu. The Real Epidemic Is Fear," *Maclean's Magazine*, September 29, 2005.
2. Public Relations Society of America website, www.prsa.org, http://psa.org/_About/overview/index.asp?ident=over1 (accessed Oct 24, 2006).
3. Edward L. Bernays, *Propaganda* (New York: Horace Liveright, 1928), 28
4. Edward L. Bernays, *Crystallizing Public Opinion* (Glacier National Park, Montana: Kessinger Publishing Co., 2004); Larry Tye, *The Father of Spin: Edward L. Bernays & the Birth of Public Relations* (New York: Henry Holt & Company, 2002); John Stauber and Sheldon Rampton, *Toxic Sludge Is Good For You: Lies, Damn Lies and the Public Relations Industry* (Monroe, ME: Common Courage Press, 2002). Facts from this section were drawn from the preceding sources that the author gratefully acknowledges.
5. Trevor Cook, Corporate Engagement Blog, trevorcook.typepad.com/weblog, derived from "Key Concepts in Journalism Studies," by Bob Franklin et al. (Thousand Oaks: Sage, 2006), and Kenneth S. Hicks, "The Anatomy of Spin: Causes, Consequences, and Cure," Rogers State University, www.rsu.edu/faculty/khicks/Essays/Spin.htm, (accessed Oct 24, 2006). Discussion of Safire's use of the term "spin."
6. Kenneth S. Hicks, "The Anatomy of Spin: Causes, Consequences, and Cure," Rogers State University, www.rsu.edu/faculty/khicks/Essays/Spin.htm (accessed Oct 26, 2006).
7. Canadian Public Relations Society Inc. website, www.cprs.ca.
8. *Oxford Canadian Dictionary*, 6th ed., s.v. "Crisis."

9. *Funk & Wagnalls Standard College Dictionary,* Canadian ed., s.v. "Crisis."

10. The official website of the United States Navy, www.navy.mil/navydata/news/ mednews/med00/med00008.txt (accessed Oct 21, 2006).

11. Steven Fink, *Crisis Management,* (New York: Backinprint.com, 2000), 56.

12. Dan H. O'Hair et al., "Crisis Communications Strategies," Department of Defense Joint Course in Communication, http://www.ou.edu/deptcomm/dodjcc/groups/ 02C2/comm%20theories.htm (accessed Nov 8, 2006). The terms for the crisis strategies are borrowed from the above article, which themselves are based upon concepts expounded in an article by W. T. Coombs, "Choosing the Right Words: The Development of Guidelines for the Selection of the Appropriate Crisis-Response Strategies," *Management Communication Quarterly,* 8(4): 447–476.

13. Ibid.

14. Ibid.

15. Ibid.

CHAPTER 2: CRISIS COMMUNICATIONS THEN AND NOW

1. "Crisis? It Can't Happen to Us," *TheHinduBusinessLine.com,* July 14, 2005, http://www.blonnet.com.catalyst/2005/07/14/11hdline.htm (accessed Oct 11, 2006); Dan H. O'Hair et al., "Crisis Communications Strategies."

2. *60 Minutes,* story on Google, aired on January 2, 2005.

3. Dan H. O'Hair et al., "Crisis Communications Strategies"; W. T. Coombs, "Choosing the Right Words," *Management Communication,* 8(4): 447–476.

4. Tamara Kaplan, "The Tylenol Crisis: How Effective Public Relations Saved Johnson & Johnson," The Pennsylvania State University, http://personal.psu.edu/users/w/x/ wxk116/tylenol/crisis.html (accessed Nov 8, 2006); Rick Atkinson, "The Tylenol Nightmare: How a Corporate Giant Fought Back," *The Kansas City Times,* November 12, 1982; Glen M. Broom, Allen H. Center, and Scott M. Cutlip, *Effective Public Relations,* 7th ed., (New York: Prentice-Hall Inc., 1994); Lawrence G. Foster, "The Johnson & Johnson Credo and the Tylenol Crisis." *New Jersey Bell Journal* 6, no. 1 (1983): 2. Facts from this section were drawn from the preceding sources that the author gratefully acknowledges.

5. Royal Bank of Canada website, www.rbc.com/aboutus (accessed Nov 8, 2006).

6. Royal Bank of Canada website, www.rbc.com/newsroom (accessed No. 8, 2006).

7. Ibid.

8. Ibid.

9. Fawzia Sheikh, *IT Business News,* "RBC's Glitch: The Post-mortem," www.itbusiness. ca/it/client/en/Home/News.asp (accessed Nov 8, 2006).

10. Royal Bank of Canada website, www.rbc.com/newsroom.

11. Ibid.

12. Erik Heinrich, "RBC's 'Perfect Storm' Has Lessons for All. Lessons Learned: Test, Test, Test. And Back Up Data," *Toronto Star*, July 19, 2004.
13. R. K. Brown. Case Study: Transaction Processing Disruption, June 2004. RBC Financial Group, Toronto. The study was an internal research project conducted by RBC for the purposes of discussion and presentation on this topic.
14. Ibid.

CHAPTER 3: IDENTIFYING AND MONITORING ISSUES

1. Sun Tzu, *The Art of War* (Oxford: Oxford University Press, 1963), 39.
2. Miyamoto Musashi, *The Book of Five Rings* (Boston: Shambhala Publishing, 2005), 20.
3. Dale Carnegie website: www.dalecarnegie.com; quotation from BrainyQuote, http://brainyquote.com/quotes/authors/d/dale_carnegie.html (accessed Nov 8, 2006).
4. Morgan Campbell and Christian Cotroneo, "Ottawa Ups Donations for Victims to $20M," *Toronto Star*, October 11, 2005.
5. Rick Winston, principal, Win-Win Communications, interview with author, March 2005.
6. Robert T. Waite, senior vice-president, Communications and Stakeholder Relations, Canada Post Corporation, interview with author, February 2005.
7. John Chartier, *CNN Money*, "Firestone, Ford under Fire," September 6, 2000, http://money.cnn.com/2000/09/06/companies/bridgestone_ford/index.htm (accessed Nov 8, 2006); E-Center for Business Ethics, "Firestone Case, Danger on the Highway: Bridgestone/Firestone's Tire Recall," www.e-businessethics.com/firestone. htm (accessed Nov 8, 2006); Legal Information Center website, "Firestone Tire Recall: Overview of the Recall," www.firestone-tire-recall.com/pages/overview.html (accessed Nov 8, 2006). Facts from this section were drawn from the preceding sources that the author gratefully acknowledges.
8. Robin Cohn, *The PR Crisis Bible* (New York: Truman Talley Books, 2001), 215.
9. Ibid.
10. Aldo Santin, "Prince Harry Evokes Condemnation," *Winnipeg Free Press*, January 14, 2005; "'Royal Idiot.' Harry's Nazi Costume Sparks EU Talk of Banning Swastikas," *Hamilton Spectator*, January 18, 2005; Rebecca Winters, "Royal Fuhrer Furor," *Time Magazine*, January 24, 2005, 47; *Newsweek*, January 24, 2005.
11. "Court Jester," *The Guardian*, January 14, 2005, http://www.guardian.co.uk/leaders/ story/0,,1390040,00.html (accessed Nov 8, 2006).
12. Tom Utley, "Someone Has Got to Stop Harry from Behaving Like a Prize Ass," *The Telegraph*, January 14, 2005.

CHAPTER 4: THE CRISIS COMMUNICATIONS PLAN

1. Ed Shiller, *The Canadian Guide to Managing the Media* (Prentice-Hall Canada, Incorporated, 2001), 39.
2. Ibid.
3. Daniel Yankelovich and Steve Rosell, "Making Trust a Competitive Asset: Breaking out of Narrow Frameworks," *Strategy + Business*, no. 35, Summer 2004, http://www.danyankelovich.com (accessed November 8, 206).
4. Robert E. Waite, Canada Post Corporation, interview with the author, January 2005.
5. Ibid.
6. Carole Howard and Wilma Mathews, *On Deadline: Managing Media Relations* (Long Point, Illinois: Waveland Press, Incorporated, 1994), 253–256.
7. John Intini, Culture, "The Resourceful Generation," *Maclean's Magazine*, January 17, 2005.
8. Margaret Wente, "Oh Danny Boy, Pipe Down," *The Globe and Mail*, January 6, 2005.
9. Peter Sandman website, www.psandman.com/col/panflu3.htm (accessed November 8, 2006).

CHAPTER 5: COMMUNICATING WITH EXTERNAL STAKEHOLDERS

1. Richard L. Oliver, "Whence Customer Loyalty?" *Journal of Marketing*, no. 63 (Special Issue), 33.
2. Mark Achbar, Jennifer Abbott and Joel Bakan, "The Corporation" (Vancouver: Big Picture Media Corporation, 2003). Based on the book *The Corporation: The Pathological Pursuit of Profit and Power*, by Joel Bakan (Toronto: Penguin Canada, 2004).
3. Joseph L. Rotman School of Management, University of Toronto, "Principles of Stakeholder Management," www.rotman.utoronto.ca/ccbe/~stake/Publications.htm, published by the Clarkson Centre for Business Ethics, Toronto, Ontario, 1999.
4. James E. Grunig, *Excellence in Public Relations and Communications Management* (Mahwan, NJ: Lawrence Erlbaum Associates, 1992), 289.
5. John McHugh, senior vice-president, Avant Strategic Communications, interview with author, March 2005.
6. Vincent T. Covello, "Seven Cardinal Rules of Risk Communication" (pamphlet), in collaboration with Frederick W. Allen, Associate Director of the Office of Policy Analysis at the Environmental Protection Agency (EPA), February 2004, Center for Risk Communication, New York, www.centerforriskcommunication.com/readings.htm (accessed Nov 9, 2006).
7. "Litter Foes Target Tim Hortons," *The Daily News*, Halifax, Nova Scotia, June 13, 2005.
8. "Sending a Recycling Message," *The Guardian*, Charlottetown, PEI, June 16, 2005;

Chris Morris, "Hot Coffee Issue," *Canadian Press*, June 13, 2005; Danylo Hawaleshka, "The Cups Runneth Over," *Maclean's Magazine*, October 24, 2004. Facts from this section were drawn from the preceding sources that the author gratefully acknowledges.

9. Rudolph Giuliani, *Leadership* (New York: Talk Miramax Books, 2002), 92.
10. John McHugh, interview with author, March 2005.
11. Ontario government website, www.mto.gov.on.ca/english/about/ (accessed Nov 8, 2006).
12. Derek Deazeley, senior manager, Ministry of Transportation, interview with author, December 16, 2005.
13. Ibid.
14. Ibid.
15. The specific example is mine, but it illustrates dynamics that have been expounded by Dr. Peter Sandman, and those dynamics are his theories. The specific dynamics illustrated were explained to me in discussion with Dr. Peter Sandman during a personal interview on December 8, 2005.
16. Elenor Snow, "Notes from a Class by Dr. Peter Sandman," Hanford Nuclear Reservation, 1993, from a class taken with Dr. Peter Sandman on risk communication, http://www.psandman.com/articles/risk.htm (accessed Nov 8, 2006).
17. Both quotes from a briefing delivered by U.S. President George W. Bush at the Mobile Regional Airport in Alabama. The quotes were posted on the White House website at www.whitehouse.gov/news (accessed Nov. 8, 2006).
18. Dr. Peter Sandman, interview with author, December 8, 2005.
19. Ibid.
20. William Leiss, *In The Chamber Of Risks: Understanding Risk Controversies* (Montreal: McGill-Queen's University Press, 2001), 28.
21. William Leiss and Douglas Powell, "Mad Cows or Crazy Communications?" (written with Amanda Whitfield), from *Mad Cows and Mother's Milk* (Montreal: McGill-Queen's University Press) 3–4.

CHAPTER 6: COMMUNICATING WITH INTERNAL STAKEHOLDERS DURING A CRISIS

1. Michael J. Epstein, Communicating with Stakeholders in a Crisis, TRG Group, Boston, Mass. www.trgusa.com/final_stakeholdercommMJE.htm (accessed Nov 8, 2006.
2. Jerry Lazar, "Foot-in-Mouth Disease," *Electronic Business*, June 2000: 118.
3. Bart Mindszenthy and Gail Roberts, "Team Leaders and the Communication Loop," *Strategic Communication Management* 5, no. 1 (2001): 28.
4. Sunnybrook Health Sciences Centre website, http://www.sunnybrook.ca/about (accessed Nov 8, 2006).

5. SARS: WebMd, World Health Organization: "Timelines on SARS Outbreak," www.webmd.com/content/Article/62/71672.htm (accessed Nov 8, 2006).
6. Craig DuHamel, "Effective Internal Crisis Communications" (thesis), University of Stirling, 2003–2004, 7.
7. Craig DuHamel, chief, public affairs and community relations, Sunnybrook Health Sciences Centre, interview with author, January 2005.
8. Ibid.
9. Ibid.
10. Ibid.
11. Ibid.
12. Ibid.
13. Craig DuHamel, interview, January 2005; Nadia Norcia, communications advisor, Sunnybrook Health Sciences Centre, interview with the author, January 2005; WebMd, World Health Organization: www.webmd.com/content/Article/62/ 71672.htm (accessed November 8, 2006); Craig DuHamel, "Effective Internal Crisis Communications." Facts from this section were drawn from the preceding sources that the author gratefully acknowledges.

CHAPTER 7: MEDIA RELATIONS DURING A CRISIS

1. NAD Bank (Newspaper Audience Databank Inc.) 2005 study on readership and demographic data, April 2005, www.nadbank.com/English/index.html (accessed Nov 8, 2006).
2. Canadian Advertising Rates and Data, CARDonline, Canadian market statistics, www.cardonline.ca/tools/cma_total_pop.efm (accessed Nov 8 2006).
3. Thomas H. Bivins, *Handbook for Public Relations Writing* (California: NTC Publishing Group, 1994), 127.
4. Marshall McLuhan, *Understanding Media*, (Cambridge, MA: MIT Press, 1994), 52.
5. Neil Postman, *Amusing Ourselves to Death*, (New York: Penguin Books, 1985), 50.
6. Marshall McLuhan, *Understanding Media*, (Cambridge, MA: MIT Press, 1994), 57.
7. Neil Postman, *Amusing Ourselves to Death*, (New York: Penguin Books, 1985), 111.
8. John Larsen, principal, Corpen Group, interview with author, March 2005.
9. Ibid.
10. Ian Taylor and George Olds, *Never Say "No Comment,"* (Toronto: LB Publishing Services), www.go4results.com/neverindex.html (accessed Nov 8, 2006).
11. Allan Dickie, former director of communications, Ministry of the Solicitor General, Ontario Government, interview with the author, February 2005.
12. Ibid.
13. Allan Dickie, interview; David Allen, Allan Dickie, Mary Clare Havey, *Derailment: The Mississauga Miracle* (Toronto: Government of Ontario, 1980).

14. Allan Dickie, interview.
15. Ibid.
16. Ibid.
17. Ibid.
18. Ibid.
19. Ibid.
20. Ibid.
21. Allan Dickie, interview; Allen, Dickie and Harvey, *Derailment*, "Welcome Home," *Mississauga Times*, November 14, 1979; "The Week They Closed Mississauga," *Toronto Star*, November 18, 1979; "Mississauga's Lost Week," *Toronto Sun*, November 18, 1979. Facts from this section were drawn from the preceding sources that the author gratefully acknowledges.

CHAPTER 8: LEADERSHIP AND THE MESSAGE

1. Tom Wolfe, *The Right Stuff* (New York: Bantam Books, 2001), 10.
2. Marlane Oliver, Toronto radio host, 680 News, interview with author, March 2005.
3. Rudolph Giuliani, *Leadership*, 92.
4. New York City website, www.nyc.gov/portal/site/nycgov (accessed Nov 8, 2006).
5. "September 11, Chronology of Terror," CNN, CNN website: archives.cnn.com/ 2001/US/09/11/chronology.attack, September 12, 2001 (accessed Nov 8, 2006); "9/11Timeline.net" (website for 9/11) www.911timeline.net (accessed Nov 8, 2006); "Attacks Timeline," Wikipedia, September 11, 2001, http://en.wikipedia.org/wiki/ September_11,_2001_attacks_timeline_for_September (accessed Nov 11, 2006).
6. Jonathan Alter, "Grit, Guts and Rudy Giuliani," *Newsweek*, September 24, 2001, 138, no. 13:53.
7. Ibid.
8. Rudolph Giuliani, *Leadership*, 110.
9. Text of Paul Martin's April 21, 2005, speech, posted on CBC.ca: www.cbc.ca/ news/background/groupaction/address_martin.html (accessed Nov 8, 2006).

CHAPTER 9: NEWS RELEASES, EXPERT TESTIMONY, ENVIRONMENTAL SCANS

1. Robert E. Waite, interview.
2. Paul Rutherford, *Weapons of Mass Persuasion: Marketing the War against Iraq* (Toronto: University of Toronto Press, 2004), 2.
3. Natrel website: www.natrel.ca.
4. Natrel statement to the media, news release, February 1, 2005, Natrel website, www.natrel.ca.
5. A statement by Natrel regarding Sealtest Brand 1% 1 litre FE 07 chocolate milk, Canada NewsWire, www.newswire.ca, February 1, 2005.

6. Ibid.
7. "Recall Affects Thousands of Milk Cartons," CBC.ca, February 2, 2005, http://www. ctv.ca/servlet/ArticleNews/story/CTVNews/20050202/sealtest_warning_milk_0502 02/20050202/; CTV.ca, February 2, 2005: "Human Error Tainted Chocolate Milk, Natrel Says," http://www.ctv.ca/servlet/ArticleNews/story/CTVNews/1107356431814_ 102765631?hub-Canada (accessed Nov 8, 2006); Philip Mascoll and Robert Cribb, "Milk Lover Mulls Lawsuit," *Toronto Star*, February 3, 2005, B3. Facts from this section were drawn from the preceding sources that the author gratefully acknowledges.
8. Word Spy (website for new or recently coined words), http://www.wordspy.com/words/tobaccoscience.asp (Nov 9, 2006).
9. "Legislation to Ban Dangerous Breed, Increase Dog Owners' Responsibility," news release posted on Canada NewsWire by Government of Ontario, www.newswire.ca, October 15, 2004.
10. "New Law Bans Pit Bulls, Increases Dog Owners' Responsibility," news release posted on Canada NewsWire by Government of Ontario, www.newswire.ca, March 2005.
11. A check of the EBSCOhost library research database revealed 194 stories relating to the pit bull ban. Source: http//www.whitbylibrary.on.ca/adatabase.php.
12. Sources are uncertain about the origins of the SWOT analysis, but it is generally credited to Albert Humphrey (died 2005) of Stanford University, who led research into Fortune 500 companies.

CHAPTER 10: THE QUESTION-AND-ANSWER DOCUMENT AND MEDIA INTERVIEWS

1. Canadian Public Relations Society, Inc., www.cprs.ca; Ian Taylor and George Olds, *Never Say "No Comment"*; Thomas H. Bivins, *Handbook for Public Relations Writing* (Sylmar, California: NTC Publishing Group, 1994); Carole Howard and Wilma Mathews, *On Deadline: Managing Media Relations,* (Long Grove, Illinois: Waveland Press, Incorporated, 1994); Ed Shiller, *The Canadian Guide to Managing the Media* (Toronto: Prentice-Hall Canada, Incorporated, 2001). These books are highly recommended supplemental reading.
2. Errol Morris (director), *The Fog of War: Eleven Lessons from the Life of Robert S. McNamara* (documentary) (Culver City, California: Sony Pictures, 2003).

CHAPTER 11: CREATING DIALOGUES AND GATHERING INFORMATION: WEBSITES AND BLOGS

1. John Shalagan, acting director, communications, Centennial College, Toronto, interview with author, October 3, 2006.
2. Donna Varrica, director, public relations, Dawson College, Montreal, interview with author, October 2, 2006.
3. Green Media Toolshed, http://greenmediatoolshed.blogs.com/gmt/2004/04/dark_

sites_publ.html, last accessed 2006/11/06; Bernstein Crisis Management LLC, http://www.bernsteincrisismanagement.com/nl/crisismgr020801.html#2` (accessed Nov 6, 2008). Both sources provided useful background reading for the writing of this section.

4. David Kirkpatrick and Daniel Roth, "Why There's No Escaping the Blog," *Forbes*, January 10, 2005; San Grewel, "Why Blogging Began," (source for data in *Star* story: blog tracking company Technorati.com), *Toronto Star*, December 13, 2005.

5. Dr. Peter Sandman, interview with the author, December 8, 2005.

6. Michael O'Connor Clarke, vice-president of business development, Marqui, interview with the author, November 25, 2005.

7. Daniel Lyons, "Attack of the Blogs," *Forbes*, November 2005, 176, no. 10:128.

8. Blogs Canada: http://www.blogscanada.ca; Public Relations Society of America, Pitching Blogs: www.prsa.org/_Publications/magazines/0802news1.asp (accessed Nov 8, 2006). Both were sources of background information for the writing of this section.

CHAPTER 12: PRACTICE SCENARIOS

1. Catherine Porter, "Fantino asks for 500 Tasers," *Toronto Star*, November 16, 2004.

2. "In Depth: Tasers," Taser FAQ, http://www.cbc.ca/news/background/tasers/, October 19, 2004, last accessed 2006/11/09.

3. Graham F. Scott, "When Stun Guns Go Bad," *Maclean's Magazine* 117, no. 34 (August 23, 2004): 44.

4. "In Depth: Tasers"; Taser FAQ, http://www.cbc.ca/news/background/tasers/, October 19, 2004 (accessed Nov 6, 2008).

5. Rachel Ross, "Taser Firm Subject of U.S. Inquiry," *Toronto Star*, January 8, 2005.

6. "Those Who Are Tasered Pose a Threat," *The Whitehorse Star*, May 27, 2005; "News Notes, Tasers," *Maclean's Magazine*, August 2, 2004, Macleans.ca, http://www. macleans.ca/topstories/canada/article.jsp?content=20040802_85623_85623, http://www.cbc.ca/news/background/tasers/ (accessed Nov 6, 2006); "Coroner's Office Probing Death of Man Hit by Police Taser," *The Evening News*, New Glasgow, Nova Scotia, May 11, 2005. Facts from this section were drawn from the preceding sources that the author gratefully acknowledges.

7. "Learning from The Blackout," *Christian Science Monitor* 95, no.184 (August 18, 2003): 8.

8. Robert Waite indicated in an interview that his comments took place at a fall Crisis Communications Management Seminar in 2003.

9. A check of the EBSCOhost library research database through the Whitby Public Library revealed 1,123 newspaper, magazine, and website articles generated from August to October 2003 on the blackout. Source: Whitby Public Library: http//www.whitbylibrary.on.ca/adatabase.php.

10. World, *Maclean's Magazine*, January 31, 2005; Justin Pope, "Harvard Chief on Hot Seat (Associated Press story)," *Toronto Star*, February 19, 2005; James Bone, "Contrite Harvard Chief Weathers Gender Storm," *The Times* (United Kingdom), February 24, 2005; "A Gray Matter," *Scientific American* 292, no. 5 (May 2005): 47; Stephen Klugewicz, "The Oppression Lobby," *American Spectator* 38, no. 4 (May 2005): 50. Facts from this section were drawn from the preceding sources that the author gratefully acknowledges.

11. "Baseball Stars Offer Drama, Few Facts at Steroids Hearing," *Kitchener-Waterloo Record*, March 18, 2005; Garth Woolsey, "Steroid Proposal Looks Like a Hit," *Toronto Star*, May 2, 2005; Hal Bodley, "Selig Flexes His Muscles to Rid Game of Steroids," *USA Today*, May 5, 2005; Geoff Baker, "Life in Needle Park," *Toronto Star*, May 14, 2005; "Baseball Notebook; Tougher Stand on Steroid Abuse," *Hamilton Spectator*, May 12, 2005; Tim Harper, "Leagues Fight Back: Anti-steroid Law Unnecessary, Bosses Tell U.S. Congress," *Toronto Star*, May 19, 2005. Facts from this section were drawn from the preceding sources that the author gratefully acknowledges.

12. Kelly Toughill, "Price of History: $9.6 million," *Toronto Star*, January 7, 2005.

13. Ibid.

14. "When There Is More Than a Fly in the Food," *Maclean's Magazine* 118, no.18 (May 2, 2005): 9.

15. "Finger Found in Wendy's Chili," *Times & Transcript*, Moncton, New Brunswick, March 25, 2005; "Woman Who Claimed She Found Finger in Wendy's Chili Has Litigious History," *Canadian Press*, April 8, 2005; "When There Is More Than a Fly in the Food," *Maclean's Magazine* 118, no. 8 (May 2, 2005): 9; "Finger Woman Said Finger She Found in Wendy's Chili Came from Husband's Co-worker," *Canadian Press*, May 13, 2005. Facts from this section were drawn from the preceding sources that the author gratefully acknowledges.